I have long considered Gerald Anderson to be the "dean" of U.S. missiology. This book is a gift to those of us who have been part of IAMS as well as to younger generations who will shape the missiology of the future. We owe Dr. Anderson a debt of gratitude for his thorough research and clear presentation.
—Stephen Bevans, S.V.D.
Catholic Theological Union

Gerald Anderson's masterly account of a half-century of IAMS is an excellent overview of how this association became the premier meeting point where world Christianity reflects on its mission and ministry. Everyone serious about missiology should read it.
—William R. Burrows
Orbis Books

Gerald H. Anderson's *Witness to World Christianity* records the fascinating history of the origin and development of IAMS. All mission scholars, missionaries, and students of mission will be enriched by this meticulously researched and well documented publication
—Sebastian Karotemprel, S.D.B.
Sacred Heart Theological College, Shillong, India

Gerald Anderson presents a finely tuned description of the evolution of IAMS and skillfully illustrates the energetic impulse infusing mission theology and practice into the future.
—Mary M. Motte, F.M.M.
Providence, Rhode Island

This brief history of IAMS is a rapid tour of key issues in global missiology over the past forty years. Only Gerald Anderson could have written such a succinct, informative, and useful account of the Association.
—Dana L. Robert
Boston University School of Theology

Gerald Anderson's history, written with all the insight of a leading participant in the organization, charts the course, not simply of IAMS itself, but also of prominent trends in Christian theology of mission since 1972.
—Brian Stanley
University of Edinburgh

This much-awaited history of IAMS is a "Who's Who" of the work and contributions of the most eminent missiologists of the past fifty years.

—James A. Scherer
Lutheran School of Theology at Chicago

Gerald Anderson has given us a grand survey of the work and witness of the IAMS. This succinct overview captures the wonderful, global vibrancy of mission studies!

—Timothy C. Tennent
Asbury Theological Seminary

Gerald Anderson's thoroughly documented history of the IAMS not only is an account of an important scholarly association but also shows how mission studies have changed from being a concern for Western scholars to a truly global venture. Being the only person who has participated in all the assemblies from the beginning in 1972, the author is uniquely qualified for this task. Highly recommended.

—Notto R. Thelle
University of Oslo, Norway

I know of no one as eminently qualified as Gerald Anderson to give us the story of IAMS. He has known all the major players personally and has, himself, been a significant figure in its development. This history reads like a "Who's Who" of Protestant and Catholic missiology of the past fifty years, and every serious student of missiology needs to read it.

—Charles Van Engen
School of Intercultural Studies
Fuller Theological Seminary

This book shows that in its forty years of existence the interest of IAMS has shifted from "missionary research" to "mission studies" as a well-established academic discipline. IAMS has become truly international, truly interdenominational, and truly interdisciplinary.

—Frans Wijsen
Nijmegen Institute for Mission Studies

# Witness to
# World Christianity

Olav Guttorm Myklebust, 1905–2001

# Witness to World Christianity

The International Association
for Mission Studies,
1972–2012

Gerald H. Anderson

with
John Roxborogh
John M. Prior, S.V.D.
Christoffer H. Grundmann

OMSC Publications
New Haven, Connecticut

Published by Overseas Ministries Study Center
490 Prospect Street
New Haven, CT 06511 USA
(203) 624-6672
www.OMSC.org

Front cover photographs (clockwise from top): Attendees at the 2008 DABOH (Documentation, Archives, Bibliography, and Oral History) conference, Balatonfüred, Hungary; Teresa Okure, S.H.C.J., at the 2000 Hammanskraal Assembly; Andew F. Walls, an IAMS Honorary Life Member (left), with Daniel Antwi of Jamaica, at the 2008 DABOH conference; and longtime member Kwame Bediako of Ghana.

Design: Dwight P. Baker, OMSC
Cover design: Daniel J. Nicholas, OMSC

ISBN: 978-0-9762205-9-6
Printed in the United States of America

# Contents

"Healing/Pneumatology" Study Group                    179
    *Christoffer H. Grundmann*

**Appendixes**

# Prologue

Forty years after the inaugural assembly of IAMS at Driebergen, Netherlands, in 1972, it is time for an initial effort to rescue, recover, and record the history of the Association. Not many of those who attended the Driebergen meeting are still living, and indeed this writer is the only person who has attended all the general assemblies.

Professor Olav Guttorm Myklebust once said that "IAMS has only a brief history, but a long past." It goes back at least to 1945, when he first suggested to a missions conference in Norway the idea of the need for such an organization.[1] Since then, as this account will show, Myklebust's grand vision of an international association of scholars for the advancement of mission studies—one that would sponsor study projects, convene international conferences, and publish a scholarly journal of high standards—has come to fruition and flourished even beyond what he imagined.

*Resources.* The IAMS archives are deposited in the Special Collections of the Yale Divinity School Library, New Haven, Connecticut, where Martha Smalley, the curator, has been most helpful, along with her assistant, Joan Duffey. Unfortunately, the archives are incomplete, especially before 1978. I have therefore relied on my own personal files and records to help fill in the gaps, as well as on information from other members, especially the former general secretaries of IAMS. Much of the reporting here is taken from the minutes of Executive Committee meetings and publications of IAMS. All the material collected for this project will be deposited in the Yale Divinity School archives.

---

1. I have not had access to the papers of Myklebust, which are now in the National Library of Norway. I have therefore drawn largely on three publications by Myklebust for this background period: *An International Institute of Scientific Missionary Research* (Oslo: Egede Instituttet, 1951); "On the Origin of IAMS," MS 3, no. 1 (1986): 4–11; and "My Pilgrimage in Mission," *IBMR* 11, no. 1 (1987): 22–23.

*Acknowledgments.* This project has been a collaborative effort in that several former IAMS presidents, general secretaries, treasurers, and editors of the journal, as well as various members, have been consulted and have provided helpful information and suggestions. Within the Association three major study group projects have been active in continuing research and consultation, which is an indispensable part of the purpose of the membership; reports of their work are included. One is Documentation, Archives, Bibliography, and Oral History (DABOH), which has been the most active and productive continuing group in the Association. I am pleased to include here an account of their work by John Roxborogh, who served as moderator for many years. Second is the project on Biblical Studies and Mission (BISAM), which has been led by Marc Spindler, David Bosch, John Pobee, Teresa Okure, S.H.C.J., and John Prior, S.V.D., the present moderator, who has written about their work for us. The third group is Healing, which deals with healing as an integral part of mission. Christoffer Grundmann, the longtime moderator of this group, tells the story of their project.

Jonathan Bonk kindly provided office space at the Overseas Ministries Study Center (OMSC), in New Haven, where the research and writing of this project could be carried out, close to the archives at Yale Divinity School. Dwight Baker and Daniel Nicholas, on the OMSC staff, gave valuable assistance in the production of the book. Edward Schroeder and John Roxborogh generously provided many of the photographs. Unfortunately, no photos were found from several of the conferences, especially in the early years.

# Abbreviations

| | |
|---|---|
| APM | Association of Professors of Mission in North America |
| ASM | American Society of Missiology |
| ATLA | American Theological Library Association |
| BIAMS | British and Irish Association for Mission Studies |
| BISAM | Biblical Studies and Mission |
| CEEAMS | Central and Eastern European Association for Mission Studies |
| CMS | Church Mission Society, London/Oxford |
| DAB | Documentation, Archives, and Bibliography |
| DABOH | Documentation, Archives, Bibliography, and Oral History |
| EMW | Evangelisches Missionswerk, Hamburg |
| IACM | International Association of Catholic Missiologists |
| IAMS | International Association for Mission Studies |
| IBMR | *International Bulletin of Missionary Research* |
| IIMO | Interuniversity Institute for Missiological and Ecumenical Research, Leiden |
| IMC | International Missionary Council |
| IRM | *International Review of Mission* |
| MARC | Mission Advanced Research and Communication Center |
| MS | *Mission Studies: Journal of the IAMS* |
| NL | *News Letter of the IAMS* |
| OMSC | Overseas Ministries Study Center, New Haven (formerly in Ventnor, N.J.) |
| SAMS | Southern African Missiological Society |
| SOAS | School of Oriental and African Studies, London |
| WCC | World Council of Churches, Geneva |

# Background

More than any other person, Olav G. Myklebust, director of the Egede Institute in Oslo, was the moving spirit and progenitor who provided the grand vision and initiative—despite skepticism, objections, and opposition from some sources—that led to the formation of IAMS.[1] In 1951 Myklebust issued a thirty-five-page booklet entitled *An International Institute of Scientific Missionary Research*, which may be considered the unofficial charter of IAMS. Six years earlier he had first suggested the idea of such an organization at a missions conference in Norway. Now he made a formal proposal in which he said that the time was ripe for the establishment of "an international association of missiologists (and others engaged in the scholarly study of mission)" that from time to time would convene "international conferences for the discussion of missionary subjects in a strictly scientific spirit" and would publish "a scholarly review of high standard."

Reactions to the proposal were mixed. In the United States it was quite favorably received, with endorsements coming from Kenneth Scott Latourette, R. Pierce Beaver, William Richey Hogg, and others. Ernest A. Payne in England and Bishop Stephen Neill in Geneva were very interested. Some Europeans, both Catholic and Protestant, such as Johannes Beckman, Thomas Ohm, and H. Dürr, were supportive. In general, however, according to Myklebust, "The response in Europe was rather disappointing." Concerns were expressed that American academic standards were not high enough and that adequate financial support would not be forthcoming; and there was uncertainty about the relationship of

1. Olav Guttorm Myklebust (1905–2001), Norwegian Lutheran missiologist, was sent to South Africa by the Norwegian Missionary Society in 1930; there he taught at the Umpumulo Teacher's College, Natal. From 1939 to 1974 he taught missions at the Norwegian Lutheran School of Theology in Oslo, where he founded the Egede Institute for Missiology and edited the *Norsk tidsskrift for misjon*. His published doctoral dissertation, *The Study of Missions in Theological Education*, 2 vols. (Oslo: Egede Instituttet, 1955–57), is a classic. See his "My Pilgrimage," *IBMR* 11, no. 1 (1987): 22–23.

1

the proposed organization to the plans and activities of the International Missionary Council.

It was particularly disappointing when the *International Review of Missions* declined to publish an article about the proposal, saying that the article did not lend itself to *IRM* publication! According to Myklebust, "Rev. Charles W. Ranson, General Secretary of the [International Missionary] Council, agreed with the editors of the *IRM*. He saw no need for the establishment of either an international institute or an international association. Even the idea of convening an international conference he was not able to endorse. Periodic meetings of this kind might in the long run fulfil a useful purpose, but at this stage 'an informal and unpretentious approach' was more desirable."[2] Fortunately, Erik W. Nielsen, research secretary of the IMC, was of another mind. He liked the proposal and offered to cooperate, despite the difficulties that might be encountered.[3]

Because of the disappointing response to the project, the Egede Institute proceeded modestly. In cooperation with Nielsen's IMC Research Department, an invitation was issued to about twenty mission professors, directors of mission institutes, and editors of scholarly mission journals in Europe to meet in Oslo in the summer of 1955 to consider the establishment of a group to be called the International Association for the Scientific Study of the Christian World Mission. For practical reasons it was decided to restrict participation in this initial meeting to European Protestants, although it was intended that the association itself should be fully international and ecumenical. According to Myklebust, this proposal "met with no success," though he gave no explanation.

*Hamburg, West Germany, 1955.* So another approach was tried. Walter Freytag from the University of Hamburg offered to invite a group of European mission scholars to meet in Hamburg later in 1955. Nielsen made the arrangements, and Myklebust—though unable to attend the meeting—prepared a "memorandum on an international organization for the scholarly study of the Chris-

2. Myklebust cites his correspondence with all of these persons regarding their reactions to the proposal. See "On the Origin," pp. 5–6.

3. This positive response was rather surprising because Nielsen worked under Ranson in the IMC. But Nielsen—a Dane—was well known and widely respected for his wisdom and integrity, and obviously he did not view the proposed new organization as a threat to the IMC.

tian world mission and the history and problems of the Younger Churches," which was circulated to all the participants in advance. The document stressed the need for "a creative international fellowship" that would be "a permanent organ of co-operation, i.e. an international association for mission studies." According to Myklebust, this meeting in Hamburg provided an opportunity for "an exchange of views on the subject but did not achieve permanent results." Unfortunately, "the continuation committee appointed by the meeting never met."

*Hamburg, 1966.* In the wake of the integration of the International Missionary Council with the World Council of Churches in 1961, and the Second Vatican Council in 1962–65, there was a sense that the old order of colonization was passing and that there was now a new acceptance of ecumenical relations. At the same time, there was increasing polarization over the role of churches in political and social processes. These issues raised new questions and made scholarly engagement and cooperation all the more essential. In short, they made Myklebust's vision more relevant.

Thus—frustrated but undeterred—the Egede group tried again in 1966 with another meeting of European mission scholars, again in Hamburg. This time the meeting was convened and chaired by Hans-Werner Gensichen from the University of Heidelberg (Walter Freytag had died in 1959).[4] The Egede Institute was represented by Nils E. Bloch-Hoell, who reminded the participants of the memorandum of 1955 and urged its adoption.[5] While the meeting did not go that far, participants did discuss "the feasibility of a larger meeting of European missiologists," which might lead to the creation of "a worldwide interconfessional missiological society." A planning committee was appointed consisting of Gensichen, Bengt Sundkler, and Douglas Webster.

*Selly Oak, Birmingham, England, 1968.* The next step was the European Consultation on Mission Studies, held April 16–19, 1968, at

4. It is noteworthy that, from the time Gensichen took a role of leadership, working closely with Myklebust, things began to move in a positive direction. As chairman of the Deutsche Gesellschaft für Missionswissenschaft (German Society for Mission Studies), Gensichen was highly regarded and influential in European and ecumenical circles of mission scholars.

5. We have no explanation for Myklebust's lack of participation in the meetings in Hamburg in 1955 and 1966. One can only speculate how the outcome might have been different, had he been present.

Selly Oak Colleges, Birmingham, hosted by President Paul R. Clifford and organized largely by Douglas Webster, who then was professor of mission at Selly Oak. In his report on the meeting, Johannes Verkuyl said that about seventy missiologists participated, including nearly all those who were teaching missiology in Western Europe. Unfortunately, there was only one missiologist from Asia, Mathew P. John from India.[6] Arnulf Camps, O.F.M., recalled that the meeting was financially supported by the Cadbury Family Trust and that, at the farewell dinner, each participant was presented with "an impressive piece of chocolate." Gensichen chaired the meeting, which was "in every respect a success," according to Myklebust. Two topics were addressed: "The Place and Task of Missiology Today" and "Presence and Proclamation as Forms of Mission." In addition to prominent European Protestants, several American and Roman Catholic scholars participated. Papers were read by Donald McGavran, R. Pierce Beaver, Bengt Sundkler, Max Warren, Hans-Jochen Margull, and Josef Glazik. Discussion and debate of contrasting viewpoints and controversial issues was candid and lively.

Andrew Walls recalls that the four Roman Catholics who were present—Camps (Nijmegen), Glazik (Münster), Charles Couturier (Paris), and Joseph Masson (Rome)—were considered "guests," but it was decided that in the future all would be participants equally, both Catholics and Protestants. No formal action was taken regarding the formation of an international association, but it was agreed to have another meeting in Oslo in 1970, hosted by the Egede Institute, "to be termed a *conference*." A continuation committee was appointed consisting of Han-Werner Gensichen, Arnulf Camps, Olav Guttorm Myklebust, Paul R. Clifford, and Stanley J. Samartha.[7]

---

6. Mathew P. John (1922–96), from Serampore College, was the William Paton Lecturer at Selly Oak during 1967–69. Apparently, he was the only non-Western participant at the consultation (interview with Andrew Walls, August 18, 2008, and e-mail from Sue John [Mathew's daughter], September 10, 2008).

7. Some papers and reports from the conferences at Selly Oak (1968), Oslo (1970), and Driebergen (1972) appeared in various journals. A list of these publications appears in *IAMS NL*, no. 4 (Feb. 1974): 9–10. Articles by Johannes Verkuyl, J. M. van der Linde, and Arnulf Camps, reporting on the meeting at Selly Oak, appeared in "De eerste europese consultatie van missiologen in Selly Oak, 16–19 April, 1968," *De Heerbaan* 21, no. 4 (1968): 205–32. Several of the papers from the Selly Oak meeting were published in *The Conciliar-Evangelical Debate: The Crucial Documents, 1964–1976*, ed. Donald A. McGavran (South Pasadena, Calif.: William Carey Library, 1977). Some of the debate at

*Oslo, Norway, 1970.* The Second European Conference on Mission Studies (as it was called), held in Oslo, August 25–28, 1970, with Gensichen presiding and Myklebust designated as secretary, was a decisive turning point. The seventy-four registered participants were predominantly Europeans, both Protestants and Catholics, but included also Stanley J. Samartha (India/Geneva), Samuel Rayan, S.J. (Cochin), Anastasios Yannoulatos (Orthodox, Athens/ Geneva), and R. Pierce Beaver (Chicago).

At the official opening the Norwegian minister of foreign affairs greeted the participants, and Gensichen delivered the keynote address. During the conference a reception at City Hall was hosted by the mayor of Oslo. The closing session included an address by the bishop of Oslo, Fridtjov Birkeli, who was also chairman of the Council of the Egede Institute. The main presentations for discussion were "Religion and Change," by Karl Henry Pfeffer (Münster) and Arnulf Camps; "Mission after Vatican II," by Samuel Rayan; and "Mission after Uppsala," by Johannes Aagaard (Aarhus). Stanley J. Samartha and Steven G. Mackie (both working in Geneva) spoke about WCC studies and discussions.

Frans J. Verstraelen recalls that, while Myklebust was eager to officially launch IAMS at the Oslo conference, there was opposition because it did not seem appropriate to launch an international organization when nearly all those present were Westerners. Therefore it was agreed that the official inauguration would take place at the next meeting.

Myklebust has described what happened: "On the last day of the meeting the Egede Institute, through its director, once more made a strong plea for the establishment of an international association for mission studies. It was proposed, seconded, and unanimously agreed to that such an association should immediately be set up. On the invitation of the Dutch members, it was decided to meet again in 1972 in Driebergen, Holland."

Andrew Walls reported in the business meeting that a group of participants had met to discuss concerns about bibliographic, documentation, and information services. They concluded that there was a need for more information about existing resources

---

Selly Oak is reported in Gerald H. Anderson, "Prevenient Grace in World Mission," in *World Mission in the Wesleyan Spirit*, ed. Darrell L. Whiteman and Gerald H. Anderson (Franklin, Tenn.: Providence House Publishers, 2009), pp. 43–52. Unfortunately, no other records of the Selly Oak meeting have been found, not even a list of the participants.

and services, and they requested that the Provisional Committee sponsor a questionnaire to this end, "and that future conferences should provide for news and discussion of documentation and other *instrumenta studiorum* for mission studies." This was the beginning of what would become a major continuing project and initiative of IAMS, known as DAB, and later as DABOH.

The meeting "recorded its disappointment that Professor Arno Lehmann, Halle, had been prevented from attending," and sent "a letter of greeting to Professor J. Glazik, Münster, in his illness." (Glazik, a prominent German Catholic missiologist, had given a paper at the Selly Oak meeting in 1968.)

Thus the Association was established in Oslo but would be formally organized and inaugurated at Driebergen. A Provisional Committee was appointed, consisting of the five persons who had planned the Oslo conference, with Andrew F. Walls (Aberdeen) as an additional member. Gensichen was elected president, Camps as vice president, and Myklebust as secretary/treasurer. One of their main responsibilities would be to draft a constitution for the new organization and also "to investigate the possibilities" for an international journal of missiology. In 1971 Gerald H. Anderson (Nashville), who was unable to attend the Oslo conference, was invited to join the Provisional Committee as a "corresponding member," since there were no funds for travel from overseas.

The Provisional Committee met briefly while in Oslo. They had a full meeting at Alverna, Netherlands, November 20–21, 1970, "the only meeting which, for financial and other reasons it [was] able to hold." A draft constitution was prepared for submission to the general meeting; "bye-laws might be developed separately as required." Myklebust would be the Association's editor, and the Provisional Committee would constitute an interim editorial board. It was agreed "to establish a working party (Mr. Walls acting as convener) to consider the suggestions made by the group on bibliography and documentation at the Oslo meeting, and to report at the next conference. Members suggested for the working party included Professors Anderson, Hopewell, Margull, Metzler, Moritzen, Promper and Turner, Abbe Bruis, and Mr. Hansen."

Further planning was carried on by correspondence and by a local committee from the newly established Dutch Interuniversity Institute for Missiological and Ecumenical Research (IIMO; Evert Jansen Schoonhoven, director, and Frans J. Verstraelen, associate director, Department of Missiology).

# I
# Driebergen, Netherlands, 1972

By the time of the inaugural assembly at the Instituut Kerk en Wereld in Driebergen, Netherlands, August 19–23, 1972, the Association had 244 members. Of these, 205 were individual members and 39 institutional members. The provisional membership fee was $3 (DM 10, £1.25) per year. A substantial program was arranged on the theme "Mission in the Context of Religions and Secularization," and 123 participants were registered, not counting several spouses who were present. While the group consisted primarily of European Protestants, there was strong Catholic participation, including several from Rome; numerous Americans, including well-known evangelicals; and at least 20 non-Western participants. It was a remarkable response after so many years of disappointment and frustration.

In his words of welcome, Willem C. van Unnik, chairperson of IIMO, mentioned that missiology was a relatively new theological discipline and was late in organizing itself. But research and reflection in this field were much needed, and he hoped this would be promoted by IAMS. Gensichen, as chairman of the meeting, noted that it was fitting to hold this inaugural assembly in the Netherlands, where in 1622 Antonius Walaeus of Leiden had founded the first missionary seminary, the Seminarium Indicum, exactly 350 years earlier. Plenary addresses on the main theme were given by the following:

Emmanuel A. Ayandele (Ibadan), "An African Viewpoint"
William D. Reyburn (London), "A Six-Continent Viewpoint"
Hans Waldenfels, S.J. (Wittlaer), "An Asian Viewpoint"
Won Yong Ji (Geneva), "Christian Witness in View of the
    Advance of Marxism in Asia"

Each address was followed by discussion in a plenary session and in groups. There were also group meetings according to spheres of interest, such as bibliography and documentation, teaching and research, and area reports.

In the business meeting, a draft constitution was presented and adopted after discussion. Charles W. Ranson (by then retired in the United States) presented the report of the Nominating Committee:

| President | Hans-Werner Gensichen (Heidelberg) |
|---|---|
| Vice president | Arnulf Camps, O.F.M. (Nijmegen) |
| Secretary-treasurer | Olav Guttorm Myklebust (Oslo) |

At-large members of the Executive Committee
Gerald H. Anderson (Nashville)
Stanley J. Samartha (Geneva)
Andrew F. Walls (Aberdeen)
Ludwig Wiedenmann (Bonn)

After discussion and voting, the report was adopted.

The offer of the Egede Institute, Oslo, to provide an office and secretarial services for the Association was gratefully accepted.

Andrew Walls presented the report of a working group on documentation and bibliography, with recommendations that were approved for this group to continue efforts to encourage the development of a comprehensive and fully ecumenical bibliography for mission studies, with standard bibliographic classification and forms of recording bibliographic information; also to ask institutions represented within the Association to cooperate in regional bibliographic coverage, to build lists of their periodical holdings, and to consider steps toward an eventual union catalog of periodicals in mission studies.

From the very outset there had been a major concern for an academic journal of mission studies to be published under the auspices of the Association, one that would be truly global and ecumenical in scope, and this objective was mentioned in the constitution. Myklebust gave a full report of steps that had been taken in this investigation and the problems they faced, mainly inadequate financial resources. The new Executive Committee was instructed to continue these investigations.

Finally, it was decided to have the next meeting of the Association in the summer of 1974, the place and dates to be determined by the Executive Committee.

The first issue of *IAMS News Letter*, edited by Myklebust, appeared in May 1973. In keeping with one of the objectives stated in the constitution of the Association, namely "to promote fellowship and cooperation among individuals and institutions engaged in mission studies and to facilitate mutual assistance and exchange of information between those engaged in such studies," the editor included articles about the newly formed American Society of Missiology and its journal *Missiology* (which had absorbed the influential smaller journal *Practical Anthropology*); the South African Missiological Society and its new journal *Missionalia* (successor to the quarterly bulletin *Missionaria* published since 1969); and the Project for New Religious Movements, headed by Harold W. Turner in the Department of Religious Studies at the University of Aberdeen. It was also announced that the next conference of the Association would be held July 29–August 1, 1974, in Frankfurt, West Germany (rather than in Vienna, Austria, as originally announced). Oddly, there was no report on the IAMS inaugural assembly in Driebergen.[1]

1. The most comprehensive published report about the Driebergen Assembly was by Frans J. Verstraelen, "Het eerste intercontinentale missiologencongres. Driebergen, 19–23 augustus 1972," *Wereld en Zending* 1, no. 5 (1972): 371–74.

# II
# Frankfurt, West Germany, 1974

The second IAMS assembly was held at the Sankt Georgen Phil-osophish-Theologische Hochschule, a Jesuit institution, in Frank-furt, West Germany, from July 29 to August 2, 1974, with 141 regis-tered participants, including about 38 from non-Western countries. The theme, "Mission in Relation to Movements of Innovation in Religion," gave attention to (1) the cultural, historical, and social roots of these movements and the spiritual and doctrinal meaning of these roots to their devotees, and (2) their significance for the understanding of Christian mission. Seminar groups dealt with movements of innovation in primal religions, Hinduism, Bud-dhism, Islam, and Marxism, and in the post-Christian West.

On the opening night President Gensichen welcomed the par-ticipants. In the course of his remarks he mentioned that one mem-ber had written a letter to the Executive Committee, criticizing the tone and content of the preliminary material announcing the pro-gram for the meeting. In responding to this criticism, Gensichen reminded the participants about the constitutional character and purpose of IAMS and clarified the distinction between a mission-ary society and a society for the study of mission. The importance of this clarification was fundamental for the young organization, so it is worth quoting Gensichen at length:

> A highly respected member of our fellowship has recently in a letter voiced some concern with regard to the program of this assembly. I quote: "Scholarship in abundance. Wise and witty remarks about movements of innovation . . . but very little mis-sionary concern, missionary methods, missionary goals, and no biblical references. The Koran and Bhagavadgita are mentioned but not the Bible. . . . I wonder whether our IAMS has fallen vic-tim to the idea of Splendid Scholarly Study, Whether the Gospel is Proclaimed or Not? Whether Men are Discipled or Not?"
>
> I know the writer, and I know that his concern is serious and that all of you here are willing to take it seriously. I feel that this is a welcome opportunity to remind ourselves of what

the Constitution of the IAMS defines as the first of the objectives of the Association—"to promote the scholarly study of theological, historical, social and practical questions relating to the missionary dimension of the Christian message." This, I think, is a very accurate description of the essential oneness of purpose to which our Association is committed: scholarly study related to the missionary dimension of the Christian message, or in other words, contextuality in order to let the text become alive and effective. We should indeed not be true to our purpose if we should concentrate exclusively on the context to the detriment of the text. But we should not be true to our purpose either if we should concentrate exclusively on the "text," on the action of God in Christ as a divine bolt from the blue, in isolation from all the other causal factors at work in history. . . . If this is true—and I believe it is—the consequences for every one of us as a missiologist, and for all of us as an Association for Mission Studies, are obvious. There can and must be no dichotomy, no separation between our scholarly and our missionary concern. Even as we are going to deal during these days with Movements of Innovation, we cannot do so apart from Him or without Him who has said, "Behold, I make all things new." As we as an Association try to live up to the objectives laid down in our Constitution, we do so within the missionary dimension, which, after all, is always greater than all our attempts to circumscribe or to confine it. Let me close with a very relevant saying of Martin Luther which may be considered as a challenge and a promise, both for the work ahead of us during these days and for the work of the Association as a whole: *Tota nostra operatio confessio est*—whatever we do should be a confession.[1]

No other comment or criticism of this nature arose throughout the meeting.

The opening address on the theme of the conference was given by Stanley J. Samartha from India, who was then director of the Program on Dialogue in the World Council of Churches, Geneva.[2]

1. The letter of criticism, dated June 18, 1974, and sent to the Executive Committee, was from Donald A. McGavran at Fuller Theological Seminary. As a member of the Executive Committee, this writer has a copy of the letter in his personal file, and also the text of Gensichen's remarks. Neither was ever published.

2. Samartha's address was published in *IAMS NL*, nos. 6–7 (May 1975): 3–11; also in *Missiology* 3, no. 2 (1975): 143–53; and a Swedish translation in *Svensk misionstidskrift* 62, no. 3 (1974): 108–14. My quotations, however, are taken from his text that was distributed at the conference.

He pointed to certain issues that emerged from the theme "which demand our careful attention," such as:

What does it mean to participate in God's continuing mission in the world today as we live together with our neighbors who belong to various faiths, cultures and ideologies? How can we be committed Christians who firmly believe that "if anyone is in Christ he is a new creation" (2 Cor. 5) and, at the same time, be open to movements of innovation, of renewal, of unfamiliar creativity among people of other faiths and ideologies? Can we be committed to the mission of the Church without being closed and be open to insights from others without being shallow? Can the word "mission" . . . be so easily connected with the words "movements of innovation" with a simple conjunction "and" without any qualification whatsoever?

In response to these questions, Samartha urged, "If we acknowledge the comprehensiveness of God's mission in the world and the activities of the Holy Spirit in history, including contemporary history, then surely the new movements we are talking about cannot be outside God's all-embracing work. The question therefore would be one of discerning the points where God is at work and of participating in his continuing mission."

He concluded: "As we struggle to understand the meaning of mission in relation to new movements, we must venture to move into new relationships with people, even though we do not know where we are being led. Nothing in the Christian life or in the history of the Christian Church suggests that there can be creativity without taking risks or newness without suffering. Our hope lies in the continuing work of the Holy Spirit in judgment, mercy, and new creation."

The conference program also included workshops on contemporary China, Christian art and architecture, and mutual missionary assistance between churches. In addition, papers were given by David Bosch ("Missiology in South Africa"), John Pobee ("Church and State in the Vasco da Gama Era"), and Wi Jo Kang ("The Influence of the 'Unification Church Movement' of Korea within the U.S.A."). There was also a session devoted to reporting on the recently held Lausanne Conference, given by a number of participants, followed by lively discussion.

In the business meeting on July 31, it was reported that the Executive Committee had met previously on three occasions, each time in Frankfurt: November 24–25, 1972; June 22–23, 1973; and (during the general meeting of the Association) July 29–30, 1974. Membership had increased from 244 (205 individual, 39 corporate) in 1972, at the time of Driebergen, to 323 (273 individual, 50 corporate) in July 1974, with members representing all six continents and all major confessions of the church universal. Five issues of the *IAMS News Letter* (*NL*), edited by the general secretary, had been published. For financial and other reasons it was still not possible to proceed with launching an academic journal of mission studies. Walls reported on the activities of the working party on bibliography and documentation (DAB). Myklebust announced his desire to retire as secretary and treasurer. Bengt Sundkler presented the report of the Nominating Committee, and the following officers were elected:

| | |
|---|---|
| President | Arnulf Camps, O.F.M. (Nijmegen) |
| Vice president | Stanley J. Samartha (Geneva) |
| General secretary | Andrew F. Walls (Aberdeen) |
| Treasurer | Paul R. Clifford (Selly Oak, Birmingham) |

At-large members of the Executive Committee
  Gerald H. Anderson (Ventnor, N.J.)
  Orlando Costas (San José, Costa Rica)
  Hans-Werner Gensichen (Heidelberg)
  Harriet Sibisi (Oxford/South Africa)

The incoming president expressed the gratitude of the Association to the retiring secretary-treasurer, O. G. Myklebust, and to the Egede Institute, Oslo. In recognition of his extraordinary contribution as a "founding father," the Association elected Myklebust an honorary life member of the Executive Committee. It was the last IAMS meeting he was able to attend.

It was agreed that the secretariat of the Association would be transferred to the Scottish Institute of Missionary Studies in the Department of Religious Studies at the University of Aberdeen, Scotland. And the office of the treasury would be established at Selly Oak Colleges, Birmingham.

In the business meeting, Orlando Costas made an impassioned intervention, stressing the desirability of meeting in a so-called Third World country, and of finding ways of increasing Third World participation. The next meeting of the Association was scheduled for 1976, and it was agreed that it would be desir-

able for future meetings to be rotated among the various continents.

The election of a new president, a new general secretary, and
a new treasurer gave momentum in a time of significant transition
for the Association.

Before the conference ended, the new Executive Committee
met with members of the old Executive on August 1, 1974. It was
agreed that the next Executive Committee meeting would be at
Selly Oak Colleges, Birmingham, November 15–16, 1974, where
the main business would be to decide on the place and dates for
the next IAMS assembly. In the meanwhile, various members were
assigned to gather information on the logistics of holding the 1976
meeting in Mexico, Costa Rica, or Scotland.

An editorial by Andrew Walls in the next issue of the *News
Letter* (nos. 6–7, May 1975) observed that the Frankfurt meeting
"was more catholic both in its international composition and in the
range of theological and confessional viewpoints than its predeces-
sors; and fundamental differences were expressed and discussed
with charity, courtesy and scholarship." In addition to reports on
the Frankfurt meeting and news of the Association, a letter from
the general secretary dated July 1975 was enclosed, announcing
that, after the preparation of the *News Letter*, the Executive Committee had decided that the next meeting of the Association would
take place August 25–31, 1976, in San José, Costa Rica, with the
theme "Tradition and Reconstruction in Mission: Where Are We in
Mission Today?"

# III
# San José, Costa Rica, 1976

In the following *News Letter* (nos. 8–9, May 1976), General Secretary Walls wrote an introduction in which he said,

> As this issue is prepared, we await the meeting of the Association in San José, Costa Rica. . . . The first meeting outside Europe, the first meeting in the "Third World," San José reflects a total shift in the Association's center of gravity. The shift is expected to be reflected in the attendance at the meeting and in the forms the discussion takes. At the center of our discussion lies the question of the very nature of mission studies. Latin America will set the tone: responses will come from the other continents. After San José, it seems safe to say, the I.A.M.S. will never be the same again.

The meeting in San José, Costa Rica, July 24–31, 1976, on the theme "Tradition and Reconstruction in Mission: Where Are We in Mission Today?" met in the Gran Hotel in the center of San José, the capital city, after original plans to meet at a Roman Catholic seminary fell through on short notice. (Some members complained that the hotel was *too Gran* for a mission conference that was concerned about issues of poverty and solidarity with the poor!) There were about one hundred participants from twenty-six countries, which included only a small number of Roman Catholics. Arrangements for the conference were organized by a local committee consisting of four institutions, under the leadership of Orlando E. Costas, director of the Latin America Evangelical Center for Pastoral Studies (CELEP) in San José, with assistance from John Kessler, who had done his Ph.D. in Utrecht and was living in Costa Rica. By coincidence, the directors of the Theological Education Fund of the World Council of Churches were meeting near San José at the same time as IAMS. In response to an initiative from Arnulf Camps, as later described by one participant, "a sudden and cordial appearance of the papal nuncio himself in mid-conference

17

dramatically papered over the difficulties [caused by the cancellation of the Catholic seminary facilities for the meeting] . . . and the nuncio said he could and would have fixed everything up for the congress—if he had known about its plans beforehand."

In the opening session President Camps, speaking in Spanish, welcomed the participants and gave a brief history of IAMS and a description of the theme and goal of the conference. This was followed by an inaugural message in Spanish by Emilio Castro from the WCC. He spoke about persecution and the suppression of human rights as the context for mission in a growing number of countries. The introductory paper on the theme of the conference was given by Orlando Costas. He described "the hopeful struggle for new forms of understanding and carrying out Christian mission in the light of the great continental challenges, and the zealous struggle to conserve the missionary heritage of our forebears."

Two series of small groups were organized that brought reports to the meeting: *geographic-cultural groups* (Latin America and Caribbean, Africa, Asia, Oceania, Europe and North America, and the Middle East) and *topical groups* (dealing with mission and culture, mission and pluralism, mission and unity, mission and political and economic order, and spirituality and mission). Short papers, with responses, were given on the nature and purpose of mission: African view (E. K. Mosothoane), Asian view (D. S. Amalorpavadass), Orthodox view (Nikos Nissiotis), and Catholic missiology in Europe (Bernward Willeke). There were also workshops on partnership in mission, women and mission, documentation and bibliography, non-Western church history, and guru movements.

In the general meeting of the Association, the general secretary reported that membership had now reached 383 (329 individual and 54 corporate members) from forty nations. The Executive Committee had met four times between assemblies, twice in Amsterdam and twice in Birmingham. (Actually, they met five times, counting the first meeting in Frankfurt on August 1, 1974.) Originally the committee had thought to have this assembly in Aberdeen, but after further consideration (with persuasive objections and promises from Orlando Costas), it was decided to meet in Costa Rica, despite considerable logistic and financial challenges. Once again the question of a journal had been considered, and it was concluded that "at this juncture a new formal journal of missiology was probably not desirable, but that the *Newsletter* should contain more information on research and cognate matters; and that the possibility of occasional papers . . . was a real possibility following the next meeting."

Several recommendations were approved that stressed "such missiological issues as mission to six continents, the necessity of recovering the central demands of the Gospel in their fullness, the centrality of the support of human rights, the importance of the struggle for just society and against racism, etc."[1] Despite the difficulties encountered in the first meeting of the Association held in the Third World, General Secretary Walls concluded his report to this meeting with a summary of accomplishments since Frankfurt:

> We recognize and thank God for work stimulated by the fellowship in Christian Scholarship provided by the Association: the informal contacts made and strengthened, the enrichment of personal contact and wider knowledge. It is pleasant to think that a meeting has taken place in Papua New Guinea this year which is in part a direct result of Frankfurt; it is certain that many members can point to things which have enriched their work, widened and improved their standards of performing it, widened their horizons or increased their appetites for fellowship, which are the result of the contacts fostered by IAMS. While the Executive Committee in giving this account of their stewardship are humbly grateful for the tangible results of the Association's actions from 1974 to 1976, they recognize that our most important assets are the invisible ones.

Once again, there was considerable turnover among the officers, with Stanley Samartha and Andrew Walls declining another term. The membership elected the following officers and members of the new Executive Committee:

| | |
|---|---|
| President | Arnulf Camps, O.F.M. (Nijmegen) |
| Vice president | Johannes Aagaard (Aarhus) |
| General secretary | Frans J. Verstraelen (Leiden) |
| Treasurer | Paul R. Clifford (Birmingham) |

---

1. "Nearly all the papers" and reports from the San José meeting were published in *IAMS NL*, no. 10 (March 1977). The appendix in that issue includes also a list of reports and evaluations of the meeting that appeared in other journals. Unfortunately, confusion appeared in some reports that referred to this as the Fourth Congress of IAMS, while others referred to it correctly as the Third Congress.

At-large members of the Executive Committee
Jonathan Chao (Hong Kong)
Larry Egan, M.M. (Maryknoll, N.Y.)
Manuel J. Gaxiola (Mexico City)
Godwin O. M. Tasie (Jos)

While the geographic representation in the Executive Committee increased to five continents, the number of women in the committee decreased from one to zero. In the year following the meeting, Larry Egan resigned from the Executive Committee for personal reasons and was replaced by Clarence Engler, also from Maryknoll, New York.

A special issue of the *News Letter* (no. 10 [Mar. 1977]) published "nearly all the papers" that were presented during the meeting in San José.

Once again the office of the secretariat relocated, this time from Aberdeen to IIMO, in Leiden, where Frans J. Verstraelen, the new general secretary, was the associate director of the Department of Missiology.

# IV
# Maryknoll, New York, U.S.A., 1978

Two weeks before he died in August 1977 at the age of seventy-three, Max Warren wrote to the IAMS general secretary, Frans J. Verstraelen, with his response to a questionnaire in preparation for the coming conference at Maryknoll. Warren was the distinguished Anglican missiologist who served as general secretary of the Church Missionary Society and wrote the *CMS News-letter* for twenty-one years. An early member of the Association, he was canon of Westminster Abbey, London, and had given a paper at the 1968 mission consultation at Selly Oak Colleges. Describing Warren as "one of the founding fathers of the IAMS," Verstraelen published his response in the *IAMS News Letter* (no. 11 [Nov. 1977]) as "The Last Will of Dr. Max Warren for the IAMS."

Q. What do you find to be the most painful experiences which challenge mission today?

A: For me speaking within the Anglican communion in general, and the Church of England in particular, there is a terrible failure of nerve about the missionary enterprise. There is doubt as to its authenticity today, and a widespread misunderstanding of history. The sudden discovery of other Religions, like arrival of an immigrant community, all this is creating confusion of mind. I have no right to comment on other Churches. But, by and large, so it seems to me the only Christians who have not lost their nerve are to be found among the most conservative groups, especially in North America.

Q: What do you think is the major theological question underlying your understanding of mission in the light of your answer to the first question?

A: There is a real need to recover a belief in the Holy Spirit, to understand him as not only influencing the individual but operating in history. There is a need to realize that the Great Commission at the end of Matthew's Gospel is only a brief summary of the implications of everything in the New Testament.

21

According to the general secretary, Warren's last book, *I Believe in the Great Commission* (1976), was "the one book that the IAMS Executive Committee wants to recommend for reading in preparation of the Maryknoll Conference: as a platform which, because of both its ecumenical and its evangelical orientation, can contribute towards overcoming the polarized positions that hinder and hamper the execution of the 'Great Commission' in our days."

It was also reported in *News Letter* 13 (Dec. 1978) that Max Warren had written "his last major missiological contribution shortly before his death." This was an essay that appeared in a Festschrift for J. Verkuyl, which included the following sentences:

> The International Association for Mission Studies, with its centre in Leiden, has for its objects the scholarly study of every subject which can have a bearing on "the missionary dimension of the Christian message"; to relate mission studies to inter-disciplinary research; to promote fellowship and cooperation on the part of all engaged in "Mission Studies"; to facilitate mutual assistance and exchange of information; to organise international conferences; and to encourage the creation of centres of research. This International Association is manifestly indispensable if the practice of Mission is to be undergirded by thorough study of all the factors which have a direct bearing on Mission today.[1]

This was a remarkable testimony to the significant role and contribution of IAMS after only five years of its existence, given by one of the most respected missiologists in the world, particularly in light of the initial resistance and objections to the formation of the Association.

The Executive Committee met in Amsterdam (Nov. 1976), Aarhus, Denmark (Mar. 1977), Selly Oak Colleges, Birmingham (Oct. 1977), Maryknoll, New York (Feb. 1978), and several times in August during the fourth assembly at Maryknoll. In addition to planning the program for the assembly at these meetings, the treasurer explained that some amendments to the constitution were necessary in order to register as a charity in Britain and that these would be presented to the General Assembly for approval.

---

1. Max Warren, "The Fusion of I.M.C. and W.C.C. at New Delhi: Retrospective Thoughts After a Decade and a Half," in *Zending op Weg naar de Toekomst. Essays aangeboden aan Prof. Dr. J. Verkuyl* (Kampen: Kok, 1978), pp. 200–201.

It was also agreed to recommend an increase in the annual membership subscription fee to $10 for individual members and a minimum of $20 for corporate members, and to hold the next assembly in 1981.

*News Letter* 12 (May 1978) was devoted mainly to articles relating to the forthcoming conference at Maryknoll, giving helpful information on the context and local setting, religion and mission in the United States, U.S. missionary outreach, and information on Maryknoll.

The IAMS Fourth Assembly was held at Maryknoll, hosted by the Maryknoll Fathers, Brothers, and Sisters, August 21–26, 1978, on the general theme "Credibility and Spirituality in Mission." The North American Association of Professors of Mission (APM) held a brief meeting immediately preceding the IAMS conference at Maryknoll. The American Society of Missiology (ASM) members joined in the IAMS meeting, with provision in the schedule for the ASM to have a session for its own business meeting, at which time Ralph Winter gave his presidential address, "Protestant Mission Societies: The American Experience."[2] The ASM also sponsored a barbecue picnic for IAMS during the conference.

The opening session on Monday afternoon featured a welcome by the president, Arnulf Camps, who reviewed the background and history of IAMS that had led up to this assembly. Then followed remarks by representatives of Maryknoll and ASM, and the IAMS general secretary, followed by a reception sponsored by Orbis Books, the publishing imprint of Maryknoll, where each participant was given a copy of Michael Collins Reilly's book *Spirituality for Mission*.

The program for the assembly included three "key lectures," given by Ulrich Duchrow ("The Spiritual Dimensions of the Scientific World"), Robert Muller ("The Spiritual Dimension of the World Order"), and Eugene Stockwell ("Spirituality and Struggle for Fullness of Life"). Members could choose among the following eight workshops:

Decasting the Ministries
Dialogue and/or Conversion
Hermeneutics of Mission
Marxism
Mission History

---

2. Published in *Missiology* 7, no. 2 (1979): 139–78.

New Religious Movements
Pluralism: Partnership or Polarization in Mission?
Religious Components of the New International World Order

Several time periods were reserved for open forums, when members could present brief papers or reports on themes and topics that were the result of their research and writing.

More than 160 participants registered for the conference. Upon arrival at Maryknoll, each person received a program workbook with more than 400 pages of study material related to the themes of the eight workshops.

In the business meeting, it was reported that the total membership of IAMS stood at 544 (488 individual and 56 corporate members). Recommendations for amendments to the constitution, as well as an increase in subscription fees, were approved. It was also decided to establish a standing committee to deal with issues of documentation, archives, and bibliography, which formally recognized what had been a major concern of IAMS from its beginning.

John Pobee presented the report of the Nominating Committee, which included increasing the number of members on the Executive Committee from eight to nine, to accommodate desired geographic, confessional, and gender representation. The following persons were proposed:

President          Johannes Aagaard (Denmark)
Vice president     Gerald H. Anderson (U.S.A.)
General secretary  Frans J. Verstraelen (Netherlands)
Treasurer          Paul R. Clifford (U.K.)

At-large members of the Executive Committee
    Ade Adegbola (Nigeria)
    Arnulf Camps, O.F.M. (Netherlands)
    Joan Chatfield, M.M. (U.S.A.)
    D. Preman Niles (Sri Lanka)
    C. René Padilla (Argentina)

After discussion and voting, the report was approved. Following his election as the new president, Johannes Aagaard thanked the members for their confidence shown toward the new Executive Committee and noted, "We should be aware of the fact that the IAMS represents the broadest ecumenical movement in Christendom, with so many confessional shades and theological orientations, meeting for discussion and mutual challenge."

Invitations and suggestions were received to hold the next General Assembly, in 1981, in Ghana, in Aberdeen, Scotland, or in Asia.

With a subsidy from IAMS, the papers and findings of the Maryknoll conference were published in the January 1979 issue of the ASM journal, *Missiology*, which was sent to all participants. It included the main addresses, workshop reports, a summary of open forum papers, and the prayer sessions, together with letters from the president and the general secretary of IAMS.

*News Letter* 13 (Dec. 1978) presented general information about what happened at the meeting, especially the business meeting, including the reports of the general secretary, the treasurer, and Andrew Walls, chairman of the working party on Bibliography, Archives, and Documentation, who gave an impassioned plea that this area of activity "can no longer be an appendage of the IAMS, that it be considered in an occasional session; that it must be a major function of the Association, requiring the allocation of a portion of its budget; implying a programme with established priorities and defined responsibilities . . . ; promoting active cooperation among the members of IAMS and the institutions they represent." At the meeting it was also decided to launch an IAMS project "Biblical Studies and Missiology" (BISAM), which would study "the importance of recent exegetical research for missiology" and reclaim the New Testament as basically a missionary document. "A first fruit of the project was the valuable publication edited by M. R. Spindler and P. R. Middelkoop on 'Bible and Mission: A partially annotated bibliography 1960–1980' (Leiden and Utrecht: IIMO, 1981), and Spindler's challenging article on 'Visa for Witness: A new focus on the theology of mission and ecumenism,' in *Mission Studies* no. 5 (1986), pp. 51–60."[3]

*News Letter* 14 (June 1979) contained reactions to the Maryknoll conference from participants that were published in various periodicals and newspapers in France, Germany, Netherlands, Pakistan, Sweden, Switzerland, the U.K., and the United States. Additional published reactions were reported in *NL*, no. 15 (Dec. 1979). A Catholic missionary concluded his report, which was published in Pakistan, "I was very happy to meet a group which

3. Joachim Wietzke, "Brief Historical Sketch of IAMS" [1993], on IAMS Web site (www.missionstudies.org), refers to the Maryknoll report in *NL*, no. 13 (Dec. 1978): 31, and also points to an article by David Bosch, "The Scope of the 'BISAM' Project," *MS* 6, no. 1 (1989): 61–69.

is going through a great deal of questioning, and still speaks so optimistically of the future, so open to the values and aspirations of people in the Third World." Michael Fitzgerald, M.Afr., reported in the *Tablet* (U.K.), "One came away with the impression that the members of the Conference were interested in mission not so much as a discipline as a vital activity of the Church." It was also noted that this meeting was a real advancement beyond earlier meetings, "as regards both organization and religious depth."

Following the Maryknoll conference, IAMS launched the BISAM, starting on regional levels. The goal was to have a task force in each continent that would develop its own format, with the common goal "to relate biblical studies to mission studies and vice versa."

# V
# Bangalore (Whitefield), India, 1982

The new Executive Committee held seven meetings: at Maryknoll and Amsterdam (1978), Aberdeen (Aug. 1979), Rome (July 1980), Bangalore (Jan. 1981), and Croydon (near London, Apr. 1981), as well as during the conference itself (Jan. 1982). At the meeting in Aberdeen it was decided that the next general conference would be held in Bangalore, India, January 4–9, 1982. It was considered wise not to have the conference at the beginning of 1981, because three major theological and missionary meetings would take place in 1980 (Third World Theologians, WCC Commission on World Mission and Evangelism, and Lausanne Committee for World Evangelization). In addition, IAMS was planning to have a con-sultation July 24–30, 1980, in Rome on the topic "Mission Studies and Information Management." Organized mainly by the DAB working party, this would involve nearly sixty participants. The program for the Rome DAB meeting was published in the *News Letter* 15 (Dec. 1979), and a report after the meeting was in *NL*, nos. 16–17 (May–Oct. 1980).[1] Since this meeting would require addi-

1. The Rome DAB meeting, July 24–30, 1980, was chaired by Andrew F. Walls, with Willi Henkel, O.M.I., as secretary. Key lectures and resource persons included Cees Hamelink, from the Institute of Social Studies in The Hague, who had published widely on the implications of advanced informa-tion technology for international communications and for the churches' par-ticipation in public communications; Robert Malloy, director of libraries at the Smithsonian Institution, Washington, D.C.; Richard Gray, from the School of Oriental and African Studies, University of London; Lajos Pasztor, director of the Vatican Secret Archives; G. O. M. Tasie, from Jos University, Nigeria; Paul Jenkins, archivist at the Basel Mission; and Stephen Peterson, librarian and archivist at Yale Divinity School, New Haven. The meeting was held in the new Pope John Paul II Aula near the Vatican Mission Library on the campus of Urbaniana University. An initial report on the meeting by Walls and Henkel is in *NL*, nos. 16–17 (May–Oct. 1980), with additional reports, actions, reactions, and a statement from the meeting in *NL*, nos. 18–19 (May–Oct. 1981). The full report of the meeting (154 pages) was produced on two microfiches and sent free of charge to every IAMS member. The present writer has often said this

tional work for the IAMS secretariat, the postponement of the General Assembly until January 1982 would allow for better preparation, in which the results of the above-mentioned meetings could be incorporated, and there would be more time for raising funds. It would also allow more time to involve colleagues in India and all IAMS members to contribute to a discussion and decision about the choice of a theme and program.

Immediately following the DAB meeting in Rome, the Executive Committee met July 30–August 1, 1980, to discuss plans for the next general conference, in Bangalore. Tentative ideas for the

**DAB consultation, "Mission Studies and Information Management," Rome, July 1980**

theme and structure of the program were discussed, but no decisions would be made until a questionnaire for suggestions could be sent to all members, and until consultation with colleagues in India could take place.

When the committee met at United Theological College, Bangalore, January 1–5, 1981, it was decided that the facilities of the college, which suffered a chronic shortage of water, were inadequate

---

was the most interesting conference he ever attended. Following the conference, participants had an opportunity to attend a general audience with Pope John Paul II in front of St. Peter's Basilica, where the pope greeted them in his remarks. Soon after the conference, Walls suffered a heart attack, but he made a full recovery following surgery.

to accommodate the IAMS conference. Instead, the conference would be held in Whitefield, near Bangalore, at the Ecumenical Christian Centre (ECC), a study center sponsored by twenty-three national churches and organizations. For serving meals to such a large group, a colorful *shamiana* (tent) would be set up outdoors, and about twenty participants would be lodged five kilometers from ECC at Kristu Jyothi College.

After a meeting with fourteen colleagues from various Indian churches, seminaries, and organizations, and with suggestions received from IAMS members, a theme was decided on: "Christ's Mission with [*or sometimes*, to] the Multitude: Salvation, Suffering, and Struggle." There would be more emphasis on Bible study, led by René Padilla, and coordination of worship would be arranged by Joan Chatfield. There would be three key lectures—by Stanley J. Samartha, Preman Niles, and Johannes Aagaard (presidential address)—with workshops and open forums. Following the conference, there would be a two-day DAB consultation, January 9–11. Study papers were sent in advance to participants who signed up for one of the nine workshops:

Ashrams and Basic Christian Communities
Bible and Mission
China and Christianity
Evangelism and the Poor
Inculturation and Theology in Context
Mission and Church Growth in India
Muslim *Dawah* and Christian Mission
Research on Religion and Society in India
Theological Study on North Indian Hinduism and Tibetan
    Buddhism

A new feature—"exposure experiences"—was arranged as a preconference option (strongly recommended) for participants coming from outside of India. Taking place in different parts of India and Sri Lanka, these would expose participants to various contexts and ministries in that part of the world for several days before the conference began. Options included programs in Colombo, Bombay, Delhi, Bangalore, and various Christian ashrams, and members could arrange their own visit according to their interest. The present writer, for example, arranged to visit the Christian Medical College and Hospital in Vellore, the Scheffelain Leprosy Research and Training Center at Karigiri, and the

Christian Ashram at Tirupattur. A time was provided on the afternoon of the first day of the conference for persons to report on their exposure experiences. The response was overwhelmingly positive, and this feature was recommended for future conferences.

The IAMS Fifth Assembly, with 120 registered participants, began on Monday evening, January 4, 1982, with President Johannes Aagaard presiding. This was the first IAMS conference in which the majority of participants (63) came from non-Western countries. Unfortunately, none of the South Africans (black and white) who were registered for the conference were able to attend, because their applications for visas were not granted by India.[2] Greetings and welcome were given by K. C. Abraham, director of the Ecumenical Christian Centre, and Russell Chandran, principal of United Theological College, Bangalore.

The keynote address was given by Stanley J. Samartha, former vice president of IAMS, who had also given the keynote address at the Frankfurt conference in 1974, and who was now living in Bangalore after serving from 1968 until 1980 as director of the WCC Program on Dialogue with People of Living Faiths and Ideologies. His topic was "Indian Realities and the Wholeness of Christ," at a time, he said, "when one era in Christian mission has ended and new forms of Christian witness are struggling to be born."[3]

With reference to the two world mission conferences held in 1980 (which he did not attend), Samartha said, "I find both Pattaya [the Lausanne meeting] and Melbourne [the WCC meeting] unhelpful in the context of Indian realities because neither paid sufficient attention to the religious dimensions of life. . . . When these religions continue to offer alternate ways of salvation, how can any world conference on mission so blindly ignore them?" It is in the struggle of the poor and oppressed people for a just society in India, and in the quest for peace within the human heart, he said, "that Indian Christians should find an entry to the heart of

2. Three of the black South Africans eventually received visas, but too late to attend the conference. So arrangements were made for them to come to India later for a two-week exposure, to "see India through black eyes," in visits to church ministries, theological colleges, research centers, development projects, and meetings with Muslims, Hindus, and Dalits in Bangalore, Madurai, New Delhi, and Bombay. A report on their visit is in *NL*, no. 20 (1982).

3. Samartha's address was published with the other papers and reports in *Missiology* 10, no. 3 (July 1982), but quotations here are taken from the text that was distributed at the time he spoke.

contemporary Indian realities to be with Christ as he struggles and suffers to bring healing and wholeness to human life." But "the church's influence seems to be marginal," he said, because of "its preoccupation with institutional matters."

After his analysis of contemporary Indian realities, Samartha concluded by expressing the hope that "perhaps both Hindus and Christians can work together towards shaping that spirituality which is at once rooted in God and is sensitive to human needs. Not competition for converts, but seeking to compensate for that which is lacking in the other, might provide the way for mutual enrichment in the future. Co-operation in the struggle against injustice could also mean sharing the pilgrimage to the mountain of peace. . . . Hindus and Christians can stand together in humility to affirm, and even to celebrate, the ultimate mystery of God."

In his plenary address, "Mission and the Peoples of Asia," Preman Niles said that a primary concern of Asian theologians was increasingly "to discover the significance of other faiths for a deeper understanding of the Christian faith." And "a central point of departure for relating to other faiths" is Christ, rather than the church or Christianity, starting from a framework of creation rather than redemption history.

In his presidential address, "The Soft Age Has Gone," Johannes Aagaard concluded, "Insofar as our witness to Christ is, in fact, a witness with the people, the *ochloi*, the multitudes, then we are in trouble, for the powers and principalities—secular as well as religious—will not forget about it. We shall not get away with it without suffering perhaps even to the utmost—our death."

The program each day began with Bible study and ended with worship. On Thursday morning, after an introduction by K. C. Abraham, there was an excursion to visit several research centers and theological colleges in Bangalore. In the business meeting it was reported there were now 576 members of IAMS (518 individuals and 58 corporate members).

A report of the names proposed for the new Executive Committee was presented by Stanley Samartha, convener of the Nominating Committee. After discussion and voting, the following were elected:

| | |
|---|---|
| President | Gerald H. Anderson (U.S.A.) |
| Vice president | Joan Chatfield, M.M. (U.S.A.) |
| General secretary | Frans J. Verstraelen (Netherlands) |
| Treasurer | Paul R. Clifford (U.K.) |

> At-large members of the Executive Committee
> Hans-Jürgen Becken (West Germany)
> Wi Jo Kang (U.S.A.)
> Sebastian Karotemprel, S.D.B. (India)
> A. Ngindu Mushete (Zaire)
> C. René Padilla (Argentina)

Invitations and suggestions for the venue of the next conference included Zimbabwe, Selly Oak Colleges (U.K.), Jerusalem, and Nigeria. Annual membership subscription fees would be raised to $15 for individual members, and a minimum of $30 for corporate members.

Reports and reactions to the conference, including the business session and the DAB meeting (with twenty-nine participants from twelve countries) were published (with photos) in *NL*, no. 20 (May 1982). A full report of proceedings and plenary lectures, including the presidential address, a letter from the general secretary, the Bible studies, exposure reports, workshop reports, and an Open Letter to the Churches, were published in *Missiology* 10, no. 3 (July 1982), which was sent to all IAMS members. At least eleven other journals in several countries carried reports on the conference; these are listed and summarized in *NL*, no. 21. Additional "Aftermath of Bangalore" is reported in *NL*, nos. 22–23, including a letter received from Johannes Verkuyl in which he expressed his concern and criticism about the report of the workshop on Christian relations with Muslims, which said that "Christian theology must complete the evolution from ecclesiocentrism to Christocentrism to theocentrism." Verkuyl maintained that this kind of evolution "without the decisive place of Jesus Christ loses the life-string of the missionary mandate." The general secretary and editor, Frans J. Verstraelen, responded by saying that "the opinions or conclusions drawn in Workshops do not express the feeling or conviction of the IAMS as a whole; the IAMS is a forum for exchange of ideas, not a body that necessarily has to reach a common opinion."

In his report on the conference (in *NL*, no. 20), Kwame Bediako (Aberdeen and Ghana) described the conference as "an important landmark." He appreciated all aspects of the meeting, he said, but for him "the highlight of the Conference was the series of Bible expositions by Dr. C. René Padilla, of Argentina, on aspects of Jesus' encounter with, and mission to, the multitudes." Also, he said, "the Conference seemed to compel the recognition that missiologists are required to do more than provide studies and papers and engage in discussions and dialogues. At the end, the agreed statement on the Harijans [the 'untouchables'] can be pointed to as a sign that IAMS avoided the temptation of being a professional, academic club, and affirmed its identity as a fellowship of Christians whose very scholarly enterprise on behalf of the Christian world mission is also the context of their discipleship, and of their commitment to Jesus Christ, Lord, and Head of the Church."

The statement on the Harijans referred to by Bediako was a letter signed by eighty participants in the conference expressing concern about the denial of "elementary human rights" to this large segment of the population in India. The letter was addressed to the National Council of Churches in India, the Catholic Bishops' Conference of India, the Evangelical Fellowship of India, the Federation of Evangelical Churches in India, the WCC, and the Justice and Peace Commission in Vatican City, asking them to take appropriate action on this issue, to bring this problem before the world press, and to request the WCC and other Christian bodies to appoint a commission to document the facts, study the causes, and present its possible remedies. The letter was published in *NL*, no. 20.

During the conference a collection from participants was received (approx. US$255) for the Employees Welfare Fund as a token of appreciation and solidarity for the workers at ECC who helped to make the meeting so pleasant.

In keeping with IAMS tradition, the newly elected officers and members of the Executive Committee met with the outgoing members after the conference ended, on Saturday, January 9, for a time of sharing—to review decisions made at the conference, identify major issues and concerns (especially finances), and discuss the way forward. Minutes of the meeting noted that "in 1982 the IAMS is bringing its first decade to an end and is starting a second one, with thanks and appreciation for those who served on the committee before, and wishing vision and strength to the new officers and members of its Executive Committee."

# VI
# Harare, Zimbabwe, 1985

The Executive Committee elected at Bangalore met next at the Overseas Ministries Study Center in Ventnor, New Jersey, in June 1982. As several members of the IAMS standing committee of DAB were visiting the United States at that time, the occasion was used for a DAB committee meeting as well, chaired by Paul Jenkins, with Willi Henkel, O.M.I., as secretary, including Andrew Walls, David Bosch, Stephen Peterson, Frans J. Verstraelen, and Gerald Anderson.

The Executive Committee decided that *IAMS News Letter* would be converted into a journal to be named *Mission Studies: Journal of the International Association for Mission Studies*, thereby to fulfill one of the original goals envisioned by Myklebust in 1951, put forward again at the inaugural assembly in 1972, that the Association should "publish a scholarly journal of high standard." In addition to scholarly articles, information about IAMS activities and members would be featured prominently, especially about DAB and BISAM projects. Frans J. Verstraelen would continue as editor to provide continuity with the splendid work he had done in editing the *News Letter*. It was a memorable moment that marked a major advance in the life and work of IAMS.[1]

It was also decided that the next general meeting of IAMS would probably take place early in 1985 in Africa. A "firm and enthusiastic invitation" had been extended by the Department of Religious Studies at the University of Zimbabwe in Harare, so it was decided to explore this possibility by sending a small delegation to visit Harare on February 2–6, 1983. The visiting team included Gerald Anderson, Frans J. Verstraelen, and John Pobee. The report of the team's visit to Harare was sent in a "Special Letter" to IAMS members, dated April 28, 1983, recommending that the next confer-

1. In the next *NL* (no. 21 [Dec. 1982]), the general secretary announced, "This will be the last time that the IAMS *News Letter* appears under this title." In fact, however, another double issue was published (*NL*, nos. 22–23 [Dec. 1983]) before the journal *Mission Studies* began in summer 1984.

ence be held at the University of Zimbabwe, January 8–14, 1985, and inviting reactions and suggestions from members.

When the Executive Committee met next at Selly Oak Colleges, Birmingham, July 7–10, 1983, it reviewed the responses from members and the suggestions of the local committee in Harare before making several decisions regarding the forthcoming conference, its theme, program, and other features.

The theme of the conference would be "Christian Mission and Human Transformation." There would be a keynote speech by the president of Zimbabwe and two key lectures, in addition to the IAMS presidential address, with eight workshops, Bible study and worship, exposure experiences before the conference, forum papers presented by participants about their research projects, an excursion to visit some institutions in Harare during the conference, films, and the usual business session for reports from the general secretary and treasurer, and elections. To those who had registered for the conference, study papers on *all* workshops would be sent beforehand. Immediately following the conference there would be a two-day DAB consultation, January 14–16.[2]

---

2. In a personal memorandum, prepared at my request while he was a senior scholar in residence at OMSC in New Haven in May 2005, Frans J. Verstraelen wrote "Some Memories of IAMS." He had been the general secretary of IAMS from the 1976 meeting in Costa Rica to 1986, before Rome (1988); he later became a professor in the Department of Religious Studies, University of Zimbabwe. Regarding the Harare conference, he wrote the following: "An interesting aspect of preparing this conference was the invitation to the (then) President of Zimbabwe to give the opening lecture. [My wife] Gerdien and I went to visit [President Canaan] Banana in State House. We were formally received, served with drinks and small pancakes by servants with white gloves. While I explained IAMS, the topic of the conference, and extended on behalf of IAMS the invitation for the lecture, Gerdien had time to survey the 'ambiance,' and she discovered a number of Banana's diplomas exhibited above a kind of fireplace. Banana in principle agreed but said that he did not know whether at the time of the conference he still would be president, because the prime minister, Mugabe, aspired to become executive president. I told Banana that IAMS wanted him to deliver that lecture, being president or not. When he gave the speech at the conference, he was still president. (At that time I could not know that Banana as honorary professor would become my colleague [at Univ. of Zimbabwe], and that later he would end up in prison.) . . . Gerdien and I visited also the Catholic archbishop of Harare, Patrick Chikaipa, to invite him for the conference. He gave the impression of being interested but he did not show up." Unfortunately, on the evening of the opening session of the Harare conference, Verstraelen tripped and fell in the parking lot as he was hurrying to the meeting. His broken spectacles cut his forehead,

Final arrangements for the conference were reviewed when the Executive Committee met in Geneva, April 9–11, 1984. Special arrangements were made for about twenty local Zimbabweans to participate in the conference, in addition to the local committee, who would be guests of IAMS. There would be a brief prayer service each morning following breakfast, and worship each evening. There would be an evening session for reports on the exposure experiences, another evening for films, and also a

**Wi Jo Kang (left), Bishop Patrick Kalilombe, and James Scherer at the IAMS assembly, January 1985, Harare**

choice of three excursions in Harare on Saturday afternoon to visit the National Archives, Catholic and Protestant seminaries, a wild game park, and national monuments. On Sunday morning participants could worship at local churches. Thursday evening would be the presidential address, followed by a reception including the local committee.

The first issue of *Mission Studies: Journal of the International Association for Mission Studies* (vol. 1, no. 1 [1984]), successor to the *IAMS News Letter*, included four articles related to topics to be dis-

---

causing a deep wound and heavy bleeding. He was taken by private car to a clinic, where they stitched the wound and told him he should stay in bed for a day or two. But the next morning he was determined not to miss the lecture by President Banana, so he sat in the back of the assembly hall with a bandage on his face, listening to the lecture and the lively discussion that followed.

cussed at the forthcoming conference in Harare, along with information about the program and logistics. The next issue of the journal (vol. 1, no. 2, also 1984) contained study papers for the eight
workshops at the conference. Myklebust wrote to the general secretary, "I am writing this letter to congratulate you and the IAMS
on the appearance of the first issue of the first volume of *Mission
Studies*. The cover is very attractive, the printing excellent, and the
content varied, enriching and thought–provoking" (Oslo, July 30,
1984). For Myklebust, the journal was the fulfillment of one of his
original goals for the Association.

The opening session of the IAMS Sixth Assembly, on January 8, 1985, with 187 registered participants and invited guests,
was held in the new lecture theater of the university. It began
with greetings and welcome to the conference by Walter Kamba,
the pro-vice-chancellor of the university, and by Anglican bishop
Peter Hatendi. Gerald Anderson, president of IAMS, responded
with appreciation for the welcome and hospitality and gave a
statement about IAMS.

An opening lecture, "Mission, Church, and State in Southern Africa," was given by Adrian Hastings, professor of religious
studies at the University of Zimbabwe, and a well-known Catholic
scholar and former missionary in Africa. In his address, Hastings
spoke about the responsibility of the church in mission to seek justice, especially for the poor, and particularly in places where there
is systemic oppression of the "native inhabitants by more powerful intruders from abroad," as in southern Africa. He cited the prophetic voices of missionaries such as Johannes Van der Kemp, John
Philip, John Colenso, John White, Shearly Cripps, Michael Scott,
Trevor Huddleston, Dennis Hurley, and Donald Lamont, and then
the voices of Desmond Tutu, Allan Boesak, and their like, who
carried on the tradition of authentic Christian witness. But they
were usually isolated, marginalized, and persecuted—"a small but
remarkable minority," while the majority "offer a seeming acceptance, if not blessing, of the *status quo*, only too characteristic of
church leadership as a whole."

Responses to his address were given by Engelbert Mveng, S.J.,
professor and head of the Department of History at the University
of Yaoundé, Cameroon, and general secretary of the Ecumenical
Association of African Theologians, and by Martin Lehmann-
Habeck, director of the Protestant Association for World Mission,
Hamburg, West Germany.

The next morning the keynote speech of the conference was delivered by His Excellency, Comrade President Canaan S. Banana. President Banana was an ordained minister of the Methodist Church in Zimbabwe, and a graduate of Wesley Theological Seminary in Washington, D.C.

When he arrived at the conference with his armed bodyguards, he was welcomed and introduced by Gerald Anderson, who was presiding. In his controversial lecture, titled "The Gospel of Jesus

**Canaan Banana, first president of Zimbabwe (left), and
Gerald Anderson, January 1985, Harare**

Christ and Revolutionary Transformation," President Banana said the Gospel of Jesus Christ is a "vibrant recipe for revolutionary transformation, and those who profess to be Christians should be agents for change—revolutionary cadres, and not docile and apologetic reformists or pragmatic liberals: which is a euphemism for fence-sitters." In colonial Rhodesia, he noted, the churches on the whole "acquiesced with the *status quo*. Though individuals from various churches were actively engaged in the efforts to change the situation, the general Church policy or attitude was to sit on the fence. . . . As such, the churches were never actually involved in the struggle on the side of the oppressed."

The church in Zimbabwe, he said, "has to dispense with the utopian idea that its primary role is to propagate the gospel, and that other issues are of secondary concern. . . . The Church's mission lies in the formulation of new theological concepts and practices that relate the people's faith to their everyday problems." The church should promote "self-determination, self-hood, and self-reliance" to overcome paternalism and dependence. "From its biblical experience, the Church can infuse a sizeable and worthwhile input into our socialist transformation process. . . . The concept of a classless socialist society is essentially theological." In conclusion, President Banana said that "the mission of the church today [is] to build bridges by bringing together antagonistic forces and turning them into positive instruments for the creation of a more humane community of nations. . . . We need a meaningful and universal dialogue which restores our distorted vision of man and society."

Following his address, President Banana entertained questions and comments from the participants, and a cordial exchange of views took place (reported in *MS* 2, no. 1 [1985]: 19–20). The tension between the state and the churches was especially evident when Bishop Hatendi expressed his concern: "We do appreciate the challenge you put to us. But the *how* can be a problem. There is no problem, as far as I am aware, in most churches with regard to socialism. But they do find a little problem when it has an adjective 'scientific,' which has been associated with atheism."

President Banana replied, "The *how* of dialogue is simple. When I speak of state and church entering into active dialogue, I am talking of dialogue at all levels, starting from local authorities. Concerning the churches' concern with the adjective 'scientific socialism,' perhaps this is the more reason why there should be active dialogue so that some of the misunderstanding can be expelled." It was a memorable occasion!

Another key lecture, titled "Doing Theology for Human Transformation," was given by Shun Govender, general secretary of the Belydende Kring in Johannesburg, South Africa. "To contextualize theology in South Africa," he said, "means that we have to radically redefine our theological mandate and transform theological reflection in terms of engagement in the life-and-death struggle of those seeking justice and peace in society." After reviewing the situation there, he said, "We are being challenged to see that Christianity in South Africa is heretical and even demonic in its comfortable co-existence with greed, exploitation and injustice. We are now learning to say that apartheid, and with it capitalism, is a Christian sin, and those who support it are living and practicing heresy. The only way to reconciliation for such people is repentance and active engagement in dismantling apartheid. Until such time no fellowship at the Communion Table is possible." To confess the faith in South Africa today, he said, requires the church "to side with the oppressed and assist them in the struggle for full and human liberation." It also means that "the churches should begin the debate for a socialist option in South Africa. Changing

David J. Bosch (left) led a discussion group
during the IAMS assembly at Harare.

apartheid cannot mean humanizing capitalism or involving more blacks in the free-enterprise programme. Rather we have to begin dismantling and rebuilding societal forms."

Responses to his address were given by Prakai Nontawasee, dean of the Faculty of Humanities, Payap University, Chiang Mai, Thailand, and by Andrew Kirk, associate director of the London Institute for Contemporary Christianity.

In his presidential address, "Christian Mission and Human Transformation," Gerald Anderson described and discussed some of the features in the global reality "that will increasingly characterize, confront, and challenge our task as we approach the twenty-first century." He discussed the threat of nuclear war, the shifting center of ecclesiastical gravity in the world to the Southern Hemisphere, the challenge of religious pluralism to mission and the need to affirm both dialogue and evangelism in witness, the challenge for witness by those living under authoritarian regimes and conditions of oppression, the need to overcome the polarization between evangelism and social justice in mission, and the internal threat in the church from "diluted faith and faltering faithfulness, of dubious disciples and timid prophets." Renewal in the church, he said, rarely comes from the ecclesial centers of power and authority; "renewal comes from the ecclesial fringes—from small, peripheral, dissident, despised, innovative, poor, creative but untidy minority movements in the church. . . . Church authorities and bureaucracies—all rhetoric to the contrary—do not really welcome renewal, because renewal means change. Therefore renewal movements are seen as threatening by the institutional church and are resisted." This was followed by a period of questions and lively discussion.

In the business meeting the general secretary reported that the Association now had 622 members (564 individual and 58 corporate members). The Executive Committee had met five times: during the Bangalore conference in January 1982; at the OMSC in Ventnor, New Jersey, June 1982; at Selly Oak Colleges, Birmingham, July 1983; in Geneva, April 1984; and during the Harare conference.[3]

Reports were given by the treasurer, Paul R. Clifford, and by Paul Jenkins, the acting chairperson for the DAB working group. New officers and members of the Executive Committee were elected:

| | |
|---|---|
| President | Joan Chatfield, M.M. (U.S.A.) |
| Vice president | John S. Pobee (Ghana/Geneva) |
| General secretary | Frans J. Verstraelen (Netherlands—on condition that the board of IIMO Leiden, where he served, would approve his continuation) |
| Treasurer | Paul R. Clifford (U.K.) |

At-large members of the Executive Committee
    Edith Bernard (France)
    Enrique Dussel (Mexico)
    Sebastian Karotemprel, S.D.B. (India)
    Takatso Mofokeng (Botswana)
    Calvin E. Shenk (U.S.A.)

After discussion and amendments, three resolutions were adopted unanimously by the conference.

• Condemnaton of apartheid in South Africa "as a sin, and consider it a Christian obligation to oppose it. Therefore, as one

---

3. The printed report mistakenly says that the committee met four times; it fails to mention the meeting in Geneva in April 1984.

consequence of our conviction, we affirm that there can be no place in the IAMS for organizations or individuals as they support apartheid."

- Expression of support and appreciation for "the courageous stand against apartheid by the South African Catholic Bishops' Conference [SACBC] and the South African Council of Churches [SACC]"; they also promised prayerful support to Archbishop Dennis Hurley during his trial in February 1985, when he would be charged for his stand and that of the Catholic Bishops' statement on police irregularities in Namibia.
- Expression of solidarity and support for "the work of the Institute for Contextual Theology in Johannesburg in its efforts to provide theological leadership in the struggle for liberation from apartheid in South Africa."

In the DAB consultation that followed the conference, participants had an opportunity to visit the National Archives of Zimbabwe. One of the memorable experiences of that visit was an opportunity to look at a journal written by David Livingstone during his expedition in Africa.

After the conference, the general secretary and the guest-editor of the Harare report, Gerdien Verstraelen-Gilhuis, had the opportunity to hand over the resolution concerning the SACBC, SACC, and Archbishop Hurley to the archbishop himself in Pretoria, and also to hand over the resolution regarding the Institute for Contextual Theology to its director, Frank Chikane. Two weeks later Chikane and several other church leaders in South Africa were arrested and charged with high treason. Immediately the IAMS general secretary sent a cable of sympathy and support to the institute and those arrested. This situation of crisis in South Africa led a large number of theologians and other committed Christians in South Africa (including several who had participated in the Harare conference) to issue the so-called Kairos Document under the title "Challenge to the Church: A Theological Comment on the Political Crisis in South Africa." A summary abstract of the document was published in *MS* 2, no. 2 (1985), along with a statement, "Why I Have Signed the KAIROS Document," by Nico J. Smith, a member of IAMS who had participated in the Harare meeting.

The official report of the proceedings, including John Pobee's biblical introduction to the theme "transformation," texts of the main lectures, reports from the eight workshops, the exposure experiences in Zimbabwe and South Africa, the open forum papers (abstracts), the colloquia on Biblical Studies and Mission (BISAM)

and on African church history, the IAMS general meeting and
resolutions, the postconference meeting on documentation (DAB),
and a list of conference participants were published with photos in
a special issue of *MS* (2, no. 1 [1985]), with a preface noting high-
lights of the conference by Gerdien Verstraelen-Gilhuis, who was
guest editor, and printed by Mambo Press in Gweru, Zimbabwe.
It was a remarkable report that was produced in timely fashion
under difficult circumstances.

**Tissa Balisuria, O.M.I. (right), of Sri Lanka, presided
at the closing Eucharist at Harare.**

Reporting on the Harare meeting continued in *MS* 2, no. 2
(1985), including six articles based on forum papers, along with
summaries of fourteen published reports and reactions regarding the conference. Simon E. Smith, S.J., in his published personal
report concluded, "If Africa itself is little changed by this IAMS
meeting, the same cannot be said of its participants!"

# VII
# Rome, Italy, 1988

The new Executive Committee met at the OMSC in Ventnor, New Jersey, June 13–16, 1985, where it was decided "that an exploratory visit should be paid to Rome, since this seemed to be the most apt place for the next conference. This exploratory visit took place November 11–14, 1985, consisting of the President (Chatfield), Treasurer (Clifford), General Secretary (Verstraelen), and Ms. Edith Bernard. This visit laid the foundation for an Executive Committee meeting to be held in Rome in April 1986 with representatives of various missiological, missionary and church institutions" (*MS* 2, no. 2 [1985]: 58). Preliminary decisions were made in Ventnor about the meeting place, accommodation arrangements, and dates: the next conference would be held in Rome, June 29–July 5, 1988, followed by a DAB meeting July 6–8. A tentative theme for the next conference was "Christian Mission Towards the Third Millennium: A Gospel of Hope." IAMS members were invited to react to this proposal and to send their comments and suggestions to the secretariat in Leiden. The Executive Committee also received reports of plans for a DAB workshop in Paris in January 1987 and of efforts to encourage working groups for BISAM (Biblical Studies and Missiology) and Healing.

In his Introduction in *MS* 2, no. 2 (1985), Verstraelen announced that "the Executive Committee has found a solution for the transfer of the IAMS Secretariat . . . from IIMO Leiden to two institutions in West Germany," with further details to be sent to all members after April 1986. The board of directors of IIMO had reluctantly decided that they could no longer provide support for the IAMS secretariat in Leiden, as they had done for more than nine years, because of their internal staffing situation and new regulations.

A special letter dated May 24, 1986, was sent to all members to inform them that "the IAMS Secretariat has been transferred to Hamburg and Aachen. Dr. Joachim Wietzke of Evangelisches Missionswerk, Hamburg, has taken over as General Secretary, while

Dr. Thomas Kramm of Missionswissenschaftliches Institut 'Missio' Aachen will take over the editorship of *Mission Studies*." This announcement was repeated by Verstraelen in his introduction to *MS* 3, no. 1 (1986). He then went on to say, "After having been IAMS General Secretary for 10 years (1976–1986) and at the same time Editor of the IAMS *Newsletter* (nos. 10–23; 1976–83) and of *Mission Studies* (nos. 1–5; 1983–86), it gives me satisfaction to be succeeded by two colleagues well qualified to continue the work and to further develop the potentialities of IAMS, which have not yet nearly been exhausted."

This was a major transition in the Association. Frans J. Verstraelen was only the third general secretary in the history of the organization; he had major responsibilities for organizing the conferences at Maryknoll, Bangalore, Harare, and Rome (until mid-1986), along with the large DAB meeting in Rome in 1980 and many meetings of the Executive Committee, while he carried on correspondence with IAMS members and simultaneously served as editor of the *News Letter* and the new journal, *Mission Studies*. At the same time he was also associate professor and associate director of the Department of Missiology of IIMO at Leiden University. With the growth of IAMS, the time had come to divide the work, and two missiologists in Germany were appointed to succeed him. Joachim Wietzke, former missionary in India and now on the staff of Evangelisches Missionswerk (EMW) in Hamburg, would be the new general secretary, and Thomas Kramm at Missio Institut in Aachen would be the editor of *Mission Studies*.

The Executive Committee met in Rome, April 20–24, 1986. It was the last Executive Committee meeting organized and attended by Verstraelen, and it was the first meeting for Joachim Wietzke, the new general secretary when this meeting ended.

An early item on the agenda of the meeting was the approval of a recommendation that came out of the meeting in Harare, namely, to establish a continuing study project "The Church as a Healing Community," similar to the already existing projects for DAB and BISAM. This was later renamed simply "Healing," to expand the scope beyond the church. This project became "a useful instrument for the exchange of relevant studies in the field of healing concepts, both in traditional and western medicine. In terms of missiology the project is geared towards the

ambitious goal of developing contextual theologies of healing."[1]
And Paul Jenkins reported on plans for a DAB meeting in Paris,
January 5–10, 1987, with the theme "Cooperation in Missiologi-
cal Indexing."

The main task for the committee in this meeting, however, was
to plan the General Assembly in Rome, scheduled for June 29–July
5, 1988. The assembly would take place at the Augustinianum,

Gerald H. Anderson (host, on left), IAMS president Joan
Chatfield, M.M., Paul R. Clifford, John S. Pobee, Sebastian
Karotemprel, S.D.B., Calvin E. Shenk, Paul Jenkins,
Edith Bernard, and Frans J. Verstraelen at the June 1985
Executive Committee meeting, held at OMSC,
then located in Ventnor, New Jersey

next to St. Peter's Square, and accommodations were reserved
at several pensions within walking distance from the conference
venue. The theme was confirmed, "Christian Mission Towards the
Third Millennium: The Gospel of Hope." Beginning on June 24,
before the conference, there would be several options for "exposure experiences" to various ministries in Rome, Paris, Frankfurt,
Berlin, and Basel. Following the conference, there would be special meetings of the IAMS projects on DAB, BISAM, and Healing.
Bible study and worship would be an integral part of the program.
Former presidents of IAMS—Gensichen, Camps, Aagaard, and

---

1. Wietzke, "Brief Historical Sketch of IAMS," p. 2, refers to project
reports of the Rome conference by H.-J. Becken (*MS* 5, no. 2 [1988]: 146–49)
and by Christoffer Grundmann (*MS* 6, no. 1 [1989]: 70–72).

Anderson—were invited to preside at the main morning sessions of the conference. In addition to the presidential address, there would be two key lectures, as well as an address by Cardinal Paul Poupard. There would be workshops, forum sessions, and interest groups. Translation from French to English, and from English to French, would be provided in all plenary sessions. A list of Sunday worship services in different churches would be offered. Also, tickets for admission to a canonization service in St. Peter's on Sunday morning would be available, and a guided tour of St. Peter's in the afternoon.

The core local committee for planning arrangements for the conference was Willi Henkel, Willie Jenkinson, Helene O'Sullivan, and Paul Jenkins. They arranged for an impressive group of about twenty-five leading missiological representatives from academic, church, and religious-missionary institutions and organizations in Rome to meet with the Executive Committee on April 22. According to the minutes, "The meeting was considered helpful in terms of making known IAMS, in creating sensitivity towards the coming congress, and in establishing personal contacts. Probably the most fruitful result was a good number of projects for exposure [the preconference experiences]."

The next meeting of the Executive Committee was in Basel, March 5–9, 1987, where they were hosted with a reception by the Basel Mission staff on Friday, March 6. Meeting with the committee were the general secretary, Joachim Wietzke; the journal editor, Thomas Kramm; Hans-Jürgen Becken, as convener of the Healing working group; Paul Jenkins, convener of the DAB group; and Martin Conway, president of Selly Oak Colleges. The meeting focused almost entirely on planning for the 1988 conference in Rome, including exposure experiences before the conference and consultations of DAB, BISAM, and Healing groups immediately following the conference.[2]

The Executive Committee met again in Rome, November 26–29, 1987, at which time details of the arrangements and program for the Rome conference were reviewed and confirmed. A working group of a dozen persons from the Executive Committee

2. Minutes of the Executive Committee meeting, April 20–24, 1986, in Rome, indicate that the next two meetings of the committee would be held in Basel (Mar. 5–9, 1987) and in Hamburg (Nov. 24–27, 1987). See a brief report on the Basel meeting in *MS* 4, no. 1 (1987): 64. The November meeting was held in Rome, November 26–29, 1987, instead of Hamburg.

and the local arrangements committee met in Rome March 3–6, 1988, to finalize plans for the conference. The Executive Committee met in Rome also on June 28, 1988, the day before the conference began, to deal with last-minute details.

Meeting in the large Aula of the Augustinianum, with more than 200 registered participants, the opening session of the IAMS Seventh Assembly began on June 29 with a welcome by the president, Joan Chatfield, and worship, followed by refreshments in

Janet Carroll, M.M. (left), Clarence Engler, M.M., Joan Chatfield, M.M., and Joan Delaney, M.M.

Arnulf Camps, O.F.M., and Willi Henkel, O.M.I. (on right)

the garden. She then gave the presidential address, "Voices to Be Heard: Mission in the Twenty-First Century," in which she said that the challenge of mission in the years ahead is to bridge "all the latent or blatant elite distinctions which sever humanity within its common fabric," and to "experience the wealth of voices yet to be heard." She commented that "the plural manifestation of this humanity is celebrated in the mission of Jesus." As the first woman president of IAMS, she warned the participants that "if voices of women are missing, cultural gaps occur which cannot be bridged retrospectively. They must be deliberately included, searched for, captured for the truth of full humanity."

Worship and Bible study on successive mornings were led by Calvin Shenk, Anna Marie Aagaard, Sebastian Karotemprel, S.D.B., and Kwame Bediako.

The first key lecture was "Hoping Against Hope? A Biblical Perspective," by John S. Pobee, who said that "the resurrection in and through Christ becomes the hope of the world. . . . Jesus Christ is a hope-creating reality. . . . In worship we experience the affirmation 'the Lord reigns,' and for precisely that reason, hope is not only possible but assured."

The second key lecture was "Future of Mission in the Third Millennium," by Enrique Dussel, in which he gave a sweeping survey of four eras in the history of Christianity. The fourth era, he said, began after the Second World War and is a period when the "missionary stage reached by Christianity is changing its meaning. We are at the end of the missionary age and at the beginning of the age of solidarity among local churches. The centripetal North-South movement has changed into a circle. . . . Now Rome learns from Latin America. Geneva from Africa. New York from the Philippines or China. It is the age of new universality." He concluded: "The missions of the third millennium of Christianity will therefore be missions towards the interior of each nation, each ethnic [group] or social class; and missions where the Spirit flows from the North towards the South, from the South towards the North, and from the South towards the South. It will be a mission with solidarity, an ecumenical, worldwide, multicentered mission respecting the differences in a common Spirit with neither center nor periphery, neither metropoles nor colonies, but with a unity, a new kind of unity: ' . . . that all may be one as you, Father, are in me, and I in you; I pray that they may be one in us, that the world may believe that you sent me . . .' (John 17:20–22)."

There was also a special lecture by Cardinal Paul Poupard, who was president of the Pontifical Council for Culture and of the Vatican Secretariat for Non-believers. His lecture, in French, highlighted initiatives of the Catholic Church since Vatican II to appreciate other cultures and religions.

In addition to these major addresses in plenary sessions, the conference program included nine workshops that met for five sessions, forums where twenty participants gave short papers on research projects, meetings of interest groups, sharing about exposure experiences, and a panel of editors of missiological journals.

Evening devotions were led by regional groups (Africa, Asia, Latin America, Europe); after devotions, the evenings were free for dinner and informal visits and gatherings. One evening a group went to share in worship and supper with the lay renewal community of St. Egidio.

Two members were appointed at the outset to give reflections at the end of the conference with their separate evaluations of what had occurred during the conference. First was Hans-Werner Gensichen from Heidelberg, the first president of IAMS.

**Johannes Aagaard (left) and John Pobee at the 1988 assembly**

**Charles Forman (left) and Joachim Wietzke in Rome**

He said there were signs that IAMS was "coming of age," reaching maturity, with the increase in membership and in the number of Third World participants and women. However, there was still an absence of Eastern Orthodox representatives, that is, Greek and Russian (there were Orthodox representatives from the Mar Thoma Church in India, including Metropolitan Geevarghese Mar Ostathios), and no participants from Uganda and Ethiopia, and very few students. He raised two critical issues: "What has this assembly done in order to uphold and strengthen the faith, the hope, the commitment of basic communities in Brazil and elsewhere, of the simple evangelists in Aberdeen and Abeokuta, in Amsterdam and Allahabad?" Finally, he reminded the assembly that "the IAMS was founded as an association for Mission *Stud-*

*ies*, and it should remain that. . . . Forum Sessions and Interest Groups should be given more attention in the future. . . . [also] the exchange about problems of the *teaching* of missions and religions in which the majority of us are engaged and to which we are going to return with new hope, faith, and love when the days of Rome lie behind us."

The other reflector was Wi Jo Kang, a Korean Lutheran who taught in Dubuque, Iowa. While he appreciated the lecture of Cardinal Poupard, he expressed disappointment that there was not

Past and current IAMS officers Gerald H. Anderson
(left), Hans-Werner Gensichen, Joan Chatfield, M.M.,
Frans J. Verstraelen, Arnulf Camps, O.F.M., Paul R.
Clifford, and Johannes Aagaard at Rome 1988

more attention to the implications of Vatican II for the future of the Christian mission, since the meeting was taking place next to the Vatican. He also felt that the major papers lacked a focus on mission toward the third millennium, and such focus was also lacking in some of the workshop sessions. The Bible studies and worship, however, were well done and much appreciated. His final comment was about the lack of evangelicals in the program. "All major presenters were from ecumenical groups and liberation theologians," he said. Some evangelical theologians should have been included "to maintain the international and ecumenical character of our association."

In the business meeting, the general secretary reported that IAMS now had a total membership of 565, with 488 individual and 77 corporate members. The decline in individual members was due largely to a decision of the Executive Committee to remove those who were delinquent in payment of their dues despite repeated requests. There was a healthy increase, however, in the number of corporate members.

Reports were received from the study groups Documentation, Archives, and Bibliography (DAB), especially about the consultation held in Paris, January 5–9, 1987; Biblical Studies and Missiology (BISAM); and The Church as a Healing Community (Healing).

**The IAMS Executive Committee elected at the Rome assembly included Guillermo Cook (left), Mary John Mananzan, O.S.B., Norman Thomas, Michael Amaladoss, S.J., President John S. Pobee, Gerdien Verstraelen-Gilhuis, and Justin Ukpong.**

Invitations to hold the next conference in Honolulu, Hawaii, or in Recife, Brazil, were referred to the new Executive Committee for consideration.

The report of the Nominating Committee was presented by the chairman, C. René Padilla. New officers and members of the Executive Committee elected at Rome were:

| | |
|---|---|
| President | John S. Pobee (Ghana/Switzerland) |
| Vice president | Michael Amaladoss, S.J. (India/Italy) |
| Secretary general | Joachim Wietzke (West Germany) |
| Treasurer(s) | Martin Conway (U.K.) and Marcella Hoesl, M.M. (U.K.), as alternate, effective January 1, 1989 |

At-large members of the Executive Committee
    Guillermo Cook (Costa Rica)
    Mary John Mananzan, O.S.B. (Philippines)
    Norman Thomas (U.S.A.)
    Justin S. Ukpong (Nigeria)
    Gerdien Verstraelen-Gilhuis (Netherlands)

Honorary members   Olav Guttorm Myklebust (Norway)
Paul Rowntree Clifford (U.K.)

The treasurer presented a proposal from the Executive Committee to increase annual membership fees for individual members to £10 and corporate members to £50. This was approved by the plenary.

There was a commemoration of those IAMS members who had died since the last conference: R. Pierce Beaver, Orlando Costas, and Charles W. Ranson.

Closing worship was a memorable eucharistic service held in the catacombs of Rome, led by Bishop Patrick Kalilombe from Malawi. Many years later Joachim Wietzke recalled that this service "was one of my most moving experiences with IAMS. At this historic site and next door to the Vatican all Roman Catholics participated in the Holy Eucharist (only one Lutheran abstained)—that for me was an eye-opener to the truly interdenominational character of IAMS."[3]

Immediately following the IAMS assembly, the DAB network had its own consultation in Rome, July 5–7, chaired by Paul Jenkins, who was retiring, and Norman Thomas, the incoming chair.

The forthcoming retirement of Paul R. Clifford as treasurer of IAMS at the end of 1988 was another significant transition. Following the Rome conference, President John Pobee referred to "the excellent work done by 'the ancient of days,' our beloved Paul Clifford," who served for fourteen years as treasurer of IAMS.[4] Clifford was honored during the Rome conference and presented with a beautiful Italian leather briefcase as a token of appreciation by the members, and he was elected an honorary life member. He had been involved with IAMS since he hosted the 1968 consultation at Selly Oak Colleges in Birmingham, where he was the president, and his years of dedicated service set a record that remains unsurpassed.

The official report of the Rome conference, with Bible studies, presidential address and key lectures with responses, workshop reports, business meeting, report of the general secretary, reflectors' reports, and list of participants were published in *MS*

3. J. Wietzke, e-mail message to author, August 21, 2010.
4. *MS* 6, no. 1 (1989): 4.

5, no. 2 (1988), and continued in *MS* 6, no. 1 (1989) with forum papers, reports on exposure experiences, and IAMS projects and activities (DAB, BISAM, Healing), plus photos of all members of the new Executive Committee. Additional papers and documentation from the Rome conference appeared in *MS* 6, no. 2 (1989) and 7, no. 1 (1990).

**President Joan Chatfield, M.M.,
honored Paul R. Clifford
for his service as IAMS
treasurer from 1974 to 1988.**

A letter from Olav Myklebust in Oslo to IAMS members, dated June 15, 1988, also appeared in *MS* 5, no. 2 (1988), expressing his "regret that for reasons of age (83)" he would not be able to attend the conference in Rome. However, he said,

> Looking back upon the last few decades, I recall with much pleasure the years 1968–1974, during which the idea of establishing a world-wide fellowship of missiologists came to fruition. . . . It has been deeply gratifying to witness the developments which have taken place since then. The results achieved have been impressive. The Association has become truly global in scope, and new vistas have been opened up. The variety and quality of the studies undertaken deserve much praise. In particular, I wish to congratulate our fellowship on its journal, which in the course of few years has become a full-fledged missiological publication—scholarly, informative, comprehensive and stimulating. The necessity of engaging in mission studies has never been more urgent than today.

Thomas Kramm continued as editor of *MS* 5, no. 2, and of the two issues of volume 6. In *MS* 7, no. 1 (1990), the name of Horst Rzepkowski, S.V.D., appeared as editor, with an explanation by

President Pobee that Missio Institut in Aachen was no longer able to provide the services of Kramm as editor, and that Rzepkowski from the Steyler Missionswissenschaftliches Institut in Sankt Augustin, Germany, would be the new editor.

# VIII
# Kaneohe, Hawaii, U.S.A., 1992

The new Executive Committee held its first official meeting at the Bossey Ecumenical Institute in Céligny (near Geneva), Switzerland, January 12–16, 1989. John Pobee, president of IAMS, was on the staff of the WCC at that time, and the committee was invited to have lunch and discussion with Emilio Castro, general secretary of the WCC during their meeting, and also to have supper on Saturday evening at Pobee's apartment. Staff members of the WCC Commission on World Mission and Evangelism reported on plans for the next world mission conference, scheduled for May 1989 in San Antonio, Texas.

A report on the Geneva meeting from Pobee appeared in *MS* 6, no. 1 (1989). After reviewing evaluations of the conference in Rome from participants, the committee began planning the next assembly. It was decided to explore the invitation from the Hawaii Christian Council to have the next meeting in Hawaii, probably in January 1992. There was also discussion of the self-understanding and profile of the Association, a review of the IAMS projects (DAB, BISAM, and Healing), consideration of whether there was room for new projects, and discussion of whether some IAMS activities could be pursued in various regions of the world. Financial concerns were also considered.

It was decided that, before any final decisions were made, some of the officers would go to Hawaii in the first week of 1990, before the next Executive Committee meeting, January 4–8, 1990, in the United States.

When the committee met in January at the Divine Word (SVD) Center in Techny, near Chicago, it began with a prayer in memory of their member Gerdien Verstraelen-Gilhuis, who had died since the last meeting. It also noted the death of John Ferguson, former president of Selly Oak Colleges and a member of IAMS.

After receiving a very positive report from the delegation that had visited Hawaii, it was decided to have the next IAMS conference in Kaneohe, Hawaii, August 4–11, 1992, on the campus of Hawaii Loa College, with the additional facilities of St. Stephen's Diocesan Center. In choosing a theme for the conference there was "a consensus that both the significance of the year 1992 and the revolutionary movements in Eastern Europe have to be captured in the phrasing of the theme. The title should have a clear biblical reference and should carry the vision of wholeness and newness." In the words of one member, "We have to highlight what the official church ignores." After a long discussion, the Executive Committee agreed on phrasing the theme: "New World—New Creation: Mission in Power and Faith."[1]

The Executive Committee met next in Hamburg, April 26–30, 1991, at the Missionsakademie. President Pobee welcomed Andrew Kirk from Selly Oak Colleges as the new co-treasurer of IAMS, taking the place of Marcella Hoesl, who had completed her term at Selly Oak. David Bosch and A. Samuelsen, who were visiting Hamburg, were invited to join the discussion.

Reports were received regarding the IAMS projects for DAB, BISAM, and Healing. The committee authorized the DAB management group to continue developing cataloging software for mission libraries and a mission thesaurus. The treasurer reported a deficit of £2,000 in the budget, but appeals for special grants for Hawaii looked promising. Horst Rzepkowski reported on plans for the next issue of *Mission Studies,* and suggestions of topics and authors for articles were offered.

The main discussion focused on planning the conference in Hawaii: the schedule, program, speakers, Bible studies, worship, workshops, exposures, regional meetings, projects, conference reflectors, and a public event with the presidential address and a banquet (or luau). A special plenary lecture on the church in the Pacific would be included. Simultaneous translation of the major presentations and plenary discussions into Spanish and French would be arranged.

David Bosch stressed "the need to give a clear focus to the forthcoming Conference and to communicate this to speakers, moderators and resource persons in advance . . . to avoid each workshop becoming an entity in itself. There is a need to define the

---

1. Explanations for the choice of the location and the theme for the next conference were given by the general secretary and the president in *MS* 8, no. 2 (1991): 127–33.

distinctiveness of the Conference in the light of the overall theme and due to the particular context we are in," he said. "IAMS is expected to provide a forum for missiologists to meet rather than to organize a missionary conference." Bosch noted that "we are in a process of fundamental revision, not only in missiology but in all sciences. We have to understand what stimulated the epistemological change in order to discover the new conceptual framework from which we can act. Otherwise we are wandering from nowhere to nowhere."[2]

Project meetings of DAB, BISAM, and Healing would be held following the conference from the afternoon of August 11 to the afternoon of August 12.

Minutes of the meeting in Hamburg reported, "On invitation of EMW there was a reception in honor of the IAMS Executive on Sunday, 28 April. More than 50 guests attended. There was an opportunity to meet members of the theological faculty of Hamburg University, church leaders and representatives of educational institutions. A welcome was extended by Peter Krusche, bishop of Hamburg and chairperson of the EMW board, and Theo Ahrens, professor of missiology and ecumenics, Hamburg. The president [Pobee] introduced IAMS and the members of the executive. David Bosch delivered the guest lecture." Bosch's talk was "The Role of the Church in Contemporary South Africa."[3]

For financial reasons, only a "rump" executive meeting was held, March 6–9, 1992, at the SVD center in Sankt Augustin, near Bonn, Germany. In addition to receiving applications for individual and corporate membership, the main business was to receive and review reports on registrations for the conference (111 so far) and finances (£85,252 in grants received), and to finalize the organization of the conference. It was decided to cancel the workshop "City and Kingdom: Mission and the Challenge of Urbanization" because only two persons had registered for it. At the same time, the workshop "Christ and the Pluralism of Religions" was oversubscribed, and some participants were encouraged to go to their second choice.

2. Executive Committee minutes, April 28–30, 1991, pp. 3–4. It is especially sad to recall that on April 14, 1992—almost exactly one year later—David Bosch died in an auto accident in South Africa. He had agreed to lead the workshop on Bible and mission at the conference in Hawaii, and he was greatly missed.

3. The revised text of Bosch's lecture was published in *MS* 8, no. 2 (1991): 147–64.

The Executive Committee met again just before the conference in Hawaii on Monday, August 3, 1992, to approve applications for membership and to make final adjustments in the conference program and organization. Despite some last-minute dropouts, there were more than 170 registrations. Special appreciation was expressed to Joan Chatfield for local arrangements, and to Jean Stromberg for coordinating plans for worship.

The Eighth Assembly of IAMS met on the campus of Hawaii Loa College in Kaneohe, Oahu, Hawaii, August 4–11, 1992. The conference theme had evolved from the commemoration of 500 years of Roman Catholic mission in the Americas, begun with Columbus. It was also the bicentennial of Protestant missionary work in Asia and elsewhere in the wake of William Carey. And it was the year of inauguration for the European Union. The theme was timely.

The opening session included a welcome, worship, and introduction to Hawaii. Members who had died since the previous conference were remembered in prayer: Gerdien Verstraelen-Gilhuis, John Ferguson, D. S. Amalorpavadass, Armand Garon, Martin Mbwana, Friedrich-Wilhelm Haack, Marie-Louise Martin, Kofi Appiah-Kubi, and David J. Bosch.

A full day was given to exposure experiences, introducing participants to aspects of traditional Hawaiian culture and to the Hawaiian Sovereignty Movement. In downtown Honolulu a woman pastor told of her work with Waikiki's prostitutes. North of Pearl Harbor, participants visited a "peace farm" that was cultivating alternatives to violence. Following these visits, there was an opportunity for reflection on the exposures.

Kosuke Koyama from Union Theological Seminary in New York City gave the keynote address on the theme of the conference, in which he noted,

> The goal of Christian mission is to create a humanity whose form is conformed to the "form of Christ." . . . The "form of Christ" is that of self-giving love. . . . The apostolic tradition proclaims that humanity is personally, communally and cosmically re-created by this "central event" of self-giving love. Self-giving, being the opposite of self-glorifying, is truly healing. The focus of this healing is on the transformation (transfiguration) of humanity. . . . The welfare of all creation is the subject of missiology. All living beings depend upon the well-being of the natural world. . . . The missiology of "individual conversion and individual salva-

tion" has distanced Christ from the community of people. It is an atomistic missiology. It goes against the basic orientation of the form of Christ. The Christian faith is, in its way of transmission, in its contents, in its life, not individualistic. The form of Christ is that of a community, and it is ever engaged in the creation of community. Christ speaks to community, and community responds.

Koyama concluded, "In *theologia crucis* we see the universal glory of the merciful and just God in the peripheralized Christ. The glory of God is revealed yet hidden in a renewed and transformed humanity created by the peripheralized Christ."[4] Following the address, there was a panel discussion chaired by Charles Forman from Yale Divinity School. The panel included participants from New Caledonia, Korea, Nigeria, Argentina, and Fiji.

Each day began with worship and Bible study led by Ana Langerak and ended with evening prayer. Several sessions were reserved for the eleven workshops and also the forums, where forty-five participants presented brief papers on their research and writing projects. Donald Senior, C.P., from the Catholic Theological Union in Chicago, agreed to lead the large BISAM workshop that David Bosch had been scheduled to lead, before his tragic death scarcely four months earlier.

On Sunday evening there was a public service of worship in the Cathedral of St. Andrew in Honolulu, which included the presidential address. Speaking on the topic "Mission from Below," John Pobee said this theme took its cue from the manger in Bethlehem and the cross on Calvary. The church, he said, "is not the goal of mission. At best the church is only an instrument of God's presence and redemptive purpose. A church that uses mission for its self-preservation will not survive. But the church that loses itself for the sake of the Kingdom will find itself enabled and ennobled beyond measure." This mission, he said, will involve community building and ecology; it will be comprehensive and holistic, it will enable those from the underside of history to tell their story, and it

---

4. While there was general appreciation for many theological insights in the keynote address, there were some feelings of disquiet that the speaker, a native of Japan, mentioned criticism of the United States for dropping atomic bombs on Hiroshima and Nagasaki but failed to mention the Japanese sneak attack on Pearl Harbor on December 7, 1941. There, only a few miles from where Koyama was speaking, more than 3,000 Americans died, which led to the U.S. declaration of war against Japan.

will be motivated by the Holy Spirit to discern God's agenda. This requires a willingness to learn from other faiths and cultures and to join in God's cosmic vision, which includes a preferential option for the poor, which is people-conscious, in a culture of hopelessness. This mission from below, he said, "means to dare to live a life of eternity in the temporal scene. That is almost impossible without conflict, pain, persecution, and martyrdom. . . . It represents a powerful testimony that the perspective from above is not the last word and is ultimately doomed to failure." He concluded that "mission from below reveals tremendous faith and power wrapped in seemingly fragile, earthen vessels. . . . [It] requires a missiology that is informed by a renewed spirituality which issues in a solidarity that commits people to solidarity with the poor and their liberation, as well as a mysticism of faith which discerns God's presence and compassion in creation."

In the business session, chaired by former president Arnulf Camps, General Secretary Wietzke reported that the Executive Committee elected in Rome in 1988 had met five times. Out of a total of 179 participants in the conference, 64 came from the Southern Hemisphere. There had been an increase in subscriptions to *Mission Studies*; in addition to IAMS members, there were now a total of 147 subscribers, mostly libraries. Those members who did not pay their dues after repeated reminders were suspended, but there were 151 new members, including 69 from the Third World. So the total IAMS membership was now 570 members (497 individual and 73 corporate). There were many registrations for the postconference workshops of the IAMS projects DAB, BISAM, and Healing, August 11–12, which indicated their indispensable role in the Association.

The report from the treasury given by Martin Conway and Andrew Kirk from Selly Oak was that "the financial situation of the IAMS is in fact much the same overall as it was in 1988," thanks to grants from twenty-three agencies, as well as from Olav Myklebust, toward the costs of the conference in Hawaii. Therefore they recommended that membership subscription dues should stay at the rate fixed for 1990, namely $21 for individual members and a minimum of $90 for corporate members.

Donald Elliot, the chairman of the Nominating Committee, presented the report and the following slate for the new Executive Committee:

President          Michael Amaladoss, S.J. (India/Italy)
Vice president     Ana Langerak (Costa Rica)
General secretary  Joachim Wietzke (Germany)
Treasurers         Martin Conway (U.K.)
                   and Andrew Kirk (U.K.)

At-large members of the Executive Committee
    Edmund Davis (Jamaica)
    Margaret F. Loftus, S.N.D.deN. (U.S.A.)
    Teresa Okure, S.H.C.J. (Nigeria)
    John Roxborogh (New Zealand)
    Faitala Talapusi (Fiji)

Honorary members  Olav Guttorm Myklebust (Norway)
                  Paul Rowntree Clifford (U.K.)

The General Assembly unanimously approved this slate. For the future, however, it was requested that the slate should be distributed in written form one day ahead of the elections, and that it should include alternative candidates.

Suggestions were made to hold the next IAMS conference in Latin America, possibly in Quito or Buenos Aires.

Comments made from the floor in the meeting included the following:

- A proposal to start another IAMS Project: "Women in Mission." The purpose would be to identify and collect materials on women missionaries and women national workers from the beginnings of the modern missionary movement.
- A resolution in support of the nonviolent Sovereignty Movement among Hawaiians. This was accepted by majority vote.
- A statement deploring the neglect of other political issues in the Pacific, e.g., the continuing colonization of Irian Jaya.
- A need to involve more representatives from independent churches and Christian minority groups.

Some of the forum papers from the conference were published in *MS* 9, no. 2 (1992). A special double issue of the journal (*MS* 10, nos. 1–2 [1993]) contained all the major presentations, Bible studies, workshop reports, IAMS projects, regional meetings, business session, resolutions, reflector's report, reports on the postconference project meetings, and a list of participants. Additional forum papers were in *MS* 11, no. 1 (1994), with additional reports from the IAMS projects DAB and Healing. The May 1993 issue of the French Catholic journal *Spiritus* (Paris) was entirely dedicated to the reports and papers of the IAMS conference in Hawaii.

On August 10, 1992, there was a meeting of the new Executive Committee with some of the outgoing committee members at the college in Kaneohe, Oahu. They appointed chairpersons of the IAMS projects: John Roxborogh for DAB, John Pobee for BISAM, and Christoffer Grundmann for Healing. Horst Rzepkowski was asked to continue as editor of *Mission Studies*. Applications for membership were reviewed, and all but two were accepted as qualified. It was felt necessary to have a thorough discussion on the criteria for IAMS membership at the next executive meeting. A proposal and budget were received from DAB that involved considerable funding for software development, which was not approved. DAB was advised that it should broaden its agenda rather than put so much of its efforts into software development.

The proposal from the business meeting of the conference to start an additional IAMS project, "Women in Mission," was welcomed. Jocelyn Murray was encouraged to prepare a detailed outline for the project.

In the Annual Report from the IAMS Treasury by Martin Conway and Andrew Kirk, dated October 25, 1993, it was stated that the Hawaii conference "was widely held to be one of the most successful in the history of IAMS, with particularly good participation from the different regions of the world."

# IX
# Buenos Aires, Argentina, 1996

The next meeting of the Executive Committee was held at Selly Oak Colleges in Birmingham, U.K., January 7–11, 1993. General Secretary Joachim Wietzke reported that the evaluations from the Hawaii conference by participants were generally quite positive. The present balance of action and reflection was considered crucial to the IAMS identity; the pattern of integrating Bible studies into the worship, and of integrating the exposure experiences into the conference, was appreciated. Encouraging reports and plans from the IAMS projects DAB, BISAM, and Healing were reviewed. Since *Mission Studies* also serves as a member bulletin, it was recommended that the journal should include more news and announcements from members and from the Association, such as progress reports on IAMS projects, news about Executive Committee meetings, and plans for future conferences.

Regarding criteria for membership, which are meant to point to a balance of action and reflection, the committee agreed on the following statement to describe the identity of IAMS. Anyone willing to subscribe to this would qualify for membership.

> As students and servants of God's mission, we affirm the essential relationship between mission theology and mission praxis. We also affirm the diversity of theology and praxis which we bring to IAMS. We are committed to learning from one another and respecting one another through fellowship, worship, discussion and debate, through sharing in special projects, exposure to issues and situations and contributions to *Mission Studies*.

Jocelyn Murray from London presented an outline of a proposal to begin the new project Women in Mission by circulating a questionnaire to a number of IAMS members, with a view to preparing a bibliography on the roles and contributions of women in mission. She was invited to serve as the convener of the project and was encouraged to develop a core group of six to eight people who would prepare a workshop for the next IAMS conference. They were given a budget of £500 for 1993 to get started.

Joachim Wietzke reported that Buenos Aires looked like a promising place for the next conference in 1996. There was an official invitation from ISEDET (a graduate institute of theological studies), and a group of local IAMS members had offered to serve as the local committee. It was felt that Buenos Aires would be a good place to study the issues of urbanization and urban mission. But there was concern about high costs and finding an adequate venue for the meeting. Hungary was also suggested as a possible meeting place. The theme of the conference would depend on the venue. Further investigation would be necessary.

The following meeting of the Executive Committee, January 27–31, 1994, in the SVD Mission Institute at Sankt Augustin, Germany, was hosted by Horst Rzepkowski, the editor of *Mission Studies*, who had recently been appointed director of the Mission Institute. The committee appointed Faitala Talapusi as the moderator of the BISAM project and confirmed the plans for DAB from John Roxborogh and for the Healing project from Christoffer Grundmann. Jocelyn Murray reported that she had not been successful in building up an international network or core group for the project Women in Mission, and she was uncertain whether she should continue. With encouragement and suggestions from the group, she agreed to carry on.

In addition to the usual matters of business, the principal item on the agenda was the venue, dates, and theme of the next conference. Wietzke had visited Hungary to consult with church leaders, and it seemed that the churches there would not yet be ready and able to host a mission conference. It was therefore decided to have the next conference in Latin America, most likely in Buenos Aires, in early 1996. The proposed theme would be "God or Mammon: Economies in Conflict." But finding an adequate facility to accommodate the conference in Buenos Aires was still unresolved. A delegation of IAMS officers would go to Buenos Aires in September to meet the local committee, as well as church leaders, and to find a suitable venue for the next conference.

By the time of the next meeting of the committee, in Washington, D.C., September 24–28, 1994, organized by Margaret (Peggy) Loftus, S.N.D.deN., the officers could report on their visit to Buenos Aires, September 20–23. Based on their report, it was decided to hold the next conference at a Catholic facility in San Miguel, near Buenos Aires, April 10–19, 1996, and to confirm the theme "God or Mammon: Economies in Conflict." Néstor Míguez would be chairperson of the local committee. Suggestions for plenary session speakers, workshops, worship, Bible studies, panels, and excursions were discussed.

This was the last meeting of the Executive Committee with Joachim Wietzke as general secretary, because he would be leaving his post at EMW in Hamburg for a new position in the church in a few months. Deep appreciation was expressed by the committee

**Jerald Gort (left) and Hans-Werner Gensichen at the IAMS assembly in Buenos Aires in April 1996**

for his nine years of devoted service to IAMS, and to his secretary in Hamburg, Carla Johannsen, and to Gillian Davis in the treasury office at Selly Oak.

Fortunately, EMW was willing to continue to provide support for the IAMS secretariat and to enable Wietzke's successor to serve in that office, if it was desired and approved by IAMS. This person was Klaus Schäfer, former missionary in India, where for five years he taught biblical studies on the faculty of Andhra Christian Theological College in Hyderabad. The Executive Committee expressed appreciation to EMW and invited Schäfer to serve as acting general secretary beginning May 1, 1995, until the IAMS General Assembly could vote on his appointment as general secretary at the conference in Argentina. It was a gracious and generous transition of great benefit to IAMS.

For financial reasons, only a rump Executive Committee meeting, limited to those committee members present in Europe, was held in Hamburg at the Missionsakademie, November 24–26, 1995. The agenda was mainly to finalize the program arrangements for the conference in Buenos Aires. Joachim Wietzke was invited to join the meeting, since he had been involved in early planning of the conference and this was Schäfer's first meeting with the committee.

Two serious issues were reported. First, two members of the Executive Committee had resigned: Peggy Loftus had been reassigned to new responsibilities in Boston and was unable to continue on the committee, and Faitala Talapusi had left the Pacific Theological Seminary in Fiji and was now involved in a new career—in sports (rugby)!

Second, it was learned in June that the Catholic facility in San Miguel, near Buenos Aires, where the conference was scheduled to be held, would not be available. When booking the IAMS conference, the sister in charge of reservations had somehow overlooked the fact that the whole building was already reserved for a meeting of the Catholic bishops of Argentina! The local preparation committee, with some difficulty, was able to make alternative arrangements for the conference to be held in downtown Buenos Aires. Participants would be housed in two hotels normally used for trade union members. Meals and plenary meetings would be held in the Swiss Centre; workshops and forum sessions would meet in classrooms of some Catholic schools in the area. In view of all the changes, it was decided that Klaus Schäfer should make a trip to Buenos Aires, February 27 to March 4, 1996, for further preparation of the conference, to meet with the local committee, and to visit the sites where the conference would be held.

Members of the Executive Committee arrived in Buenos Aires on April 9, 1996, so they could have a meeting on April 10 with the local committee on arrangements, before the opening session of the Ninth IAMS Assembly that evening.

There were 129 registered participants from 37 countries. The somewhat lower attendance was attributed to the higher costs for travel to South America, the schedule of meeting in April, when those from the Northern Hemisphere were still in the midst of the academic year, and the fact that there were few local members of IAMS. On a positive note, at least 50 percent of the participants were from the Third World.

The opening service was in the Iglesia del Salvador. There was a liturgy in Spanish and English of celebration and worship, with Michael Amaladoss, S.J., president of IAMS, presiding, and Juan Carlos Scannone, S.J., preaching a homily based on Luke 16:1–15. Each morning the program began with worship and Bible study. C. René Padilla and Mariam Terese Winter, M.M.S., each led three Bible studies. Padilla's text was Leviticus 25. Israel, he said, was to be the people that incarnated shalom and justice. He emphasized

**C. René Padilla and Miriam Therese Winter, M.M.S.,
led Bible studies in Buenos Aires.**

that peace is the fruit of justice and that without justice there will be no peace. Latin Americans, he said, say that external debt is eternal debt; it is institutionalized injustice. He concluded that the present world economic order is leading to disaster and that the church in its mission is called to be prophetic. Unfortunately, we have no record of Sister Winter's Bible studies.

Ulrich Duchrow, professor of systematic theology at Heidelberg University, delivered the keynote address on the conference theme. He offered a broad criticism of the global capitalist economy, which divides people and lowers ecological standards. The situation, he said, is especially devastating for most people in the

Third World, because the Western capitalist powers control the system to their own benefit for maximum profit. He proposed a multiple strategy of saying No to the totalitarian global goal of capital accumulation and of "developing a new vision; experimenting with small-scale alternatives; and intervening prophetically in order to tame the political economy at all levels, where possible." He concluded: "Christians, churches, and church organizations are called and empowered by the Spirit to be salt, light, and leaven in our different contexts and in a global community.

**Frans J. Verstraelen (left) and Klaus Schäfer in Buenos Aires**

If we join God's struggle with the poor for a just alternative as witnessed throughout the Scriptures in our own threatened situation, people will rejoice and praise God. If we don't, we betray our mission. That is the choice before us. Let us pray humbly to God: 'Thy kingdom come.'"

In his presidential address, "Mission in a Postmodern World: A Call to Be Countercultural," Michael Amaladoss said, "Though there is much talk of mission, a convincing new vision that one could propose, relevant to the postmodern world, seems lacking." He proposed that "Jesus' good news of the reign of God projects an alternative vision of community. . . . The challenge of mission today is therefore to be a countercultural community that will embody in itself the values of life, community, and transcendence so as to witness to and to promote the reign of God in the world." This will require a paradigm shift, he said, that enables us to have a

> perception of the believers of other religions as allies in a common struggle with Mammon. . . . Our theological reflections are still coming to terms with this shift, with questions turning around the uniqueness of Christ. . . . I suggest that the discourse about the uniqueness of Christ is often a hidden discourse about the uniqueness of Christianity and about our desire to

**Michael Amaladoss, S.J., gave the presidential address at the IAMS assembly in Buenos Aires.**

> be the sole "possessors" of Christ. I think that we will not solve such questions without a real experience of working with other believers in our common fight with Mammon. . . . Then we may discover that Christ is present, enabling the people, wherever the power of Mammon is challenged. Our mission to witness to this presence does not allow us to claim exclusive rights to it. What is more postmodern than such an experience of pluralism and a call to dialogue in the context of mutual respect and collaboration?

In the lively discussion with the speaker following his address, there was appreciation for his thoughtful analysis of the current cultural crisis and his proposal for a "countercultural community." There was also, however, a concern expressed that this vision for mission apparently had no place for evangelism or need for conversion to Christ, but only a calling to work together and dialogue with people of other faiths to counter the forces of Mammon.

During one day of the conference, participants had the opportunity for exposure experiences to visit mission projects being carried out by church groups in the Greater Buenos Aires region. These included care for homeless men and women, care for persons with HIV/AIDS, orphanages and homes for children at risk and street children, institutions of theological education, and programs of rehabilitation from drug addiction as well as rapidly growing neo-Pentecostal churches.

Participants could choose from eleven workshops, and there were forum sessions where forty short papers on research projects related to the conference theme would be presented.

The business meeting of the association included a memorial tribute to those who had died since the last conference: Theodore E. Bachmann, Joseph Lévesque, P.S.S., Ido H. Enklaar, Katherine B. Hockin, Bengt Sundkler, and Evert Jansen Schoonhoven. Edward Schroeder presented the report of the Nomination Committee. The following were elected:

| | |
|---|---|
| President | Chun Chae Ok (Korea) |
| Vice president | Paulo Suess (Brazil) |
| General secretary | Klaus Schäfer (Germany) |
| Treasurers | Martin Conway (U.K.) |
| | and Andrew Kirk (U.K.) |

Regional representatives

| | |
|---|---|
| Africa | Teresa Okure, S.H.C.J. (Nigeria) |
| Asia | Joy Thomas (India) |
| Europe | Graham Kings (U.K.) |
| North America | Tim Huffman (U.S.A.) |
| Latin America | Jerjes Ruiz (Nicaragua) |

Horst Rzepkowski, who was unable to attend the conference, was reappointed as editor of *Mission Studies*.

Klaus Schäfer reported that there were invitations from three places for hosting the next IAMS conference: Jerusalem, Edinburgh, and Pretoria. Participants indicated a preference for Pretoria; the new Executive Committee would consider all the invitations and make a decision.

Martin Conway introduced the following resolution on associate membership: "The IAMS Conference agrees that for an initial 4-year period (to be reviewed by the next conference) a new separate category of *Associate Member* shall be created. Associate membership will be open for not more than four years exclusively to students engaged in post-graduate research at a doctoral or equivalent level, recommended by the student's supervisor and one (other) IAMS member. The membership fee will be half that of normal membership." It was additionally noted that associate membership is a distinct category of membership; the criteria for membership are not affected in any way by this proposal. After some discussion the conference adopted the resolution.

**The Executive Committee elected in April 1996 at the IAMS assembly in Buenos Aires were Klaus Schäfer (left), Chun Chae Ok (president), Martin Conway, Jerjes Ruiz, Tim Huffman, Teresa Okure, S.H.C.J., Andrew Kirk, Joy Thomas, and Graham Kings.**

A summary statement at the end of the conference concluded: "Looking back on the ninth IAMS conference, we see issues that have moved us and elements of a vision that will sustain us in mission. We also feel a frustration that we were not able to move further in our analysis, that our proposals were not as concrete as we would have liked. We see now through a glass darkly, knowing only partly (cf. 1 Cor. 13:12), awaiting the full revelation of God's Reign. Our struggle in mission for the economy of God in this world will continue."

The closing worship was celebrated in a communion service in the Anglican Cathedral. The Anglican bishop of Buenos Aires presided, and the sermon was delivered by José Míguez Bonino. After the worship and lunch on April 18, the three IAMS projects—DAB, BISAM, and Healing—met separately, concluding their business on April 19.

As was customary, there was a joint meeting of the old and new Executive Committee members on April 18. Because of time pressure, there was only a brief agenda: (1) a brief evaluation of the conference, sharing first impressions; (2) reviewing and approving applications for membership; and (3) agreement to have the next meeting of the Executive Committee January 10–12, 1997, either in Hamburg or in Birmingham.

During the Buenos Aires meeting, Jan Jongeneel from Utrecht proposed to the European regional group that they should discuss the possibility of having a European regional meeting every four years, between general meetings of IAMS. It was agreed, and the first European regional conference was held at Stavanger, Norway, in 1998. The success of that meeting led to further meetings in Halle in 2002, and in Paris in 2006. Full documentation of the first European regional meeting was published in a special issue of *Swedish Missiological Themes* (86, no. 4 [1998]), and proceedings of Halle 2002 appeared in the same journal (90, no. 4 [2002]). This European initiative followed the successful organization of the British and Irish Association for Mission Studies (BIAMS), which was established in 1989 and inaugurated in 1990; it meets regularly and publishes both a newsletter and the proceedings of its conferences. The IAMS Executive Committee encouraged these initiatives but decided that no formal institutional or financial connection with IAMS would be possible.

A double issue of *Mission Studies* (13, nos. 1–2 [1996]) contained the major addresses, Bible studies, workshop reports, a selection of forum papers, report of the business session, the Healing project meeting, the summary statement in the closing session, and a list of participants at the Buenos Aires conference. Sadly, however, it also contained an editorial by Klaus Schäfer announcing that the editor of the journal, Horst Rzepkowski, had died suddenly on November 25, 1996. He had been the editor since 1990 and had prepared this double issue shortly before his death. Two other members had also died: Everett N. Hunt, Jr., and Eugene Stockwell.

# X
# Hammanskraal, South Africa, 2000

The new Executive Committee met January 9–12, 1997, at Selly Oak Colleges, Birmingham, where the members were welcomed by Martin Conway, who was president of the colleges and also co-treasurer of IAMS. A time of shared memories and appreciation for Horst Rzepkowski was observed by the committee.

In evaluating the Buenos Aires conference, some felt that the days were too full, and therefore opportunities for unhurried conversations were limited; there was a need to ask what the real aim, purpose, and priority are in coming together in conference, and this question related to the self-understanding and identity of IAMS as an association. In an initial sharing on the reformulation of the IAMS identity, the committee stressed that IAMS is

- a genuinely international association
- interested in sharing thinking and being in dialogue (geared to publications and conferences)
- a meeting place between institutions of mission and mission practitioners and academic missiologists
- contextual in character

It was reported that interest in the proposed IAMS projects "Patristics and Mission" and "Women in Mission" had not advanced because of lack of response from members. Further efforts would be made to encourage these initiatives.

It was decided to approach Stephen B. Bevans, S.V.D., at Catholic Theological Union in Chicago, to be the new editor of *Mission Studies*, with Robert J. Schreiter, C.PP.S., as associate editor.

Pretoria, South Africa, was the preferred venue for the next IAMS conference, in 2000. Negotiations with a local committee would be pursued.

As Martin Conway would retire in summer 1997 as president of Selly Oak Colleges, he would then also retire from the IAMS treasury, where he had served since 1988. Since this would be his last meeting with the Executive Committee, President Chun Chae Ok expressed the deep gratitude of IAMS for his dedicated service, and a resolution of appreciation to Martin and to Selly Oak Colleges from the committee was recorded. Andrew Kirk would serve as treasurer until the next conference could confirm his appointment.

It was reported that plans were underway in Rome to organize a new mission organization: the International Association of Catholic Missiologists (IACM). While there was regret about this

Robin Morgan (left) and Edward Schroeder

Jan Gorski (left) and Stephen Bevans, S.V.D.

initiative for the establishment of a parallel organization to IAMS, it was hoped there could be collegial cooperation.

The Executive Committee met next in Hamburg, January 28–February 2, 1998, at the Missionsakademie and was hosted by EMW. They were joined by Stephen Bevans, who had accepted the invitation to be the new editor of *Mission Studies*, and by Willem Saayman of the Southern African Missiological Society (SAMS), who was especially invited to take part in the planning process for the next IAMS conference, which would be held in South Africa in 2000.

As a continuation of the earlier discussion about the IAMS

identity, it was suggested that it would be important to have someone write a history of IAMS, to be reminded of what it has been,
as a basis for discussions about what it might be in the future. This
also involved preliminary discussions about the best location for
IAMS archives.

**Kwame Bediako (left) and
John Pobee at the IAMS
assembly in Hammanskraal**

**Teresa Okure, S.H.C.J.,
introducing *To Cast Fire upon
the Earth: Bible and Mission*,
the IAMS book she edited,
Hammanskraal 2000**

The rest of the meeting dealt largely with planning for the
next conference. Klaus Schäfer had already visited South Africa
and met with members of SAMS, which resulted in the invitation
for Willem Saayman to take part in this planning process for the
conference.

It was decided to hold the next conference in the Megawatt
Park Conference Centre near Johannesburg, January 21–28, 2000,
on the theme "Reflecting Jesus Christ: Crucified and Living in a
Broken World." After participants had two days of exposure to
the South African ecclesial, cultural, political, and economic realities, the conference would focus on various aspects of the theme
in four plenary presentations and various other forms of study
and interaction. In contrast to previous conference programs,

what were formerly called workshops were now described as mission study groups, underlining the missiological orientation of the group work. Sixteen such groups would be offered. (Later, three of the groups would be canceled because of inadequate registrations.)

There would be no separate meetings of IAMS projects or interest groups outside the main conference program; instead, these would be incorporated into the mission study groups, and the

**Women in Mission study group at Hammanskraal**

facilitators of the current projects DAB, BISAM, Healing, Patristics and Mission (later called Mission in the First Millennium), and Women in Mission would take responsibility for planning a mission study group. Instead of "forum papers" there would be a session called Research Reporting, where reports on some major—though not individual—research projects would be presented. Also, two sessions were scheduled for regional meetings; one would focus on the theme of the conference, and the other on common interests related to mission studies and IAMS as an association. Two optional features in the conference would be a session where a panel of mission journal editors could speak about their editorial focus and features, and a session that would focus on specific interests of missiological teaching (curricula issues, teaching methods, the role of missiology in faculties, etc.).

Fortunately, there was a strong committee for local arrangements in South Africa, mainly within SAMS, to assist with preparation and planning for the conference.

Klaus Schäfer informed the committee that, because of restructuring in EMW, it would not be possible for them to continue to host the IAMS secretariat after the next conference, and that he would not be able to continue as general secretary. EMW, however, would continue to support the cause of IAMS as much as possible. The committee received this news with regret, but also with gratitude to EMW for their support over the last fifteen years, and with

**Truth and Reconciliation Bible study group**

appreciation to Klaus for his devoted service since 1995. A process would begin by talking to institutions and persons that could be in a position to take over the secretariat following the conference in South Africa.

Thanks largely to the work of John Roxborogh in New Zealand, IAMS now had a Web site that provided a wealth of information about IAMS, its history, projects, membership forms, journal, officers, and plans, as well as links to other Web sites for mission resources.

When the Executive Committee met next—in Rome, January 27–31, 1999—there was an opportunity to meet with Sebastian Karotemprel, S.D.B., the acting president of the new IACM (and a former member of the IAMS Executive Committee), for a cordial discussion of common concerns in the two associations.

In addition to routine business, most of the committee meeting was devoted to planning the conference in South Africa: the worship, the celebration on the concluding evening (it was hoped that Nelson Mandela might greet the conference), plenary speakers, facilitators of the mission study groups, the exposure program ("a very essential aspect for the success of the conference") around

Pretoria and Johannesburg, Bible studies (which would take place in small groups instead of being led by a Bible study leader in the plenary), reporting on major research projects, regional meetings, and the business session and elections.

As happened before the conference in Buenos Aires, so it happened again just a few weeks before the conference in South Africa: the conference venue had to be changed. The secretariat sent a

**John Roxborogh (left) and Edmund Davis**

notice to the registered participants that the Megawatt Conference Centre had raised its prices and demanded additional payments, which the Executive Committee decided were unacceptable. The local committee therefore arranged for the conference to meet instead near Pretoria in Hammanskraal at a former Roman Catholic theological seminary that was now the Hammanskraal campus of the University of Pretoria. It turned out to be quite an attractive and congenial setting, with good facilities for accommodations, dining, chapel, and meeting rooms.

The committee met again upon arrival for the conference on January 20, 2000, to finalize program arrangements before the conference began the following day.

The conference began with a worship service led by Klippies Kritzinger from the faculty of missiology at the University of South Africa (UNISA), and each morning began with a short worship service, followed by a plenary address.

The first plenary address, "Proclaiming the Crucified Christ in a Broken World: An Asian Perspective," was by A. J. V. Chandrakantan, a Catholic priest from Sri Lanka who was teaching at the Toronto School of Theology in Canada. He spoke about the atrocities being committed against Tamils in the "broken world" of contemporary Sri Lanka and said it was the duty of Christians to speak the word of truth to the powers that be, that they stop "this indescribable suffering of the innocent."

The second plenary address, "The Gratuitousness of the Presence of Christ in the Broken World of Latin America," was given by Paulo Suess, a German Catholic missionary in Brazil and vice president of IAMS. He spoke about the importance of developing a Latin American missiology that is not just *for* the poor and indigenous, but *with* them as well. "The experience of Jesus Christ crucified and living in the poor," he said, "lends wings to our imagination and sandals to the reasons of our hope."

**Sergei Shirokov (left), Gerald H. Anderson,
and Vladimir Fedorov at Hammanskraal**

A plenary address entitled "The Crucified Reflected in Africa's Cross-Bearers" was given by Tinikyo Sam Maluleke, professor of African theology at UNISA. He described a "picture of popular African Christology" in which "African Christianity is a broken Christianity." He spoke of "the need and scarcity of hope in Africa. Hopelessness is in a sense one of the greatest indicators of Africa's brokenness." In this context, he said, "we come to appreciate the reality and worth of Jesus' brokenness for ourselves."

Another presentation on the theme in the African context that described the meaning of brokenness for women in Africa was given by Philomena Njeri Mwaura, from Kenyatta University in Nairobi, Kenya. She spoke about the paradox that African women experience when the church has been at the same time both an instrument of liberation and one of entrapment as it has ignored certain sectors of the very group it claims to speak for. It is therefore not surprising that women are drawn to African Independent Churches, where the gifts of women are welcomed.

In her presidential address "Mission in a New Millennium," Chun Chae Ok from Ewha Woman's University in Seoul, Korea, described several characteristics for mission in the new millennium. It should be a cooperative effort, should involve youth and women, should be holistic and ecological, should celebrate life and overcome

**Annemie Bosch and Martin Conway**

**Anneliese Gensichen, President Chun Chae Ok, and Annemie Bosch at Hammanskraal**

violence, should preach Christ and be in harmony with actual living, should be the activity of local churches, should work for unity, and should be committed to reconciliation of human and cosmic wounds.

The business session of the conference began with commemoration of those who had died since the last conference: Horst Rzepkowski, S.V.D., Lesslie Newbigin, Josef Glazik, M.S.C., John Fleming, William A. Smalley, Anton G. Honig, Jr., Everett N. Hunt, Jr.,

**Chun Chae Ok delivered the presidential address at Hammanskraal.**

Norman A. Horner, Guillermo (William) Cook, Joseph Levésque, P.S.S., John C. Bennett, J. Christy Wilson, Jr., Eugene L. Stockwell, Harvie Conn, and Hans-Werner Gensichen.[1]

There was a special welcome and recognition given to Annemie Bosch, the widow of David Bosch, and to Anneliese Gensichen, the widow of former IAMS president Hans-Werner Gensichen.

1. Gensichen died on March 26, 1999. In 1995, on his eightieth birthday, a special tribute to him was published in *MS* 12, no. 1 (pp. 3–4), recalling how he had helped to "overcome the difficulties standing in the way of the realization of the ideals of Myklebust. In a prudent, amiable and faithful way he acted as a midwife during the meetings held in 1966, 1970 and 1972. Moreover he was president of the Association until 1974, and was a member of the Executive Committee until 1976." Along with Myklebust, Gensichen was truly a "founding father" of IAMS, together with Arnulf Camps, Andrew Walls, and Paul Clifford.

The general secretary reported that the Executive Committee had met four times since the last conference: January 1997 in Birmingham, January 1998 in Hamburg, January 1999 in Rome, and just before the conference in South Africa. IAMS's membership stood at 608: 523 individual, 77 corporate, and 8 associate members, and additional applications had been received. A total of 222 persons had registered for this conference.

Some amendments to the constitution were recommended by the Executive Committee and were approved after discussion by the members. Looking to the future, the Executive Committee "particularly felt the need to write the history of IAMS, but we have not yet succeeded to interest somebody to do this rather major job"!

Klaus Schäfer then informed the members that, following this conference, EMW in Hamburg would no longer be able to host the IAMS secretariat, and he would not be able to continue as general secretary, because of restructuring of EMW and reduction of their staff. The Executive Committee had been informed about this situation, but there was not yet a decision about a new person and place for the secretariat. In the meanwhile, Schäfer was willing to continue as acting general secretary until a new person was designated by the new Executive Committee. The assembly recorded its appreciation to EMW and to Schäfer for their support and service.

The following persons were elected as the new officers and members of the Executive Committee:

| | |
|---|---|
| President | Paulo Suess (Brazil) |
| Vice president | Darrell L. Whiteman (U.S.A.) |
| Treasurer | J. Andrew Kirk (U.K.) |
| Journal editor | Stephen B. Bevans, S.V.D. (U.S.A.) |
| General secretary | Klaus Schäfer (Germany), pending the new appointment, to be announced |

Regional representatives

| | |
|---|---|
| Africa | Christopher O. Oshun (Nigeria) |
| Europe | Klaus Schäfer (Germany) |
| North America | William R. Burrows (U.S.A.) |
| Oceania | Catherine Rae Ross (New Zealand) |
| Latin America | Emilio M. Monti (Argentina) |

The conference ended, as it began, with a service of worship. Canon John S. Pobee from Ghana, a former president of IAMS (1988–92), was the preacher.

There was the customary joint meeting of the members of the old and new Executive Committees toward the end of the conference. Much appreciation was expressed to SAMS and members of the local committee for all their work, which was so important in the success of the conference.

There was a tragedy following the conference when the Kenya Airways plane carrying one of the participants, Efemie Ikenga-Metuh from Nigeria, crashed into the Atlantic Ocean off the coast of Abidjan, Ivory Coast, on January 31, resulting in Ikenga-Metuh's death. He had served on the "Listening Committee" that reported

**Robert Schreiter, C.PP.S. (left), and William R. Burrows**

in the final session of the conference, and he submitted a paper that was published as the lead article in *MS* 18, no. 1 (2001). His death was a great sadness for all those who had enjoyed his fellowship in the conference.

The proceedings of the conference were published in a double issue of *Mission Studies* 17 (2000). In his editorial in that issue, Stephen Bevans said that the conference in Hammanskraal was "one of the most rewarding gatherings in which I have ever participated." In particular, he mentioned "connecting and re-connecting with colleagues and friends, experiencing the South African reality in the immersions, the smooth organization and the gracious hospitality afforded to us by our South African hosts, . . . the amazing harvest of editors of missiological publications who presented reports about their respective journals; the evening devoted to reports on current research projects undertaken by individuals and missiological centers; the powerful performance by the local group of actors on the last evening of the conference; and the times of worship—particularly those graced by members of local congregations and choirs. One of my most vivid personal memories was the visit of my exposure group under the leadership of Rev. Nico Smith, to the Vortrekker Monument in Pretoria—a chilling experience of the power of myth in a culture!"

**Local choirs led morning worship at the IAMS assembly held at Hammanskraal in January 2000.**

In the same issue of the journal was a letter from IAMS president Paulo Suess. He reported, "After having been hosted for fifteen years at EMW in Hamburg, IAMS secretariat has moved to Areopagos in Denmark, after consultation with our new Executive Committee and officially since September 11. . . . In Hamburg on September 11, I welcomed Birger Nygaard, former Secretary of the Danish Missionary Council and now staff member of Areopagos, as the new General Secretary of IAMS. In a small celebration, the outgoing and the new secretary were present. . . . In Hamburg was also signed an agreement of mutual understanding between Areopagos and IAMS. To say farewell on a windy summer day could be a little melancholic, but wasn't. Now we are again en route. The archives will follow in a container."

# XI
# Port Dickson, Malaysia, 2004

As reported in the editorial in *MS* 18, no. 1 (2001), "From January 25 to 30, 2001, members of the IAMS Executive Committee met at the Maryknoll House in New York City, U.S.A.. Except for a brief meeting towards the end of the Hammanskraal Conference the previous year, this was the first time that the new Executive had met. . . . Our new general secretary, Birger Nygaard, ran a superbly organized meeting. . . . I can assure the membership that IAMS is in very good hands!"

At the meeting in New York, the committee first spent some time identifying issues that were strengths, weaknesses, opportunities, and threats for IAMS. It noted how the global context for mission and missiology has changed since 1970, with there now being a real need for a truly global network of missiologists. In an afternoon session the committee met with local mission leaders at a gathering where Lamin Sanneh from Yale Divinity School spoke about his most recent book, *Abolitionists Abroad*.

In addition to routine matters of organization and business, the committee discussed preliminary plans for the next international conference, to be held in 2004, somewhere in Southeast Asia, since only one conference had been held in Asia (India), with a theme appropriate to the context. The general secretary would explore the possibilities and report to the next meeting in January 2002, when decisions would be made on location, theme, and dates.

Reports from DAB, BISAM, and Healing groups were received, with thanks. As there were no reports from the groups on patristics or on women in mission, their continuation would be dependent on status reports from them.

The Executive decided to appoint the following honorary life members: Arnulf Camps, Gerald H. Anderson, Joan Chatfield, C. René Padilla, Stanley J. Samartha, and Willem Saayman.

Stephen Bevans announced that he planned to retire from editing *Mission Studies* in 2004, so the committee needed to start think-

87

ing about his successor. Also, Andrew Kirk said that he would retire as treasurer after the 2004 conference.

Plans presented by John Roxborogh were approved for a joint IAMS-IACM conference for Archives, Documentation, and Oral Histories at the Pontifical Urbaniana University in Rome, July 8–13, 2002. The theme would be "Rescuing the Memory of Our Peoples," with a focus on action for saving church and mission archives. Roxborogh, who was also the Web site administrator, reported that in a typical week there were 644 visits to the IAMS Web site.

The next meeting of the Executive Committee was held in Prague, at the International Baptist Theological Seminary, January 29–February 4, 2002. Great appreciation was expressed for Stephen Bevans's work as editor of the journal, as he reported on discussions with Brill in Leiden about publishing *Mission Studies* and administering subscriptions. The committee reviewed names of possible candidates to be the new editor when Bevans retired in 2004, and there was conversation about the possibility of an electronic version of the journal.

After consideration of invitations to hold the next conference in Hong Kong, Korea, Indonesia, and Malaysia, the committee chose Malaysia as the venue for the 2004 conference. It was chosen because the location offered several complex missiological challenges and because all the components of a good framework (local committee, affordable travel expense, and affordable conference facility) were present. The general secretary was asked to work on the details with the local committee in Malaysia and to decide on the dates and venue as soon as possible.

The Executive Committee spent considerable time in discussion before deciding that the theme of the 2004 conference would be "The Integrity of Mission in the Light of the Gospel: Bearing the Witness of the Spirit." Tentative suggestions/decisions were made about plenary addresses, speakers, program, worship, Bible study, mission study groups, optional sessions, research papers and projects, exposure programs, regional meetings, translation policy, and so forth. The general secretary was asked to be in dialogue with the local committee about these suggestions to get their opinions in light of the local/regional context and possibilities. A representative of the Malaysian local committee would be invited to the 2003 Executive meeting.

Quite a remarkable consultation on the theme "Rescuing

the Memory of Our Peoples," with forty-four participants from twenty-five countries, was held in Rome, September 29–October 6, 2002. It was organized by the core group of DABOH (Documents, Archives, Bibliography, and Oral History, the new name for DAB) and convened by John Roxborogh, with Sebastian Karotemprel, S.D.B., as the local host. Major presenters were Andrew Walls, Archbishop Francesco Marchisano, Martha Smalley, Rosemary Seton, Kwame Bediako, Jean-Paul Wiest, Ana Bidegain, Jonathan Bonk, Klaus Schäfer, William Burrows, and Paul Jenkins. Others presented case studies and documentation projects. A notable outcome of the meeting was production of *Rescuing the Memory of Our Peoples: Archives Manual*, compiled by Martha Smalley (Yale, New Haven) and Rosemary Seton (SOAS, London), which was published in 2003 and was later translated into Korean, Chinese, French, Spanish, Portuguese, and Swahili. It can be downloaded

**Executive Committee meeting in 2003 in Paris**

as PDF files at www.omsc.org/archivesmanual.shtml. The group also produced a fresh statement, "Archives and Mission for the Twenty-First Century." In some ways this was a sequel to the DAB working party theme "Mission Studies and Information Management," explored in Rome in 1980.

The Executive Committee met in Paris, January 28–February 2, 2003, at the guesthouse of the Protestant Churches in Paris. Birger Nygaard informed the committee that Areopagos would not be able to continue financing the secretariat after 2004, and it was unlikely that he would be able to continue as general secretary. The experience of frequent changes of the secretariat raised a number of issues related to the structure of IAMS, while all agreed that the goals of IAMS should remain unchanged.

Allan Anderson, formerly of the Selly Oak Colleges but now at the University of Birmingham, would be recommended to take over as treasurer of IAMS at the 2004 conference, when Andrew Kirk retired. Lalsangkima Pachuau would be the new editor of *Mission Studies*, with J. Jayakiran Sebastian, Cathy Ross, and Paulo Suess as associate editors from 2005. It was approved in principle that publication of the journal would be turned over to Brill Publishers in Leiden as of January 2004, subject to acceptable contract terms.

News about the inauguration of the Central and Eastern European Association for Mission Studies (CEEAMS) at Budapest in November 2002 was warmly received, and CEEAMS was challenged to host the next IAMS assembly, in 2007 or 2008.

It was decided to change the requirement for IAMS membership to a focus on whether the applicant is "research active" (demonstrated by publications within the last five years) as the primary criterion for admission of new members. Such change was not to be regarded as a lowering of the academic profile and quest of the association. This change would make the "associate member" category obsolete; it would therefore be recommended to the assembly that this category be deleted from the constitution.

Philip Siew, chair of the local planning committee in Malaysia, was present in order to discuss matters related to the forthcoming conference in 2004. The dates for the conference would be July 31–August 6, 2004, and it would be held at the Regency Hotel in Port Dickson, Malaysia.

Discussions and decisions for the 2004 conference, including program structure and schedule, speakers, budget, and participants, were on the agenda for the meeting. Plans included exposure experiences, worship, Bible studies, plenary sessions, testimonies, study groups, interest groups, optional sessions, research papers to be tabled, research reporting, regional meetings, and cultural celebrations. The next meeting of the full Executive Committee would be on July 30, just before the Malaysia Assembly at Port Dickson.

However, a meeting of the officers was held at the Maryknoll House in New York City, April 29–30, 2004, which featured eighteen hours of intense discussion. Klaus Schäfer was invited to join the meeting because of his previous conference-planning experience when he was general secretary. A main focus of the meeting was on further planning for the conference in Malaysia, fund-raising, and allocation of subsidies. The issue of the future of the secretariat had major attention, along with reports from the general secretary, the treasurer, and the editor of the journal. It was reported that a major purging of the membership files took place as addresses were given over to Brill for mailing the journal; 240 members had not paid their dues for 2003; 51 of these were maintained on the membership list, for they were expecting to pay their dues. The officers welcomed the offer of At Ipenburg in Holland to serve as Webmaster of the IAMS Web site for 2004–6.

The Executive Committee met on July 30 at Port Dickson to review plans for the conference. A major consideration was a proposal to appoint Frans Dokman, at the Missiological Institute of Nijmegen, Netherlands, as the new general secretary. Negotiations were underway, but there would be no public announcement at this time.

An informal meeting was held on July 31 before the conference with representatives from sixteen regional mission associations and networks to share information and learn from each other about the activities of each association. The primary objective was to strengthen relations and for IAMS to clarify its function as networker and bridge-builder in relation to other associations around the world.

With over 200 attendees from 44 countries, the Eleventh General Assembly of IAMS, meeting in Port Dickson, Malaysia, began on Saturday afternoon, July 31, 2004, with a welcome by President Suess and orientation by Philip Siew, followed by worship. During the worship, a Chinese Christian orchestra played Christian hymns on traditional instruments. The preacher was Bishop Paul Tan Chee Ing, S.J., who spoke about the need for evangelism in the contemporary missiological endeavor.

After dinner the keynote address on the theme of the conference—"The Integrity of Mission in the Light of the Gospel: Bearing the Witness of the Spirit"—was given by Hwa Yung, director of the Centre for the Study of Christianity in Asia at Trinity Theological College, Singapore, and former principal of the Malaysia Theological Seminary (Seminari Theologi Malaysia), in Seramban. (He would soon become the bishop of the Methodist Church in Malaysia.)

Hwa Yung focused on the extraordinary growth of the church in the Two-Thirds World, particularly in China, and gave attention to some of the factors that draw people and communities to Jesus.

These include "signs and wonders," with healing and deliverance from "supernatural powers"; the power of the Gospel to change individual and personal circumstances; and the Gospel as providing the spiritual foundation for building a new society. "Can the church of today," Hwa Yung asked, "maintain its integrity in the face of the colossal spiritual, physical, and sociopolitical needs in the world if it holds back from obeying the call of the triune God to mission? Can it speak of being a church that bears the witness of the spirit if it shies away from the ministry of liberation and the proclamation of Christ as the universal Savior?"

Following this opening session, participants had two full days of local exposure to the historical and contemporary culture and religious setting of Malaysia, where Christians compose only 7 percent of the population. On Sunday they could worship in local churches, then chose a visit to Buddhist centers, Hindu temples, a native-people village, or a social ministry organization, or they could visit the historic city of Melaka (Malacca), which is known as the gateway of Christianity to Malaya, China, and Southeast Asia.

The following day was a full program, with Islam as the focus. All delegates were bussed to the large, modern mosque in Putrajaya, the Malaysian government's new administrative city, then to the International Institute of Islamic Thought and Civilization (ISTAC) and the International Islamic University of Malaysia (IIUM), where they met with Islamic scholars for discussion. A sign at the entrance to the university said, "The mission of IIUM is to achieve: Integration, Islamization, Internationalization, and Comprehensive Excellence." A university official explained that by "Islamization" they mean, "to recast the world of knowledge according to the worldview of Islam; to put spiritual and ethical values into knowledge." By "Integration," they mean that "secularization has done great damage to knowledge, and we need to integrate religious knowledge with scientific knowledge. It is a project," he said, "to indigenize knowledge." The university, founded in 1983 and sponsored by the government of Malaysia, had 13,000 students. The day ended in Kuala Lumpur, where participants visited the Petronis Twin Towers, which at that time were the tallest buildings in the world (and were designed by an architect from New Haven, Connecticut!).

Each day the conference began with worship and Bible study led by Robert Solomon, bishop of the Methodist Church in Singapore and former principal of Trinity Theological College, Singapore. This was followed by plenary sessions each morning, with two speakers—one Catholic and one Protestant—from each continent in dialogue on what integrity of mission means in their continental setting. Significantly, in no case was there any clear disagreement or a major difference in approach.[1]

The first morning the focus was on Asia. Chun Chae Ok, president of IAMS from 1996 to 2000, and now professor emerita of Ewha Woman's University in Seoul, Korea, spoke about mission in Asia from a woman's perspective, which she described as a unique contribution. It is "mission from the poor to the poor . . . often hidden and veiled . . . a mission of emptiness and a mission of comforting." The reality, she said, "is that women in mission without names and in most cases without writings have been vehicles of the Gospel in the Korean churches and in other Asian churches. Their roles have been justice-making and life-giving without any demand for reward or recognition. They are always behind and hidden in life-giving work. It is their experience of life being given as a gift from God and their love for life itself that makes it possible for them to give without ceasing as seen in a life of a mother for her children." Yet "women's leadership in mission societies and in the mission fields is not encouraged. . . . The existence of a female majority in the world church must no longer be ignored. Rather, it should be celebrated and become a source of inspiration for a more authentic form of mission."

She was followed by Leo Kleden, an Indonesian who was a member of the SVD General Council in Rome. He affirmed that "God's reign is deeper and greater than the church. . . . The reign of God is actively present within the church but is not identical with the church." He also acknowledged that "people of different faith communities, of different cultures and religions in their own way have experienced the saving act of God. Of course they are in need of full redemption and ultimate salvation. Mission, therefore, is no longer a one-way traffic." This awareness, he insisted, "will slowly, but radically, transform our way of thinking and doing mission."

The following morning the focus was on Latin America. The two presenters were Peruvian Tito Paredes from the Latin American Theological Fraternity and Mexican Eleazar López Hernández,

---

1. In addition to the published papers in *MS* 24, no. 2 (2007), I have drawn on the reporting in a news release about the conference prepared by Martin Conway for the media news service of the World Council of Churches.

who served in El Centro Nacional de Ayuda a las Misiones Indí-
genas. Both speakers highlighted the revival of ancient "Indian"
cultures and the way that the churches are learning to heed the
theological wisdom of the indigenous peoples, without compro-
mising biblical teaching.

Next day the focus was on Africa. Philomena Njeri Mwaura,
from Kenyatta University in Nairobi, Kenya, described Africa's
current troubles, where the perennial problems of corruption,
impoverishment, and oppression of the masses through inept governance have created a "bleeding continent." In this context, she
gave five suggestions for enhancing the integrity of mission in the
light of the Gospel:

- View the church as mediator of peace, reconciliation, and
  healing.
- Provide visionary leadership for discipling the nations.
- Prepare courageous and effective leaders committed to evangelization and ecumenism.
- Recognize that, in a pluralistic context, religions and denominations can fulfill their prophetic role only in collaboration.
- Commit to mission as Shalom to the marginalized, especially
  to women in Africa.

Tite Tiénou, from Burkina Faso and teaching in the United
States, saw the present challenges facing Africa as providing "the
greatest opportunity for a fresh and creative examination of issues
related to the integrity of mission in the continent." He discussed
the following three points:

- Africans can turn marginalization into a resolve to find intra-
  African solutions to African problems.
- Africans may be able to think realistically about nation build-
  ing and development.
- Churches in Africa have a window for being hope-generating
  churches.

The final focus was on Europe. Edith Bernard, a French Catholic laywoman from the Pontifical Mission Aid Societies (Missio-
France) in Paris, and Parush R. Parushev, a senior Bulgarian Baptist now teaching at the International Baptist Theological Seminary
in Prague, Czech Republic, speaking of their different contexts
agreed in substance:

- Mission means responding to the Holy Spirit's call into the body of Christ.
- Mission also means responding, in ways appropriate to the context, to God's transforming presence in serving the needy, working for peace and justice, embracing the neighbor, proclaiming the Good News, and making disciples.
- Integrity of mission requires a holistic involvement with the local context by "the followers of the Way of Jesus Christ, as an authentic witness for the Kingdom of God, bringing hope in cultures of fragmentation and despair" (Parushev).

**Paulo Suess delivering his presidential address in Port Dickson**

In his presidential address, Paulo Suess, a Catholic priest of German origin who had long been identified with the original peoples of Brazil and with various movements of liberation theology, focused on what the Holy Spirit is saying to today's Christians as

> they encounter the Spirit side by side with the oppressed, the excluded, and the marginalized . . . who reveal the unrecognized God in the world. . . . The universality of mission today has to be understood as an alternative to the globalization under the dictates of a social-Darwinistic liberalism. . . . Mission and missiology are universal, and their universality is an aspect of the integrity of mission because it does not exclude anybody. Christians

do not have the status of a "redeeming class," or of an "elected race." . . . Hope for redemption and liberation is given us because of the hopeless. It is because of the universality of victims that our mission is universal. Mission follows the suffering servant of God into the most remote areas of the world. . . . The missionary project in its contextual universality can be understood as an alternative to cultural colonization and social exclusion.[2]

Afternoon and evening sessions in the conference were given to thirteen study groups, optional sessions for reports on research projects, regional meetings, and interest groups for DABOH, BISAM, Healing, and Women in Mission (WIM).

During the conference, when announcements were made by the local host, Philip Siew from Malaysia Theological Seminary, who was very short, he would be lifted up by a tall professor from Denmark so he could be seen and heard by the 200 participants. Someone described this as the "elevation of the host"!

General business meetings of the Association were held during the conference on August 3 and 5. Some amendments to the constitution and byelaws were approved to simplify election procedures; Oceania was separated from the Asia region to form a distinct region; and the category "associate member" (for doctoral students) was eliminated—based on the premise that the primary criterion for membership is that the applicant is "research active," and by definition doctoral students are research active, so they qualify to be full, individual members.

Birger Nygaard, as general secretary, reported that "negotiations with a new host for the secretariat and a new General Secretary candidate were in process, and if concluded with a positive result, an announcement can be expected by October 2004. It was explained that this was a similar situation to that of four years ago, when negotiations had not been concluded at the time of the Conference. The negotiations and decisions were handled by the Executive [Committee]."

Nygaard also reported that, as of 2004, the administration of the journal publication, subscriptions, and membership fees would be handled by Brill Academic Publishers, Leiden. This should significantly reduce the workload of the treasury and the secretariat.

As of July 2004 the total membership of IAMS was 424 mem-

2. The presidential address was not published; I have therefore relied on the reporting by Martin Conway cited above.

bers: 361 individual, 46 corporate, 12 associate, and 5 honorary. Of these, 43 percent were from Europe, 30 percent from North America, 10 percent from Asia, 8 percent from Africa, 5 percent from Latin America, and 4 percent from Oceania. Since the last conference, 21 members had died. Their names were not listed in the minutes, but the present writer knew the following who had died: honorary life members Olav G. Myklebust, Stanley J. Samartha, and Paul R. Clifford; other members Nils Egede Bloch-

**Worship service at the IAMS assembly in Port Dickson**

Hoell, William J. Danker, Carl F. Hallencrutz, Daniel J. Harrison, Adrian Hastings, George A. F. Knight, Karl Müller, S.V.D., Ludwig Munthe, Jocelyn M. Murray, Alan P. Neely, William M. Pickard, André Seumois, O.M.I., Eric J. Sharpe, David M. Stowe, John V. Taylor, Harold W. Turner, Johannes Verkuyl, and Marcello Zago, O.M.I.

The assembly recommended that the new Executive Committee accept the invitation of the CEEAMS and the Protestant Institute for Mission Studies to host the next IAMS conference in Budapest. It also recommended that the Executive Committee accept the invitation by the Church of Scotland and the Centre for the Study of Christianity in the Non-Western World at the University of Edinburgh to play an active supporting role in the processes being planned leading up to the celebration of the 2010 centenary of the Edinburgh 1910 World Missionary Conference.

The retiring treasurer, Andrew Kirk, and the retiring editor, Stephen Bevans, presented their reports, and the assembly expressed appreciation for their service to the Association. The

Nomination Committee, chaired by Paulo Suess, presented a slate of candidates for officers and members of the new Executive Committee, which was discussed and unanimously approved for election by the assembly, as follows:

| | |
|---|---|
| President | Darrell Whiteman |
| Vice president | Philomena Njeri Mwaura |
| General secretary | Birger Nygaard, pending the new appointment, to be announced. |
| Treasurer | Allan Anderson |
| Journal editor | Lalsangkima Pachuau |

Regional representatives
| | |
|---|---|
| Africa | Philomena Njeri Mwaura (Kenya) |
| Asia | Hwa Yung (Malaysia) |
| Europe | Anne-Marie Kool (Hungary/Netherlands) |
| North America | Jonathan Bonk (Canada) |
| Oceania | Susan Smith (New Zealand) |
| Latin America | Tito Paredes (Peru) |

Three honorary life members had died since the last conference, and three new ones were appointed in recognition of their special contributions to IAMS: John Pobee, Ghana, president, 1988–92; Frans J. Verstraelen, Netherlands, general secretary, 1976–86; and Andrew F. Walls, Scotland, general secretary, 1974–76.

There was an extra plenary session on the last morning, in response to requests from members, to discuss the topic "The Future of Missiology as an Academic Discipline." The session was coordinated by Stephen Bevans, the retiring editor of the journal. There was a lively discussion, but no papers or publications resulted.

Finally, Dale T. Irvin from New York Theological Seminary had been assigned the task of listening in at the conference as a participant and of reflecting on what he had heard, and to think about what he had not heard, during the conference. At the end of the conference, he was invited to report on his reflections. Irvin noted how important the local immersion experiences were, especially the face-to-face meetings in Islamic institutions of higher learning, and "the manner in which Islamicization was offered to us self-consciously as an alternative globalizing narrative or framework, a meta-narrative that challenges and yet is closely related to the meta-narratives of both Christianization and globalization." Throughout the week, he said,

I heard the conference searching for the right tone for our approach to Islam, as well as to the other religions of the world. . . . I found unresolved the tensions that exist among evangelization, dialogue, witness, and presence as being the primary task of Christian missions, or between models of pluralism versus exclusiveness concerning salvation. . . . The other [metanarrative] that we encountered through the week was that of globalization. . . . What seemed to me to remain inadequately reflected upon during the week was the degree to which globalization is a local cultural reality here in Malaysia and elsewhere throughout the world, and the degree to which it has become the medium of global theological gatherings such as ours. . . . I don't have any suggestions for how we respond to this challenge, but I think we ought to do more reflection as an Association upon the questions posed by globalization today, and upon the effects of our near-exclusive use of English as the medium of communication.

"We talked several times," he said, "about the issues of mission and the poor, but without much depth of reflection. Issues of gender inequalities in mission and in mission studies seem to me to be likewise underaddressed in our work as an Association on the whole. I heard a great deal of sensitivity to these issues all week long. . . . I commend the Association for its efforts to address these concerns and would hope that we continue in our commitment to do so forcefully."

He continued:

One of the areas of great ambiguity that I encountered all week concerns the colonial heritage and the lingering impact of Western forms of thought and identity in missions. I thought this week that there is still much work to be done in decolonizing missions. And what about the issue of secularization? On the one hand, we criticize the West for its secularization, rationalism, and scientific worldview. On the other, some of us at least are attracted to the West for its institutions and wealth and leadership. Separating the wheat from the tares . . . is not easy. It has been part of the project of postcolonial history. I certainly think it is a task that mission studies must continue to press.

Regarding the theme of the conference, Irvin observed, "Time and time again I heard integrity pointing away from the church and toward Jesus Christ, a theme that has been heard in mission studies for the better part of a century. But I also consistently heard something else. I heard articulated an effort to link mission to the church in a fresh way, and not just leave it at communicating the Gospel. I think this is significant. Over the past fifty years, due in part to the influence of the concept of *missio Dei*, mission theory has tended to move in the opposite direction, away from a focus on the church and toward a focus on Christ. I wondered this week if a shift is not in the making."

The issue of mission studies as an academic field, he noted, "is elusive and some would say still insufficiently defined. One of the purposes of IAMS is to provide professional academic credibility for its members. This is the reason for the concern to maintain the academic level required for membership. The heart of any academic discipline resides in the rigor and depth of its methods. . . . Our desire is to be deeply spiritual and deeply academic at the same time. The challenge is how to do so."

Finally, Irvin spoke about "the integrity of IAMS as a society. . . . From attending this meeting, I would be tempted to say that the ecumenical movement's efforts to realize the unity given to us in Christ has been achieved. . . . *You genuinely like one another*. That is critical for maintaining the overall integrity of this association. . . . Integrity at this level assures the Association has a future."

Ezra Kok, the principal of Malaysia Theological Seminary, presided at the communion service in the closing worship. Music was arranged by Eileen Khoo, and Cathy Ross, from New Zealand, was the preacher.

The new Executive Committee met with the old Executive briefly right after the election on Thursday evening, August 5. At that meeting the old Executive handed over a number of issues in process for the new Executive to pay special attention to.

It was announced in an editorial in *MS* 21, no. 2 (2004), that the proceedings of the Port Dickson conference would be published in a special volume within the next year. Because of various circumstances, that did not happen. Three years later, eight of the main plenary presentations were published in *MS* 24, no. 2 (2007).

# XII
# Balatonfüred, Hungary, 2008

The new Executive Committee had its first official meeting on Friday night, August 6, 2004, at Port Dickson before the conference ended. Meeting with them was the new general secretary candidate (whose name was not mentioned publicly or in the minutes). They decided that the next meeting of the committee would be held in the Netherlands, January 30–February 1, 2005, at a location to be decided. Tentative dates for meetings in January 2006 and January 2007 were discussed.

It was decided to have a history of IAMS written. Klaus Schäfer would be contacted to see if he had the time and interest to do it. If he declined, then Gerald H. Anderson would be commissioned to write the history. No honorarium would be paid.

A draft Memorandum of Understanding was approved in principle for the next IAMS secretariat, concerning both the place and the person. It would be circulated to all the other parties, and a final version would then be sent to the Executive Committee for approval. After approval, it would be announced to the membership. The agreement would be for a four-year period and could be negotiated for renewal after three years.

A preliminary discussion about the next conference took place. It was decided to pursue the invitation to go to eastern Europe in August 2008.

A circular letter to IAMS members, dated December 21, 2004, was sent by Birger Nygaard, the outgoing general secretary, in which he reviewed the events of the Port Dickson conference. He also announced that Frans Dokman, at the Nijmegen Institute of Missiology, had agreed to serve IAMS with secretariat functions over the next period of years. One of the oldest missiological institutes in Europe, Nijmegen is part of the theological faculty at the Radboud Catholic University of Nijmegen, in the Netherlands. One of the founding fathers of IAMS, Arnulf Camps, was the head of this institute for nearly thirty years. The actual handing over of

101

the secretariat from Copenhagen to Nijmegen took place November 1–2, 2004.

It was not surprising that the next Executive Committee meeting was held at Mennorode, a Mennonite conference center in Elspeet (near Nijmegen), Netherlands, January 30–February 1, 2005. Committee members arriving the night before the meeting began were welcomed by Frans Wijsen, director of the Nijmegen Institute of Missiology, where the IAMS secretariat was now located. Birger Nygaard, the outgoing general secretary, gave a report on the outcome of the 2004 Port Dickson conference and the transfer of the journal management and publication to Brill. Frans Dokman, the new general secretary, reported on the transfer of the secretariat from Copenhagen to Nijmegen, and on his participation in the IACM conference in Cochabamba, Bolivia. He had also met with people at Brill regarding the journal. Visa problems prevented Kima Pachuau, editor of the journal, from attending the meeting, but he sent a report announcing that Stephen Bevans had been appointed as senior contributing editor.

It was decided to transfer the IAMS archives to the Day Missions Library at Yale Divinity School in New Haven, which is near the home of Gerald Anderson, who agreed to write a history of IAMS.

The next IAMS conference was set to take place in or near Budapest August 9–16, 2008, on a theme yet to be decided. (The dates were later changed to August 16–22, 2008.) It would be the first IAMS conference to be held in central and eastern Europe.

A major issue for discussion was the role and relationship of IAMS to the forthcoming conference in 2010 at Edinburgh. A delegation from IAMS will participate in a planning meeting at Edinburgh in June 2005, so a decision was deferred on the precise nature of the participation of IAMS until after that meeting.

There was also discussion coming out of the meeting at Port Dickson with representatives of regional associations for mission studies about the role and relationship of IAMS to the growing number of regional associations and networks. Based on the discussion here, Frans Dokman will prepare a memo on how to develop better relationships with the regional associations.

On Monday evening an informal "high tea" was arranged with about twenty-five Dutch missiologists. During this occasion Arnulf Camps, one of the founding fathers of IAMS, was invited to give his views on the future of missiology. Darrell Whiteman congratulated Camps, whose eightieth birthday was the next day, and presented him with an early gift from IAMS. This occasion was especially meaningful, as it turned out, because Camps died just a year later, on March 5, 2006. He had been a wise, winsome, and constant supporter of IAMS since the meeting at Selly Oak, Birmingham, in 1968, and had served two terms as president.[1]

The first IAMS electronic newsletter was sent from the secretariat to all members, dated March 2005. It introduced all the members of the Executive Committee and contained a message from Presi-

**Discussion group in Balatonfüred in August 2008**

dent Darrell Whiteman, reporting on the meeting of the Executive Committee in the Netherlands at the end of January. He announced the dates and place of the next IAMS General Assembly, to be held in Hungary in 2008, and the tentative plan for participation in the Edinburgh 2010 conference. There also was news of the Web-based directory of IAMS members; all members were invited to enter their contact data and academic profile into the directory, located on the IAMS Web site at www.missionstudies.org.

In November 2005 General Secretary Dokman sent a report to the Executive Committee about his recent visit to Budapest to assess the local situation for the IAMS assembly in 2008. He met with church and academic leaders and with board members of the

1. See his obituary in *MS* 23, no. 1 (2006): 5–7.

Protestant Institute for Mission Studies (PMTI), whose director was Anne-Marie Kool. She was also on the local planning committee, as well as a member of the IAMS Executive Committee, so she would be a key person in planning and organizing the conference. In general, Dokman said, there was enthusiasm among the local leaders he met for holding the IAMS assembly there in 2008, and a hotel had been selected as the site for the assembly. Some local organizational and personnel issues needed to be resolved, however, before making a final decision about going to Budapest in 2008. The Executive Committee could continue this discussion and make a final decision at their next meeting.

The year 2006 proved to be a very difficult time in the history of IAMS because of several unfortunate circumstances. The Executive Committee met at the OMSC in New Haven, Connecticut, January 27–February 1, 2006. Darrell Whiteman, president, resigned from the committee for personal reasons. The Executive Committee then appointed Vice President Philomena Njeri Mwaura as president and Jonathan J. Bonk as the new vice president.[2]

Frans Dokman and Anne-Marie Kool reported on progress with the local planning committee in Budapest regarding logistic and financial arrangements, local involvement, the missiological topics for the conference, and a hotel that was selected as the venue. After considerable discussion, the theme decided on for the Budapest 2008 conference was "Human Identity and the Gospel of Reconciliation: Agenda for Missionary Churches in the Twenty-first Century." The goal of the Budapest Assembly would be "to identify and explore ethnic, gender, political, and religious dimensions of human identity as challenge, opportunity, and obligation for Christian churches in mission."

Dokman also reported on his meetings with the planning group for the Edinburgh 2010 celebration, which led to a wide-ranging discussion regarding the significance of Edinburgh 2010 for IAMS. Plans were still in flux for the celebration, and it was decided that "after the IAMS 2008 conference it may be necessary to refine and redefine some of the IAMS goals set for 2010."

It was agreed that, "generally speaking, IAMS was as strong and healthy as were its study groups," several of which were active and involved between conferences. It was expected that DABOH,

---

2. See the announcement of this action in the Editorial Note in *MS* 23, no. 1 (2006): 1.

BISAM, Healing, and possibly others would have sessions during the conference in Budapest.

The committee visited the Day Missions Library at Yale Divinity School, which houses the IAMS archives, and were given a presentation about the library by Martha Smalley, the curator of special collections. They also had a discussion with Gerald Anderson about the IAMS history that he was commissioned to write.

The next meeting of the committee would be in Budapest, January 26–30, 2007.

Anne-Marie Kool and Jan A. B. Jongeneel

A second setback for IAMS came in April 2006, when Frans Dokman became seriously ill. When it became apparent that he would not be able to continue as the general secretary of IAMS, he resigned in June. The loss of two key leaders in such a short period posed a serious challenge for the Association. The Executive Committee had a teleconference on May 27, 2006, to discuss means to manage the secretariat during an interim period and to carry forward the planning for the conference in 2008.

After consultation with Frans Wijsen, director of the Nijmegen Institute of Missiology, which hosted the IAMS secretariat, the Executive Committee appointed Jan van Butselaar as the new general secretary, who agreed to serve until January 2009. Van Butselaar was already a member of IAMS and was well known as a Dutch missiologist. He had served as a missionary in Rwanda from 1975 to 1983 and then was general secretary of the Netherlands Missionary Council from 1983 to 2001.[3]

---

3. See the announcement of his appointment in *MS* 23, no. 2 (2006): 170.

In October 2006 a letter went to all IAMS members from President Philomena Njeri Mwaura in which she reported on the changes in leadership and expressed appreciation to both Darrell Whiteman and Frans Dokman for their service and a hope for their continued involvement in IAMS. She welcomed Jan van Butselaar as the new general secretary, announced the plans for Budapest 2008, and referred members to the IAMS Web site and the current issue of *MS* for further information on the theme of the conference and guidelines for writing papers.

Teleconference meetings of the Executive Committee were held on November 29 and December 8, 2006, to discuss issues related to the new secretariat.

With its new leadership, the Executive Committee met January 26–30, 2007, in Budapest at the Károli Gáspár University of the Reformed Church in Hungary where Anne-Marie Kool was professor of mission studies. On Sunday morning, the members participated in a worship service of the Gazdagrét Reformed Church in Budapest, where Hwa Yung, bishop of the Methodist Church in Malaysia and keynote speaker at the 2004 Port Dickson Assembly, was the guest preacher.

Jan van Butselaar presented a report of his activities as general secretary for the period from August 15, 2006, to January 15, 2007. Immediately after his appointment in August, he attended the Conference of European Missiological Associations in Paris. Then in November he went to Budapest to meet with the local committee that was planning arrangements for the conference in 2008. He was encouraged by the warm reception he received from local leaders, but they were astonished when they learned that the hotel that was the proposed venue for the conference had been sold and would no longer function as a hotel. It brought back memories of what happened in Costa Rica (1976), in Buenos Aires (1996), and in South Africa (2000), when the planned venue for the conference was suddenly not available. Fortunately, the local committee in Budapest still had time to find a new venue.

He also visited with Brill in Leiden to discuss some problems with publication and distribution of the journal, and the transfer of funds to IAMS. The contract with Brill would come up for renewal in November 2007, and the Executive Committee would need to decide what action to take. The discussions were very fruitful, and a new contract was drawn up wherein IAMS took back the responsibility for handling the membership fees and would pay Brill only for the publication of *Mission Studies*—as had been the arrangement before 2005.

In December van Butselaar represented IAMS at a meeting near London of the planning committee for the celebration of the Edinburgh World Missionary Conference in 2010. He came away with a feeling that the conference would be more limited than was originally envisaged and that "more work has to be done to create

Jan van Butselaar, general
secretary, at Balatonfüred

a coherent program." He also stressed to the Executive Committee that "our first concern has to be the [IAMS] Assembly in 2008."

Up to this time, van Butselaar spent one or two days each week in the office in Nijmegen and worked other days at home. He had a secretary in Nijmegen who worked half a day each week in the IAMS office. Clearly more assistance would be needed as the workload increased once they began organizing the conference in Budapest.

The treasurer reported that "the funds of IAMS were now quickly dwindling, so that careful use of financial means is needed."

A large part of the meeting dealt with preparation of the forthcoming assembly in 2008. It was decided to amend the theme slightly to "Human Identity and the Gospel of Reconciliation: An Agenda for Mission Studies and Praxis in the Twenty-first Century." The dates would be August 16–23, 2008.

Since the original meeting venue in Budapest would not be available in 2008, an excellent alternative site had been found in Balatonfüred, a popular summer resort town outside of Budapest, at a hotel on the shore of Lake Balaton. The Károli Gáspár University of the Reformed Church in Budapest agreed to function as the official host for the assembly, and it designated its officer for external affairs, Ms. Niké Skárosi, to function as assembly director for all practical matters. The local planning committee would be responsible for all local arrangements.

A program and schedule for the assembly was developed, with a list of proposed speakers and respondents.

Regarding the Edinburgh 2010 celebration, it was decided that IAMS would cooperate fully in the preparation of the event by delegating its general secretary to serve on the planning committee and by setting apart one plenary session at the 2008 assembly to focus on the legacy of Edinburgh 1910.

The committee was made aware that attention should be given to where the IAMS secretariat would be located after 2008. Would it continue in Nijmegen, or should other possibilities be considered?

In October 2007 the general secretary again visited Budapest, where he met with members of the local planning committee. They went to see the conference venue in Balatonfüred and were very pleased with the facilities and location for the assembly in 2008.

He had two meetings in 2007 with the planning committee for the Edinburgh 2010 conference, one near London, and the other in Edinburgh. He also attended a meeting in Poland of the IACM to strengthen IAMS's relationship with it.

The next meeting of the Executive Committee was held at Fuller Theological Seminary, Pasadena, California, January 25–29, 2008, where they were hosted by the provost of the seminary, Sherwood Lingenfelter, and his wife. On Sunday the members participated in a service at the cathedral of the Church of God in Christ in Los Angeles and then were given a tour through Pentecostal history in Los Angeles by Cecil Robeck from the seminary.

It was reported by the treasurer that, "although the finances are still healthy, there is some concern for the future developments in the light of the coming assembly." For the 2008 budget, "a shortfall is foreseen."

The editor of *Mission Studies*, Lalsangkima Pachuau, reported that he and the general secretary had visited the publisher Brill in November 2007 to discuss some problems, and that the relationship had improved, so the contract with Brill would be renewed for the period 2009–13. Pachuau agreed to serve another term of four years as editor, and the committee renewed his appointment with great appreciation.

The committee voted to encourage the new Executive Committee to be present at the Edinburgh conference in June 2010.

The main part of the meeting was devoted to further preparation of the forthcoming assembly. In response to the call for papers, ninety abstracts had been received and were being reviewed. In addition to several plenary presentations, with respondents, there would be parallel sessions of interest groups, regional group meetings, exposure trips to various mission sites, worship and Bible study, and time for recreation and informal discussion, in addition to a business session.

The Executive Committee met next on August 15, at Balatonfüred, just before the opening of the assembly. Anne-Marie Kool, chair of the local committee, urgently requested additional funding for local conference operations, since costs in Hungary had increased 10 percent since January 2007, when the budget was drafted. Almost 100 participants received some subsidy, and 20 percent more participants were coming than expected and had to be transported on the exposure excursions. Also the local committee was involved in additional tasks of registration, planning, and program. An additional €9,800 was therefore approved, representing a budget increase of 40 percent.

An invitation had been received to hold the next IAMS conference at Wycliffe College, which is affiliated with the University of Toronto, Canada, and the offer would be recommended to the General Assembly for approval. Cathy Ross, at CMS in Oxford, would be recommended as the new general secretary, and David Emmanuel Singh, at the Oxford Centre for Mission Studies, would be recommended as the new treasurer, for approval by the General Assembly. Eleven applications for membership were approved.

This being the last official meeting of the Executive Committee for 2004–8, President Mwaura "expressed her thankfulness to the members of the committee for their hard work in the past four years" and closed the meeting with prayer.

The Twelfth General Assembly of IAMS, meeting at Balatonfüred, Hungary, on the theme "Human Identity and the Gospel of Reconciliation: Agenda for Mission Studies and Praxis in the Twenty-first Century," began on August 16, 2008. After dinner on Saturday evening, the opening session started with a welcome by President Mwaura and worship, led by Péter Gáncs, bishop of the Lutheran Church in Hungary, and by Ferenc Szücs of the Reformed Church and rector of the Károli Gáspár University of the Reformed Church in Hungary. This was followed by greetings from local church and academic leaders, a film about Hungarian history, and a performance by a folk-dance group.

On Sunday morning, participants were taken in buses to worship in various churches in Budapest, followed by a city tour. With the exception of Tuesday, the program each day began with worship and Bible study, followed by a plenary presentation and sometimes a respondent.[4]

On Monday the theme was "Religious Identity and the Gospel of Reconciliation: A Central European View," presented by Hungarian sociologist Miklós Tomka. He described the situation before Communism, when "a hierarchical class structure and feudal conditions . . . existed in most countries of Eastern and Central Europe." Then came Communism, which "discredited previous social identities, obstructed and hindered community relations, and transformed individuals into solitary, dependent servants of the political machinery. . . . The collapse of the Communist dream buried those identities from the socialist or Communist past," but "the process of individualization, which is instrumental in the emergence of modern identities, is still in its beginnings." Now, he said, "the genuine vocation of religion is to strengthen human values, to help stabilize personal identity, to diminish social conflict, to promote reconciliation and human understanding by leading and relating people to God. . . . The first step to reconciliation is the healing of wounded identities." In conclusion, he noted, "One aspect of religious identity which can lay the foundation for reconciliation" is the religious insistence on "human sinfulness. . . . The realization of one's own failures plus the trust in God's forgiveness and God's help in overcoming one's wickedness puts reconciliation in a new dimension. . . . This is not yet reconciliation but can begin the disposition and willingness for it. And this is no small step." It was a powerful contextual reflection on the theme of the conference.

The respondent to Tomka's presentation was C. René Padilla, a New Testament scholar from Buenos Aires and an honorary life

4. The plenary presentations and responses mentioned in the following paragraphs were published in *MS* 26, no. 1 (2009). The address by Wi Jo Kang was not published, and no copy of the response to his paper by Norberto Saracco, from Buenos Aires, Argentina, exists in the records of the conference.

member of IAMS. He agreed with Tomka's analysis and added
an important emphasis: "The fact remains, however, that there is
not true healing for the oppressor without their liberation from the
evil of oppressing others, and there is no healing for the oppressed
apart from their liberation from oppression."

The next day was devoted to exposure trips for everyone. Participants could choose to visit a variety of Roma/Gypsy mission
projects; a meeting with representatives of the Jewish community and see the second largest synagogue in Europe; an exhibi-
tion showing the terrifying realities of both the Nazi and Communist dictatorships, where a pastor and member of Parliament
would speak about the experience of the churches in the time of
anti-Christian ideological dictatorships; or an urban mission that
ministers to 30,000 homeless people in Budapest. The DABOH
group would visit several church archival centers in Budapest and
end with a visit to the Central and Eastern European Institute for
Mission Studies of the Károli Gáspár University of the Reformed
Church in Hungary. A highlight for this group came during their
visit to the National Lutheran Archives, where they saw the original handwritten last will and testament of Martin Luther (signed
in Wittenberg, January 6, 1542), attested by the signature of his
friend Philipp Melanchthon.

On Wednesday the plenary theme "Ethnic Identity and the
Gospel of Reconciliation" was presented by Lalsangkima Pachuau, the editor of *MS*. His main point was that "there is only one
reconciliatory work and that is God's, and God's people are called
to the ministry of God's reconciliation in the world." However,
he said, "In the history of the institutionalization of the church,
it has been the self-centeredness of the church that stands in the
way of God's mission. . . . Christian mission (or God's mission) is
by nature other-centered, lacking which the church fails to express
its raison d'être, that is, its missional call. . . . The other-centered
formation of the selfhood of God's people reflects God's missional
purpose."[5]

Thursday's plenary theme, "Mission and Human Identity in
the Light of Edinburgh 1910," was presented by Brian Stanley,
professor of world Christianity and director of the Centre for the

5. There was a response to Pachuau's presentation by Peter Murungo
Kanyandago, from Kampala, Uganda, but no copy exists in the records of the
conference.

Study of World Christianity at the University of Edinburgh. He began with two bold claims of Christian theology as a motivation for Christian mission: "first, that the propagation of the Gospel of Christ offers the best prospect for reconciliation between human beings; and second, that human beings find their identity most completely by being 'in Christ.'" He then examined criticisms of these claims from a representative non-Christian (Jonathan Sacks) and a Christian theologian (Stanley J. Samartha). Stanley responded to their criticisms and, while repenting for "the repeated failure of the church throughout history to live out the truth of the Gospel of reconciliation," said he would still support the two Christian claims he proposed. The World Missionary Conference in 1910, he acknowledged, was "an event which graphically illustrates the fallibility of Christian thinking on the theme of human identity." But despite "all the archaic and unacceptable accents which [their] words carry to our ears, they surely convey something of the wonder of the final biblical vision of a new Jerusalem, a new city of God in which the identity of a divided humanity is made whole by incorporation in Christ."

Robert Schreiter, professor of theology at the Catholic Theological Union in Chicago, responded to Stanley's presentation. He discussed the consequences of taking reconciliation as a motivation for Christian mission, proposed a better way to deal with the unavoidable universalizing claims of religious traditions, and suggested some of the distinctive practices and disciplines needed if the Christian doctrine of reconciliation is to inform Christian mission. He concluded: "Can reconciliation be a paradigm of mission? Can it lead us to a new humanity that is at once true to our grounded identities yet at a new place if we are able to come together? . . . If reconciliation as mission is practiced according to the biblical insights into reconciliation, and not just proclaimed via the practices that have dominated mission in the last half millennium, then I think we may come to a new place, to a transfigured humanity, true to ourselves, and true to the God who created us."

The plenary theme on Friday morning was "The National Identity of North Korea and the Theology and Praxis of Reconciliation," presented by Wi Jo Kang, a Korean-born professor at Wartburg Theological Seminary in Dubuque, Iowa. He reviewed the military and political events that led to the division of Korea between north and south at the Thirty-eighth Parallel following World War II, a decision he described as "a national tragedy in historic proportion" for the Korean people. Less than five years later the Korean War broke out, which was a "direct result of the division created by the Thirty-eighth Parallel." The Korean War proved that "reunification cannot be achieved by military means! If Korea is to be reunified, there must be different means other than military, through the means of reconciliation." He then recounted that, "to achieve a peaceful reunification of Korea, thoughtful Korean Christian leaders and organizations emerged as a powerful force of reconciliation and peace movements . . . [with] the initiative coming from Korean Christians living abroad." Gradually in the 1980s and 1990s there were meetings of Christian leaders from North

Robert J. Schreiter, C.PP.S. (left), and Stephen B. Bevans, S.V.D.

and South Korea and from abroad, with some even going to North Korea as apostles of peace and reconciliation. In 1988 the National Council of Churches in [South] Korea proclaimed that the year 1995 would be the "Year of Jubilee for Peace and Reunification." Unfortunately, "The Jubilee year of 1995 came and went without reaching the goal of reunification, however the theological movement of reconciliation by Christians gained momentum." In June 2000 South Korean president Kim Dae Jung went to Pyongyang, where he met with Chairman Kim Jong-Il and issued a declaration regarding their desire for reunification of the country in the near future. In 2001 President Kim Dae Jung was awarded the Nobel Peace Prize in recognition of his efforts to achieve peace in the peninsula through national reconciliation. Kang concluded, "Korean Christians are serious about their calling to carry out the message of reconciliation and to practice a ministry of reconciliation." In 2002 Christian leaders in South and North Korea issued a joint prayer to be used in the Easter services that year. The prayer concluded with these words: "Bless the churches in South and North Korea and revive in us the spirit of peaceful reunification. Through the reconciliation of South and North Korea, help us to make a contribution for the peace of East Asia and protect the lives of the human community throughout the world." The prayer, said Kang, "acknowledged the global implications of reconciliation and peace in Korea."

In her presidential address, Philomena Njeri Mwaura gave "An African Reflection" on the theme of the conference. She observed that the numerical growth of Christianity in Africa "has not translated into a transforming spirituality that fosters Christian and national identity." Partly, she said, this is due to "the implanting of a divided Christianity by different denominations from different countries with diverse political agendas[, which] has left a lasting adverse mark on African Christian identity." Added to this is the problem of ethnocentrism. This was illustrated by the crisis in Rwanda, which "was ethnic in its manifestation, and the role of the church in it is illustrative of the magnitude of ethnic animosity that characterizes the church in some parts of Africa." She charged that "the nature, integrity, and identity of the church have been brought into question. . . . The church in Africa has failed in some respects to promote an authentic Christian identity that transcends barriers of ethnicity." The needed ministry of reconciliation, articulated by Paul, requires the church in Africa to be prophetic, vigilant, intrusive, and in solidarity with the marginalized. "The future of the African church," she argued, "depends on how it negotiates difference and reunites divided people into one family, a people of God who stand up for justice and promote and live the Gospel value of love of neighbor."

In addition to worship, Bible study sessions, and plenary presentations, there were eight parallel study groups that members could choose to attend, where eighty-five short papers were presented during seven sessions: BISAM, DABOH, Ethnic Ministries and Mission, Globalization and Mission, Healing and Pneumatology, History, Interreligious Relations, and Women in Mission. There was also a session for a meeting of young missiologists, as well as a time for regional group meetings; each of these groups would elect one of their members to serve on the Nomination Committee and would nominate three of their group for the new Executive

Committee, in order of preference. This was also a time to discuss ways to strengthen relations between IAMS and regional associations and networks.

In the general business meeting of the Association, the members stood while a list of members of IAMS who died since the last conference was read by the president: Arnulf Camps (a founding father and former president), Johannes Aagaard (former president), Kwame Bediako, Heribert Bettscheider, S.V.D., Frederick H.

**Philomena Njeri Mwaura following her presidential address to the IAMS assembly in Balatonfüred**

Bronkema, Walbert Bühlmann, O.F.M. (Cap.), Clyde Cook, Kwesi A. Dickson, Ralph E. Dodge, Jacques Dupuis, S.J., John Richard Grey, Per S. Hassing, Paul G. Hiebert, William Richey Hogg, David A. Kerr, Larry Keyes, Kosuke Koyama, James Kraakevik, Leny Lagerwerf, Louis Luzbetak, S.V.D., Donald E MacInnis, John Orme, Andrew C. Ross, Nico Smith, Charles Taber, Ralph Wiltgen, S.V.D., Ralph Winter, Hans Wisen, and Diana Witts.

Reports of the general secretary, the treasurer, and the editor were received, discussed, and accepted with gratitude. It was noted by the general secretary that "membership [of IAMS], now well over 400, is still increasing." The treasurer drew attention to "some significant changes in expenditure. . . . The main reason for this was the changeover in 2005 from a Secretariat where all expenses were covered by the hosting institutions to one where IAMS was principally responsible for the costs."

An amendment of article 5 in the constitution of IAMS was proposed by the Executive Committee, and after some discussion of the wording, the following sentence was added: "The Executive Committee of IAMS manages the affairs of the Association between general meetings of the Association."

The report of the Nominating Committee for a new Executive Committee was presented by the chairperson, Darrell Guder:

| | |
|---|---|
| President | Jonathan J. Bonk (New Haven) |
| Vice president | Mika Vähäkangas (Helsinki) |
| General secretary | Catherine Rae Ross (Oxford) |
| Treasurer | David Emmanuel Singh (Oxford) |
| Journal editor | Lalsangkima Pachuau (Wilmore, Kentucky) |

| Regional representatives | |
|---|---|
| Africa | Rose Uchem, M.S.H.R. (Nsukka, Nigeria) |
| Asia | Ken Christoph Miyamoto (Kobe, Japan) |
| North America | Paul Kollman, C.S.C. (Notre Dame, Indiana) |
| South America | Mariel Deluca Voth (Argentina; studying in San Diego, Calif.) |
| Oceania | Gerard Goldman (Thornleigh, Australia) |
| Europe | Mika Vähäkangas (Helsinki) |

There was a discussion regarding the tradition that the president and vice president of IAMS should belong to a different confession (Protestant/Catholic). It was argued that this should no longer be an issue in our ecumenical times, especially not in academic circles. In a secret ballot, the new Executive Committee was elected as proposed. In addition, Jan A. B. Jongeneel from Utrecht was elected as an honorary life member in recognition of his publications and other academic contributions to the advancement of mission studies, and also for his initiation of the European meetings of IAMS members.

It was reported that invitations to host the next IAMS conference in 2012 had been received from Wycliffe College at the University of Toronto, Canada, and from Abuja, Nigeria. The matter was referred to the new Executive Committee to make a decision.

A request was registered for the continuation of the study group Women in Mission, with a suggestion to change the name to Gender in Mission. Another study group—Young Missiologists—was in process of formation. Other areas of interest could be identified by the Executive Committee in order to involve as many members as possible in the IAMS study groups.

With no other business on the agenda, the meeting was closed with prayer by the new president of IAMS, Jonathan Bonk.

After dinner on Thursday evening, there was an opportunity for members to take a boat ride on Lake Balaton, followed by wine tasting from local vineyards.

On Friday afternoon there was a plenary for evaluation and summation of the conference, followed by a closing worship service, led by Bishop László Német from the Roman Catholic Church

**Former and current officers in Balatonfüred, August 2008.
Seated left to right, Martin Conway, Andrew F. Walls,
Philomena Njeri Mwaura, Gerald H. Anderson.
Standing, left to right, Darrell L. Whiteman,
Jan van Butselaar, Allan Anderson, Andrew Kirk,
John Roxborogh, and Jonathan J. Bonk.**

of Serbia. This was followed by a farewell lakeside dinner, with a musical program celebrating the cultural diversity of the participants in the conference.

Following the conference, Anne-Marie Kool, chair of the local committee in Budapest, sent a summary report, noting the conference "had 234 participants, plus local committee members, visitors and 12 stewards, representing 48 countries. 188 people visited 49 churches on Sunday. 252 persons participated in eight exposure visits on Tuesday during the conference, traveling 3,000 km.; 24,650 photocopies were made; two national TV channels in Hungary reported on the conference, twice there were live interviews on the national radio, and a number of national newspapers published articles on the conference."[6] A few years later she reported on the impact of the conference, "The consultation has had a great influence on [CEEAMS]. About fifty people of our region participated. It was the first time ever that an IAMS General Assembly was held in formerly Eastern Europe. The participants, stewards, the churches visited by the participants, and the Károli University as hosting institution, as well as the site visit hosts, still speak about this milestone."[7]

On October 7, 2008, Jan van Butselaar sent a farewell letter to the Executive Committee, with "the last greetings from the IAMS Nijmegen office! End of this month, my duties as general secretary will be fully assumed by my successor Cathy Ross," in Oxford. He had received "many enthusiastic messages from participants who thanked us for the excellent conference [at Balaton]."

---

6. Anne-Marie Kool, e-mail message to author, August 26, 2008. See also the Editorial in *MS* 25, no. 2 (2008), which included some reflections on the Balaton conference.

7. Anne-Marie Kool, e-mail message to author, December 1, 2011.

# XIII
# Toward Toronto, Canada, 2012

From January 8 to 11, 2009, the newly elected Executive Committee had its first meeting near Oxford, where the secretariat had been relocated to the Church Mission Society offices. This was especially appropriate since the newly elected general secretary of IAMS was Cathy Ross, director of the Crowther Centre for Mission Education at CMS. Also the newly appointed treasurer was David Singh, who was based nearby at the Oxford Centre for Mission Studies. During their time in Oxford the committee visited the offices of CMS and had afternoon tea with staff.

As President Jonathan Bonk later explained in a letter to IAMS members, the committee reviewed IAMS finances during the meeting and realized that the reserve funds of the Association were "at dangerously low levels, sufficient only to cover operational expenses for another year," and "necessitated severe cuts to our operating budget." This situation arose because of a number of unanticipated events. In his letter to "Fellow Members of IAMS" after the committee meeting in Oxford, Bonk said:

1. The cost of the Secretariat over the past four years had to be borne almost entirely by IAMS. For the first time in its history, the Association was obliged to pay a stipend to the General Secretary, who stepped into the breach when Frans Dokman suffered serious health problems and resigned. Dr. van Butselaar kindly came out of retirement to take up the work, but IAMS was thus obliged to compensate him for his time and effort.

2. It was the wish of the 2004 Assembly at Port Dickson that the next conference be convened in Eastern Europe. Accordingly, the 12th Assembly was convened in Balatonfüred this past August [and] attracted approximately 280 mission scholars from around the world. Although the local hosting committee budgeted as carefully as they could, a number of unanticipated expenses were incurred, mostly relating to transportation and accommodation for participants from Africa, Asia, and

even parts of Eastern Europe who had no way of paying their own expenses.

3. Finally, IAMS funds were held in US dollars, and the Executive continued to follow the pattern of budgeting in US dollars. Unfortunately, the American economy proved to be much less stable than all of us had been led to imagine. The result was an exchange rate that profoundly affected IAMS. The Balaton conference budget was calculated in US dollars, but actual expenses associated with the conference had to be paid in Hungarian forints, the local currency. As a result, instead of the expected surplus, the conference generated a deficit. In years past, surplus funds generated by our conferences have enabled us to move forward with a modest financial buffer in the bank to cover IAMS operational expenses between conferences. The Port Dickson Assembly, for example yielded a surplus of $13,000. The Lake Balaton Assembly, in contrast, suffered a shortfall of more than $26,000, leaving the operational reserves severely depleted, and risking the survival of IAMS as we know it.

It was later reported by the treasurer that, when all the final expenses for the Balaton Conference were paid, the shortfall was actually about $42,000!

To deal with this situation, the Executive Committee found ways to reduce the cost of the secretariat by at least one-third. They also agreed to meet by Skype, e-mail, and telephone, rather than—as had been customary—to convene annually in a central location as they did in January. This would save IAMS a substantial amount of money.

There was also a need to update and correct the IAMS membership database, as much of the information was out-of-date, and most members had not yet paid their dues for 2009. So members were requested to update their membership profile and pay their annual dues, following instructions on the IAMS Web site. Members who did not pay their dues would not receive the *Mission Studies* journal.

Finally, President Bonk appealed to the members for a one-time gift over and above the annual membership dues to carry on the work of IAMS in these difficult circumstances.

In the meeting at Oxford the Executive Committee took action to contract Tom Peek at CMS to redevelop the IAMS Web site. And after reviewing evaluations of the conference at Balaton, they began to discuss plans for the next assembly, in 2012. It was decided to accept the invitation to hold the meeting at Wycliffe College in Toronto in August 2012 on a theme related to issues of God's mission, human migration, and the movement of peoples. Initial discussion was held about the size and structure of the conference, resource persons, fund-raising, budget, and plans for future issues of *MS*.

It was agreed that an electronic newsletter should be issued twice yearly—as was initiated originally by Darrell Whiteman in March 2005—to supplement whatever appeared in *MS* and on the Web site.

The meeting ended with Evensong at Christchurch Cathedral on January 11.

Thereafter in 2009 the Executive Committee had meetings by teleconference on June 4 and September 28. The financial situation was still serious but started to improve. The publishing contract with Brill had expired, and there were issues to be resolved. A report was received about the successful DABOH workshop that was held in May in Lima, Peru, on the topic "Recovering the Memories of Our Peoples." The workshop was attended by eighteen pastors, church leaders, missionaries, and graduate students of missiology.

Planning the shape and content of the Toronto conference was undertaken to sketch out a conceptual framework and calendar, with provisional goals and deadlines for stages of preparation. Names of resource people, Bible teachers, theologians, and missiologists who had special interest in the theme were suggested. The length and size of the conference, firm dates, and budget were considered. On December 15 Jonathan Bonk had an initial meeting with a group of church and academic representatives in Toronto to form a local committee to discuss issues of logistics in hosting the conference, such as facilities, transportation, excursions, visas, translation, and liaison with churches and government agencies.

In January 2010 President Bonk sent a letter to IAMS members informing them about developments during the past year and outlining what was ahead in planning for Toronto 2012. He expressed appreciation to the Nijmegen Institute "for hosting the secretariat for so many years," to CMS in Oxford "for agreeing to become the new home of the secretariat," and to the "Oxford Centre for Mission Studies, where David Singh is encouraged and facilitated in his role as our Treasurer." Forty-eight new members had joined since the Balaton conference.

As another cost-saving measure, IAMS would not be paying the cost for two of its three delegates to the Edinburgh 2010 meeting in June. Cathy Ross and Jonathan Bonk would have their expenses covered from other sources, so that IAMS would be required only to subsidize the registration expenses of David Singh and his travel from Oxford.

During 2010 the Executive Committee had teleconference meetings on January 15, July 12, October 8, and December 10. Major decisions and developments in these meetings included the following:

- The contract with Brill for publishing *Mission Studies* was extended to 2012.
- Kima Pachuau indicated his intention to step down as *MS* editor after the Toronto conference; the search for his successor began immediately.
- By exercising better control over expenses and greater emphasis on increasing income, the deficit in 2010 improved significantly over 2009.
- Ann Chow in Toronto, who had considerable experience in managing arrangements for Christian conferences, was contracted as event manager for the Toronto conference.
- The name of the study group Women in Mission was changed to Gender in Mission.
- Dates for the Toronto conference were confirmed for August 15–20, 2012; the theme is "Migration, Human Dislocation, and the Good News: Margins as the Center in Christian Mission."

In September 2010 President Bonk sent a letter to IAMS members informing them about activities and decisions of the Executive Committee, in which he announced the dates and theme of the Toronto Assembly, which will "explore the profound missiological dimensions of human migration and dislocation, past, present, and future. We will attend especially to the many repercussions of widespread contemporary human movements for the theory and practice of mission. We welcome papers on mission and diverse aspects of human mobility from across the disciplines. These can touch upon a range of themes, including ethnicity, race, gender, HIV-AIDS, human rights, violence, poverty, nationalism, other religions, and ecclesiastical tradition."

Bonk also reported that a program design group for DABOH met in Rome, May 26–29, 2010, to plan for their participation in the 2012 General Assembly in Toronto. At that meeting, it was resolved "to ratify Marek Rostkowski, O.M.I., director of the Pontifical Missionary Library, Rome, to be a co-chair of the DABOH Study Group, effective from July 2010, for an eight-year term. This would bring DABOH more in touch with the Roman Catholic Church and the non-English speaking worlds. . . . DABOH also decided to commission a book project—a manifesto—on the *theology of memory*, to be published soon after the IAMS 2012 Toronto General Assembly. The goal of the book will be to make the theological case for being faithful stewards of memory for the sake of evangelization. . . . These two resolutions were the concrete outcome of the 2008 Balaton resolution to strengthen ties with Roman Catholic counterparts, and to pay greater attention to the theological foundation of archives."

In a teleconference meeting of the committee on December 10, 2010, Ann Chow, the event manager for the Toronto Assembly, was welcomed and thanked for the work she had already done. It was decided that a core group of the committee would meet with the local hosting committee in Toronto in mid-2011. Then the whole Executive Committee would meet with the Toronto hosting committee in early 2012, and again three days before the conference begins in August 2012. The committee had extensive discussions about the program design elements of the Toronto conference, speakers, and group leaders, as well as regarding the need to establish criteria and limits for those who apply for a subsidy to attend the conference.

In September 2010 Cathy Ross left her position at CMS in Oxford. Fortunately, she continued to reside in Oxford, where CMS was willing to maintain the IAMS office that would enable her to continue as general secretary of the Association. She was now teaching at Regents Park College in Oxford, and at Rippon College, Cuddesdon.

When the Executive Committee had a teleconference on February 7, 2011, they were pleased to hear from the treasurer that IAMS ended the year 2010 in the black for the first time since the 2008 Balaton conference. A conservative budget for 2011 was adopted, and all members were urged to assist in fund-raising for the Toronto conference. There was further discussion about potential plenary speakers and leaders for Bible study and worship at the conference. Guidelines were discussed for a conference subsidy formula and a subsidy application form, with priority given to IAMS active members from poorer countries who have an academic position and have paid their dues.

Jonathan Bonk, Cathy Ross, Paul Kollman, and Mariel Deluca Voth met in Toronto, April 13–15, 2011, with key members of the local hosting committee, including Ann Chow. All logistic aspects and details were discussed, and responsibilities were assigned for dealing with the schedule and other issues. The conference was planned for a maximum of 180 participants; about 40 would require visas, and 30–40 would receive some financial assistance, depending on the amount of funding available.

On May 10, 2011, the Executive Committee had a teleconference to hear a report about the meeting in Toronto. A provisional conference program and schedule were drafted that aimed to reflect a missiology of migration, for the story of the human race and migration is also the story of mission. It would include geographic, gender, ethnic, and religious representation. The opening welcome will be from the First Nations people of Canada. There will be provision for exposure experiences and church visits, Bible study and worship, plenary addresses, study groups, and parallel sessions for interest groups.

It was reported that Kirsteen Kim, a well-known missiologist who teaches at Leeds Trinity University College, has agreed to be the next editor of *Mission Studies*, and John Prior, a long-time missionary in Indonesia, is willing to serve as associate editor. The committee voted to recommend them to the assembly in 2012 for formal ratification, along with great appreciation to Kima Pachuau for his years of outstanding service as editor.

President Bonk sent a letter dated May 10, 2011, to the "IAMS Family," informing them about the latest developments in planning the program and arrangements for the Toronto Assembly, including fund-raising efforts and guidelines for those who apply for subsidy. He reported that the total current membership was 523 (plus 7 honorary members), but only 120 had paid their yearly membership fees of €30. He urged all members to pay on the IAMS Web site; if just 200 members were to pay their dues for this year, IAMS revenues would increase by €6,000. The budget for the Toronto Assembly, he said, was approximately $100,000 smaller than was budgeted for the last assembly, due largely to this being a shorter conference; in addition, the cost of food, facilities rental, and ground transportation will be substantially less than it was for similar services at Lake Balaton.

When the committee had its next teleconference on September 19, 2011, there was much to report. The inaugural issue of *IAMS Matters*, an official bimonthly electronic newsletter, was sent this month. In addition to messages from the president, the general secretary, and the treasurer, there were updates from all the study groups and links to various IAMS Web pages, with the latest news about plans for Toronto 2012.

The second number of *IAMS Matters* (Nov.–Dec. 2011) gave a Web link to the basic program for the Toronto conference and announced that in November the conference Web page would go online, where members could register for the conference. President Bonk advised that "registrations will be capped at 180, due to budgetary and logistical considerations." So far, $76,600 in pledges and actual contributions had been received, but an additional $99,400 was needed to support the conference budget of $176,000. The newsletter also contained an interesting DABOH update about the newly established "Global Digital Library on Theology and Ecumenism," which provides a single online library of theological resources available free of charge on the Internet, with multilingual access to full-text content, not only references, including journals, magazines, books, dissertations, and news documents on theology and ecumenism, open to all. It is based in Geneva, Switzerland, where the program executive of GlobeTheoLib is Stephen Brown (e-mail brown@globethics.net).

In another teleconference meeting of the Executive Committee, on November 28, 2011, there was evidence of momentum in planning and programing for the Toronto Assembly. The registration form for the conference and the Toronto Assembly Web site were ready and would be active online in December. The cost for general participants at the conference is CA$1,050 for registration, room, and meals.

Conference speakers include:

- M. Daniel Carroll Rodas, from Denver Seminary, whose latest book, *Christians at the Border: Immigration, the Church, and the Bible* (2008), is a biblical-theological orientation to Hispanic immigration;
- Daniel G. Groody, a Holy Cross priest, scholar, teacher, and award-winning author and film producer, who directs the Center for Latino Spirituality and Culture at the Institute for Latino Studies at Notre Dame University;
- Jehu Hanciles, born in Sierra Leone, director of the Center for

Missiological Research at Fuller Theological Seminary, and
the author of *Beyond Christendom: Globalization, African Migration, and the Transformation of the West* (2008);

- Mojúbàolú Olúfúnké Okome, born in Nigeria, a professor
at the City University of New York's Brooklyn College, with
thirty years' experience working on international development issues;
- Emma Wild-Wood, director of the Henry Martyn Centre in
the Cambridge Theological Federation, who has taught in
Congo and Uganda as a CMS mission partner and written
*Migration and Christian Identity in Congo (DRC)* (2008).

Study groups at the conference will include BISAM; DABOH;
Environment; Gender; Healing and Pneumatology; Interfaith Relations; Migration, Religion, and Identity; and World Christianity.

David Singh, treasurer, reported that "IAMS at the moment is
in a comfortable position and should be able to cover the conference (if within budget) and enable the future of IAMS to grow." A
budget report will be ready when the committee meets in Toronto
in March.

Lalsangkima Pachuau informed the committee that the next
issue of *Mission Studies* would focus on the theme of the Toronto
Assembly. He also reported that he will hand over his responsibilities to the new editor in January 2013.

The third issue of *IAMS Matters*, January–February 2012, gave
updates on the Toronto Assembly, including an introduction to
each of the plenary speakers and members of the hosting committee and a description of the exposure trips at the assembly.

The full committee met in Toronto with the local hosting group
March 2–4, 2012, to confirm the program and local arrangements.
The Executive Committee will also arrive in Toronto on August 12
to review conference plans and make any necessary adjustments
in arrangements before participants arrive on August 15.

# Epilogue

Forty years after the 1972 Driebergen Assembly, the Thirteenth IAMS Assembly convenes at Wycliffe College in Toronto, Canada, on August 15, 2012. IAMS has done what Olav Myklebust envisioned: it has become an international and interdenominational network association of individuals, organizations, and centers that are engaged in the scholarly study of the Christian world mission. It provides mutual encouragement, fellowship, and dissemination of information for the advancement of scholarship about world mission and the encounter of the Gospel with cultures and religions worldwide. It is not a sending or promotional agency—that is, not itself a mission organization—but an association for the study of mission. This was also the reminder from David Bosch, when he said, "IAMS is expected to provide a forum for missiologists to meet rather than to organize a missionary conference." At the same time, he noted that "we are in a process of fundamental revision, not only in missiology but in all sciences."[1]

As Birger Nygaard once observed, in the years since IAMS was founded, "tremendous developments have taken place in the area of mission studies. A number of national, regional, and denominational associations have emerged. Missiology has become a well-established academic discipline. Thousands of missiology graduates are now functioning in all parts of the world. IAMS has played its important little role in these developments." At the same time, he said, "these very positive developments pose challenges to what IAMS should be in years to come. What is the role and function of IAMS in relation to other missiological associations? What does the continued growth of Christianity in the Southern Hemisphere mean to the priorities of IAMS? How does electronic communication change the ways in which we should publish research findings and relate as a global community of mission scholars? What is the advocacy role of IAMS in the broader

---

1. See p. 59, fn. 2.

spectrum of theological scholarship?"[2] These issues still continue to shape the agenda of the IAMS.

In conclusion, this writer has three lasting impressions from his study. First, IAMS has flourished because it has had courageous, creative, and committed leadership that has been diversified in geography, gender, and church/theological traditions.

Second, while it has been faithful to Myklebust's original vision, the IAMS has expanded its scope. For instance, IAMS began as a predominantly Eurocentric, white, male organization. Today it is truly global, with strong membership of women (still a minority, but increasing). It has had international assemblies around the world: four in *Europe* (Netherlands, Germany, Italy, Hungary), three in *North America* (United States [New York, Hawaii], Canada), and two each in *Africa* (Zimbabwe, South Africa), *Asia* (India, Malaysia), and *Latin America* (Costa Rica, Argentina). Several areas of the world, however, have not (yet) hosted an assembly: East Asia (Japan, South Korea, China), the Middle East, and Oceania; nor has the United Kingdom been a host country. Also, the themes and issues of the assemblies have expanded. For instance, it is hard to imagine that the theme of the Toronto Assembly would have been featured in one of the early assemblies.

Third, while IAMS has flourished, it is a vulnerable organization, due largely to structural weaknesses caused by the frequent shift of offices and its dependence on hosting agencies or academic institutions, with quick turnover of officers.[3] In a period of economic recession, many mission organizations and churches are less able to contribute to its support. And while the number of IAMS members is increasing, many are often unable to pay their membership fees. The Association has therefore been forced to modify its traditional means of administration and meetings and to adopt a less costly style of consultation and communication, utilizing more electronic forms of contact. Four features, however, remain essential for the organization: the international assemblies, the study/work groups, the scholarly journal, and the newsletter, although these may not always remain the same in format, frequency, and makeup.

Finally, looking back over the record of these forty years, we

2. *MS* 17, no. 1 (2000): 11.

3. Joachim Wietzke, e-mail message to author, August 21, 2010, suggested some of these observations.

are able to say with gratitude and confidence that truly "IAMS matters," where members witness together to address the challenges of vast new developments and opportunities in mission studies, "so that God may be glorified in all things through Jesus Christ" (1 Peter 4:11).

# Addenda

# Rescuing the Memory of Mission: The Story of "Documentation, Archives, and Bibliography"

## John Roxborogh

The Documentation, Archives, and Bibliography (DAB) mission workgroup within IAMS had its origins in a meeting, in Oslo in 1970, which led to the formation of IAMS two years later.[1] For over forty years it has facilitated international cooperation, conferences, and statements to help publicize the importance of documentation for mission studies. It has contributed to the production of *Rescuing the Memory of Our Peoples: Archives Manual* (2003), which has been translated into Chinese, French, Korean, Portuguese, Spanish, and Swahili.[2] For a number of years DAB invested much effort in a major project that attempted to design and develop software for sharing bibliographic resources on mission. The challenge of "rescuing the memory of our peoples," set for DAB in 2001 by the IAMS Executive Committee, remains a key statement of the purpose of the workgroup.[3]

DAB has sought to bridge the worlds of professionals and institutions, researchers, administrators, educationalists, church

---

1. See www.library.yale.edu/div/RTMmanuallinks.html. Since 2003, DAB has been DABOH: Documentation, Archives, Bibliography, and Oral History. I am indebted to many people who helped with valuable input for this account of DABOH's interesting story, but special thanks are due to Gerald Anderson, Paul Jenkins, and Martha Smalley.

2. Martha Smalley and Rosemary E. Seton, *Rescuing the Memory of Our Peoples: Archives Manual* (Oxford: IAMS; New Haven: OMSC, 2003). Available in Chinese, English, French, Korean, Portuguese, Spanish, and Swahili. See "RTM Archives Manual—Additional Links," August 3, 2006, www.library.yale.edu/div/RTMmanuallinks.html. Also available from www.omsc.org/archivesmanual.shtml.

3. There was some inconsistency in usage between "rescuing the memory of our people" and "rescuing the memory of our peoples." The plural was intended to convey concern for minority groups.

leaders, and laypeople who from conviction or necessity find themselves guardians of the oral and written stories of the mission of the church in Asia, Africa, Latin America, and the Pacific. It has facilitated the writing, translation, and promulgation of guidelines. In 1997 it set up the first IAMS Web site. It has supported IAMS members seeking to come to terms with the challenge and promise of information technology and has, like the community of IAMS as a whole, been a place of respectful encounter, informed exchange, and deep fellowship.

When DAB began, its primary concern was to provide a stimulus to the collection of data needed for mission studies with an initial focus on non-Western Christianity. Before the age of computers, bibliographies compiled by experts were the major distributable guides to journals and books in libraries. Archives and documentation centers, whether in an academic or mission setting, held unique manuscripts and archival collections as well as oral histories and more ephemeral evidence of the life of the church—reports, clippings, pamphlets and papers, and other missiologically rich "grey literature." The practice of creating distributable finding aids for archival collections was developing in academic settings, but mission archives and missionary libraries often documented their published and archival holdings only in informal ways. If Christian mission was going to have the apparatus that its serious study demanded, there was need for shareable finding aids and citation systems across diverse categories of material in diverse settings.

It is part of the story that, at the point that DAB most energetically sought to provide these systems by defining subject categories and bibliographic specifications and by commissioning computer software, it did not succeed. From 1988 to 1992 the "DAB project" aimed to develop and in due course market a universal mission studies database. Although the process was well informed, there was a failure to appreciate quite what was involved, and by mid-1992 it was clear that the project was outside the core mission of IAMS. The Association was hardly alone in coming to recognize that the realization of a technological dream can be frustrated. The need remained, of course, but it became increasingly possible to make use of affordable systems developed by the information technology industry. Mission studies may have seen itself as singular among the theological disciplines in the range of resources it sought to preserve and reference, but it was less unique in the wider world, which eventually provided tools that were generally and globally accessible.

The purpose, however, not the technology, remains the proper concern of IAMS. The work of DAB continues, as every generation concerned with the critical study of Christian mission seeks to address the task of recording the present and recovering the past with evidence that can be revisited by others.

## Beginnings

The decision to form an international association for mission studies and to appoint a provisional committee was taken at the European Conference on Mission Studies, meeting in Oslo in August 1970. The vision was for a body that would be scientific and scholarly in its discussions and publications. This demanded the ability to locate and identify the objective data without which rigorous study could not take place. Andrew Walls summarized the report of a group of members, including himself, who had expressed their concerns about bibliographic, documentary, and information services:

> The group had concluded that there was a need for more information in systematic form about existing resources and services and requested the Provisional Committee to sponsor a questionnaire to this end; urged that institutions compile and exchange lists of periodical holdings; that institutions adopt, after due consultation, a standard form for recording bibliographical information; that a comprehensive bibliography for Mission Studies was desirable, with careful determination of its relationship with existing projects; that institutes should meanwhile seek at least local or national comprehensiveness with a view to exchange of information; and that future conferences should provide for news and discussion of documentation and other *instrumenta studiorum* for mission studies.[4]

4. Andrew F. Walls, "Minutes of a Meeting Held During the European Conference on Mission Studies in Rönningen Folkehögskole, Oslo, on Thursday 27th and Friday 28th August 1970," August 29, 1970, pp. 2–3, http://missionstudies.org/archive/3exec/1970Aug-A_meeting-Oslo-Norway.pdf. Walls recalled that the term *instrumenta studiorum* was used by other disciplines such as patristics. As mission studies sought to establish itself as a new discipline, it was important to clarify the instruments for study that it needed. Paul Jenkins reports in "Rome Working Party DAB: Report, Actions, Reactions," *IAMS NL*, nos. 18–19 (Oct. 1981): 9, that this ongoing need became the underlying question of the 1980 Rome Conference.

The Provisional Committee met at Klooster Alverna, Netherlands, in November 1970, and "Bibliography and Associated Activities" was a significant item on the agenda. It was agreed that Andrew Walls convene a working party to follow through on the suggestions made at Oslo and that links be established with the *Bibliographia Missionaria*, published annually since 1935 by the Pontifical Missionary Library.[5]

IAMS was finally launched in Driebergen in August 1972, and the next meetings were held in Frankfurt in 1974, San José in 1976, and Maryknoll, New York, in 1978. These all included further workshops on documentation and bibliography. The working party advocated "documentation, bibliography, and archives" as a major function of IAMS as a whole, and planning began for a major consultation in Rome in July 1980.[6] In 1974 the Lausanne Conference and the research group MARC pioneered the use of computers to process statistical data and information about Christianity around the globe, and there was growing awareness that the implications of computer technology for common standards and information sharing needed to be explored.[7]

It was not self-evident where the boundaries either of mission studies or of its sources lay. Andrew Walls reported in 1974 that the working party saw "little usefulness in comprehending items on evangelism in western countries, nor indeed every item which could be represented as having relevance to Christianity in Africa and Asia (e.g., every article on the Theology of Paul written by, say, Indian theologians, or every commentary on, say, the Church and alcoholism by Afrikaner church leaders)."[8] An immediate focus

5. Andrew F. Walls, "Minutes of a Meeting of the Provisional Committee of the International Association for Mission Studies, Held at Klooster Alverna, Netherlands 20–21 November 1970," 1970, p. 2, http://missionstudies.org/archive/3exec/1970Nov-Provisional_Cmte-Alverna-Netherlands.pdf.

6. The objective was that concern for documentation, bibliography, and archives appear "not as an appendix but as belonging to the aims of IAMS." F. J. Verstraelen, "Minutes of IAMS Executive Committee Meeting March 25–27, 1977, Aarhus, Denmark," September 26, 1977, p. 2, http://missionstudies.org/archive/3exec/1977-Aarhus.pdf.

7. MARC, the Mission Advanced Research and Communication Center (not to be confused with "Machine Readable Cataloguing), was founded in 1967 and merged into World Vision Resources in 2003. Steven Haas, "MARC to Make Transition, Retain Its Mission," *MARC Newsletter* 3, no. 4 (Nov. 2003): 1.

8. Andrew F. Walls, "International Association for Mission Studies

was identified in the history of non-Western Christianity and in critical studies of mission from the West. Although such concerns already found expression in the bibliographies of the *International Review of Mission* and *Bibliographia Missionaria,* much more was needed. The collections of the Missionary Research Library in New York and the library of the Pontifical Urbaniana University in Rome were important, but the need was for centers around the globe, not just in the West. In 1967 funding for the Missionary Research Library in New York had been withdrawn, a worrying reminder of the fragility of even Western institutional commitment.[9]

## DAB Rome, July 24–30, 1980

The first Rome DAB conference is remembered as one of the most significant that many of the participants ever recall attending. The gathering of fifty-seven registered participants from fourteen countries was chaired by Andrew Walls, and the host was Willi Henkel, O.M.I., who was also secretary. Held in the recently constructed John Paul II Aula in the grounds of the Pontifical Urbaniana University and adjacent to its famous Pontifical Missionary Library, there was a strong sense of place and of occasion. Participants felt the weight of a "communications revolution, perhaps even more momentous in its consequences than the invention of the alphabet."[10] The papers were outstanding, though it became part of DAB folklore that, having been microfiched with the best technology of the day, they were then easily mislaid, if not lost altogether. In 2004 the conference report was reprinted in conventional format, and it is now available online.[11]

Concern was expressed about the Eurocentricity of the par-

Report of the Executive Committee, 1972–1974," 1974, http://missionst udies.org/archive/3exec/1972-1974.pdf.

9. Cecilia Irvine, "Documentation of Mission in the Nineteenth and Twentieth Centuries," *Missiology* 4, no. 2 (Apr. 1976): 196.

10. Andrew F. Walls and Willi Henkel, O.M.I., eds., *Mission Studies and Information Management: Report of a Working Party Organized by the Committee on Documentation, Bibliography, and Archives of the International Association for Mission Studies, Held in the Urban University, Rome, 24–30 July 1980* (Leiden: IAMS, c/o Interuniversity Institute for Missiological and Ecumenical Research [IIME], 1980), p. ii, www.ttc.edu.sg/csca/arch-pres/dab1980.pdf.

11. www.ttc.edu.sg/csca/arch-pres/dab1980.pdf.

ticipants, but the global scope of their interests and wide denominational spread was also clear. There was a balance of attention among philosophical, practical, and technical issues. Recommendations included investigation into microform technology and a handbook to be titled "Appropriate Technology and Procedures for Local Church Archives in the Third World." Duplication was a concern, as was the need for coordination and use of common standards in bibliographic projects. In referencing the same article, "one center gave 3 key-words, and another 61."[12]

The meeting called on churches worldwide to cooperate in partnership in preserving, organizing, and making their oral and written archives available.[13] The need for surveys of existing collections and a directory was also highlighted.

Arthur Glasser, from Fuller Theological Seminary, later wrote of the "rather determined group" who had brought the event together, and of the visits, papers, and inspiration, which included special mention at a papal audience. In *Missiology* he reiterated the appeal for "archival decentralization with scholarly collaboration."[14]

## IAMS Bangalore, India, 1982

The next DAB meeting was a two-day consultation following the IAMS conference in January 1982, during which the chair passed from Andrew Walls to Stephen Peterson, who at the last minute was unable to attend. As in every gathering, the role DAB should play was a real question in the face of persistent needs and changing environments. Considering the needs in the Indian context also raised the question of whether DAB was "just another" funding agency—or were networking and awareness to be its greatest contributions? Paul Jenkins, archivist at the Basel Mission, considered DAB to be "in the business of raising consciousness" and that tasks requiring financial commitment would be more difficult. DAB saw

12. Paul Jenkins, "Documentation, Archives, Bibliography Meeting 14–16 January 1985, Harare," *MS* 2, no. 1 (1985): 138.

13. Stephen L. Peterson and Paul Jenkins, "Future Steps in Church and Mission Archives," in *Mission Studies and Information Management*, ed. Walls and Henkel , pp. 131–33; later circulated as "Statement on Missionary and Church Archives."

14. Arthur Glasser, "Archival Alert—Rome 1980," *Missiology* 8, no. 4 (1980): 389–95.

opportunity for twenty Third World documentation centers, but a proposal to seek sponsorship did not pass the core group.[15]

Discussions continued. In December 1983 DAB was noted as "an important concern" of IAMS, and it was reported that Stephen Peterson and David Bosch had visited the Religion Index offices of the American Theological Library Association (ATLA) in Chicago.[16] They examined the ATLA Religion Index thesaurus and its suitability for missiology, as well as computerization and the possibility of assistance. They recommended exploring "a missiological database within the services and programs of the Religion Index." This "would receive indexing input from several worldwide centers of mission study and documentation. The database could be used for specialized bibliographies, customized literature searches, and printed bibliographical tools." It was hoped that linking with an existing provider like ATLA would avoid the need for DAB itself to get involved in computer programming and development of a new thesaurus.

In July the IAMS Executive agreed to fund further explorations and asked for a report for the forthcoming meeting in Harare, as well as a session "DAB Issues in an African Context."

## IAMS Harare, Zimbabwe, 1985

Papers presented at Harare included "Archives and the Re-orientation of African Church History" and reports on the archives of the Methodist Church of Zimbabwe, the United Methodists, Catholics, and Evangelical Lutherans. Time was spent at the Zimbabwe National Archives and in discussing the work of oral history programs.[17] The core group now consisted of Paul Jenkins, Willi Henkel, Sigvard von Sicard, and Leny Lagerwerf, with Stephen Peterson, Gerald Anderson, and Andrew Walls in the wings. All except von Sicard had shared the experience of Rome in 1980.

Paul Jenkins noted the felt tension between hope and reality.[18] DAB was "a good network," but it had no finances. A handbook

15. Paul Jenkins, "Report on DAB," *MS* 2, no. 1 (1985): 131.

16. "DAB Concerns," *NL*, nos. 22–23 (1983): 48.

17. Jenkins, "Documentation, Archives, Bibliography Meeting 14–16 January 1985, Harare," pp. 135–38.

18. Jenkins, "Report on DAB."

had been produced[19] and information had been collected on the practicalities of microform media. Tropical humidity and archives without air conditioning were ongoing concerns. Several long-running bibliographic projects were using 3" × 5" index cards and typeset publications. Andrew Walls maintained the bibliography in the *International Review of Mission* (*IRM*), which had begun in 1912. Willi Henkel and the Pontifical Urbaniana University Library produced *Bibliographia Missionaria*, begun in 1935. David Bosch and the Southern African Missiological Society organized the production of abstracts for each issue of their journal *Missionalia*. Missio Aachen (Thomas Kramm) had its own program and thesaurus, and that of Centre de Recherche Théologique Missionaire in Paris (Joseph Lévesque, P.S.S.) had reached its third revision. Over time, these publications themselves raised further issues of classification and indexing. The founding father of IAMS, Olav Myklebust, had compiled an index to the *IRM*, and Lesslie Newbigin revised the categories to reflect awareness of his era that "the home base is everywhere."[20]

Stephen Peterson proposed a central mission documentation database with a standard bibliographic format, but allowing centers to use their own subject descriptors.[21] The aim was to be able to distribute both bibliographies and documents. A necessary step would be to identify possible centers and interested people and to evaluate a pilot project. ATLA's religion indices were among the possible databases, but costs and the nature of any potential relationships were issues. "While the time-saving of coordinated analysis looks attractive, is this practicable in view of the different interests of the different centers and in view of the deeper problems of translating key-words from one language to another?"[22]

Further questions focused on who the users would be and whether they could cope with the data generated. Mission's lack of conceptual boundaries was an intractable issue—"mission should not be narrowly conceived, but it had to be defined. The range of literature of relevance to the missiological quest was wide indeed."

19. Sven Hedenskog, *How to Arrange Archives* (Uppsala: Church of Sweden Mission, 1984).

20. A. Christopher Smith, *International Review of Mission: Index, 1912–1990* (Geneva: IRM, 1993), p. vii.

21. Jenkins, "Documentation, Archives, Bibliography Meeting 14–16 January 1985, Harare," p. 140.

22. Ibid., p. 139.

Duplication was still an issue, as were the means of communication and delivery between centers and contributors. Experience with computers was giving a better sense of what appeared to be within reach, but electronic exchange demanded common standards, and "uncoordinated application of PCs and Macs added to the difficulties."[23]

Agreement was reached to cooperate with Emory University on a bibliography of mission and church-related periodicals in Africa. The microfiche distribution of Harold Turner's material on new religious movements was noted as a model for returning data to its sources.[24] Turner had also had to design a taxonomy to cope with missiological information that challenged inherited conceptual frameworks and to find ways of doing something practical with the resources available. The Year Book on Race Relations in South Africa was an example of documentation on a specific issue. As Paul Jenkins commented, "We cannot have too much documentation of grassroots Christian belief and practice in Africa."[25]

## DAB Paris, January 5–10, 1987

The question of indexing was immediate. At the request of the IAMS Executive, a workshop was held in Paris in early 1987.[26] Institutions and publications represented included the American Society of Missiology (Norman Thomas), ATLA (Albert Hurd), *Bibliographia Missionaria* (Willi Henkel), the Centre de Recherche Théologique Missionaire (Joseph Lévesque and Edith Bernard), the Centre for the Study of Islam at the Selly Oak Colleges (Sigvard von Sicard), the Maryknoll China Project (Sue Perry), Interuniversity Institute for Missiological and Ecumenical Research (IIMO,

23. Paul Jenkins and Willi Henkel, "DAB Workshop in Paris, 5th–9th January 1987," *MS* 3, no. 1 (1986): 100.

24. Harold W. Turner, "'And brought forth fruit a hundredfold': Sharing Western Documentation Resources with the Third World by Microfiche," *IBMR* 9, no. 3 (1985): 110–14.

25. Paul Jenkins, "The Roots of African Church History: Some Polemic Thoughts," *IBMR* 10, no. 2 (1986): 70.

26. Paul Jenkins, "Documentation, Archives and Bibliography Network (DAB) Co-operation in Missiological Indexing: The Search for Common Ground," *MS* 4, no. 1 (1987): 71–84; Joseph Lévesque, "Atelier de travail, Paris janvier 1987," *MS* 5, no. 2 (1988): 134–36.

Leny Lagerwerf), the *International Review of Mission* (Andrew Walls), Missio Aachen (M. Nienhaus), Missio Munich (W. Kaminsky), and *Missionalia* (David Bosch).[27] A. Ngindu Mushete and K. Tshimanga came from Kinshasa, M. Pereira from Colombo, Bernard Anderson from the Heras Institute in Bombay, and Eduardo Bierzychudek from ISEDET in Buenos Aires.[28]

By any standards, this was a substantial gathering with expert input. Taking seriously issues highlighted at Harare, it recommended cooperation between the *International Review of Mission* and ATLA in producing a list of periodicals of missiological interest, and between *IRM* and *Bibliographia Missionaria* on the harmonization of their indexing practices. It determined basic specifications for computer work-stations[29] and formats for exchange of data, as well as a missiological macro-thesaurus to facilitate cooperation among centers using different thesauri and languages. The group still had in mind the problems of computers, as indeed of documents, in the tropics. The meeting expressed recognition of issues raised for missiology by video and audio tape media as well.

Each center had its strengths, personalities, and areas of interest and expertise. Bilateral cooperation seemed easier than multilateral agreement of any depth. The ATLA could receive information and help with software but was not able to key in other people's data. Computers produced areas of both compatibility and incompatibility. Although computerization was now a global phenomenon, questions of politics and power were of missiological concern.

The group saw itself as "people building up databases," and it wanted to bring "grey" literature into mission studies, as well as to identify what was relevant in other genres of writing.[30] Inadequacy

27. David J. Bosch, "The State of Co-operation in Missiological Indexing Now" (unpublished paper presented at the IAMS Workshop on Co-operation in Missiological Indexing, Paris, 1987).

28. Instituto Superior Evangélico de Estudios Teológicos.

29. An "IBM PC-AT" using the database software dBASE III+ was recommended. In the sequence of personal computer development designed by IBM, the "AT" had become a common standard by 1986 and was replicated globally. It is odd, given its successful use by Joseph Lévesque, that the meeting did not also commend the freely available CDS/ISIS database software designed by UNESCO in Paris for developing countries.

30. *MS* 4, no. 1 (1987): 82.

of time and resources were exacerbated by confessional and geographic diversity. A sense that the world was moving under one's
feet and of not being able to respond appropriately caused uneasi-
ness. When different systems were being developed by different
centers in different languages, could or should their differences be
resolved? Whose responsibility was it to do so? Was it a task for
IAMS-DAB, or was their role just one of championing the needs and
facilitating learning?

## IAMS Rome 1988

The energy from Paris flowed into a wider DAB forum following the IAMS conference in Rome in July 1988. Papers in English and in French provided reminders of the significance of
mission archives for secular and cultural history. Heinz Hunke's
keynote address updated the challenges of documentation in an
electronic age.[31] John Pobee called attention to oral theology and
traditions.[32] Jean-Paul Wiest and Sue Perry reported on using a
database to cross-reference Wiest's comprehensive research on
Maryknoll in China.[33] Norman Thomas picked up the concern
about tape media.[34] The convener, Paul Jenkins, reported that the
1980 statement on archives and documentation had been widely
quoted; it had "even found its way into one or two social science
periodicals."

The meetings sustained the sense of urgency. Christian
Deutsch, a youthful programmer who, almost stereotypically,
looked the part, demonstrated database software, though what had
been specified just eighteen months earlier was already becoming
obsolete. One concern was the amount of data and labor involved
in implementing the vision, which led to a decision to allow a
smaller number of essential database fields, thirty-two, instead of
an optimal fifty-four if MARC (Machine Readable Cataloguing)

31. Heinz Hunke, "Documentation for a New Millennium of Mission,"
*MS* 6, no. 1 (1989): 73–86.
32. John S. Pobee, "Oral Theology and Christian Oral Tradition: Challenge to Our Traditional Archival Concept," *MS* 6, no. 1 (1989): 87–93.
33. Jean-Paul Wiest, "The Maryknoll China History Project," *IBMR* 9,
no. 2 (1985): 50–56; Susan Perry, "Computerized Data Retrieval: The Maryknoll China History Project," *IBMR* 9, no. 2 (1985): 61.
34. "Projected Media in Mission Archives and Documentations," *MS* 5,
no. 2 (1988): 136–41.

standards were to be followed.[35] Plans envisioned for data to be entered locally then sent to a central location for redistribution.[36]

Perhaps the full import of what was being contemplated was not quite appreciated; by being concerned with data found in materials ranging from published books and academic journals through grey literature and other occasional documentation to the unique items deposited in archives, DAB found itself trying to apply the same set of cataloging standards to an expansive and heterogeneous array. Archivists might be accused of harboring other people's stories, but they did have a respect for the terms in which people told them and knew that their finding aids ought to reflect these terms. Paul Jenkins was aware of the importance of other disciplines and new sources for fresh understanding but was also troubled by the conceptual and practical limitations of culturally bound classification systems.[37]

## From Rome to Hawaii 1992

At Rome the chair was taken by Norman Thomas, who was involved in editing a joint American Society of Missiology and IAMS annotated bibliography of books on mission that would follow the specified standards and use the software. In March 1990 Patrick Lambe, then librarian at the Selly Oak Central Library, became coordinator and spent three weeks in the United States visiting many people associated with DAB, including Norman Thomas, Gerald Anderson, Stephen Peterson, and Douglas Geyer of ATLA.[38] When the project group met again in Basel, the prospect of compact discs addressed the problem of information distribution.[39] Later, a meeting at Selly Oak in Birmingham made progress with the macro-thesaurus and software, and the programming

35. See "MARC Standards (Network Development and MARC Standards Office, Library of Congress)," August 26, 2010, www.loc.gov/marc/.

36. *MS* 5, no. 2 (1988): 145.

37. Paul Jenkins, e-mail to John Roxborogh, "IAMS/DAB History," April 7, 2011.

38. Patrick Lambe, Librarian's Report, Selly Oak Central Library, 1990, p. 5.

39. Stephen L. Peterson, "North American Library Resources for Mission Research," *IBMR* 15, no. 4 (1991): 155–64. Later taken further by A. Christopher Smith, "Mission Research and the Path to CD-ROM: Report on the Global Quest to Share Information," *IBMR* 19, no. 4 (1995): 146–153.

begun by Christian Deutsch was continued by Richard and Sue Fairhead.

Despite IAMS's concern about the financial implications, success seemed within reach, and further efforts were made to raise funds. Norman Thomas provided a detailed overview of the rationale and progress,[40] and DAB became committed to a project for developing software for distribution. It had moved beyond just formulating standards or facilitating cooperation. The goal of producing licensed software was set for the next IAMS international conference, to be held in Hawaii in August 1992.

Meantime, the role of coordinator shifted from Patrick Lambe to Stan Nussbaum. During a meeting in Basel in November 1991, Norman Thomas e-mailed John Roxborogh in New Zealand. The encouraging new possibilities of economical global communication and data exchange seemed confirmation of the project's feasibility and value.

Each of these meetings reported progress, yet the incremental changes in goals obscured just how far the aims of the project had moved. A viable product was always just over a horizon, requiring further investment and the evaluation of promising new software.

The need driving the project was indisputable—how else would researchers be able to check that they had identified all relevant sources? If IAMS did not champion and coordinate access to global material of missiological relevance, who would? Bibliographic theory and technology were emerging concerns for theological librarianship, as reflected in the start, late in 1992, of the *Journal of Religious and Theological Information*. Other disciplines faced similar issues, and some of them, such as medicine and education, already had their centralized databases and were moving toward online delivery.[41] Missiology had not yet sensed that a different paradigm altogether might be needed or that another academic discipline might be the one to provide it.

Looking back on what was involved in two highly technical areas—formulating international standards for bibliographic

40. Norman Thomas, "Documentation, Archives, and Bibliography (DAB): Progress Report," *MS* 7, no. 2 (1990): 237–43.

41. For instance, AskEric began in 1992 as an online service of the U.S. Department of Education Educational Resources Information Center. See "Educational Resources Information Center—Program, Organization, History," n.d., http://education.stateuniversity.com/pages/1939/Educatio nal-Resources-Information-Center.html.

descriptions, and designing software to use them[42]—it may seem remarkable how DAB came to believe that it was within its reach to specify and configure database software, sustain its development in a rapidly changing environment, successfully obtain international agreement, raise sufficient capital, and with a group of volunteer researchers and academics from different languages, cultures, and churches, successfully coordinate the collection, management, and distribution of accurate electronic data in a universal format. Yet the project was in many respects eminently plausible, the database was eventually developed to a professional standard, and a way forward around the difficulties of the thesaurus did eventually emerge. These, however, were not the only issues.

An article from that period entitled "The New Age of Documents" indicated that problems in setting international standards were common, and that what was needed in the face of marketplace realities was daunting.[43] IAMS did not have the resources demanded by a situation that posed a challenge even for sizable businesses with expertise in the field. In 1992 only a very few were beginning to foresee ways that the Internet might provide a different model of ways information could be organized and shared.

As planning for the next IAMS conference progressed, personal circumstances required Norman Thomas to withdraw, and in mid-1992 the IAMS Executive approached John Roxborogh to take over as chair. By this time the coordinator, Stan Nussbaum, had joined Global Mapping International (GMI) in Colorado Springs, where Richard Fairhead had already moved to benefit from collegial support.[44] GMI was dedicated to placing information technology at the service of Christian mission. If it was willing to take

42. See Ross Harvey and Philip Hider, eds., *Organising Knowledge in a Global Society: Principles and Practice in Libraries and Information Centres*, Topics in Australasian Library and Information Studies 23 (Wagga Wagga, N.S.W.: Charles Sturt Univ., Centre for Information Studies, 2004).

43. John Warnock observed, "Most attempts to define standards by committee are plagued by the need to reach agreement among many different interest groups and factions. Compromises are made, and the result is often a 'paper standard' that is too abstract and complex to be practical. . . . [This] in no way implies that the members . . . are not trying to do the right thing." And "Computers should not be the center of our attention—the information should." John E. Warnock, "The New Age of Documents," *Byte* 17, no. 6 (1992): 260.

44. Stan Nussbaum, e-mail to John Roxborogh, "Draft paper," June 26, 2010.

over the database development and if IAMS members supported GMI by purchasing copies, it would provide an appropriate home at least to the information technology side of the project. During the Hawaii conference it was agreed that the project should be formally handed to GMI.

## From Hawaii to Buenos Aires 1996

The decision involved some grief, and DAB had to rediscover other dimensions of its mission. IAMS wondered what there was to show for its financial commitment, though the possibility that GMI could see the project through to a viable outcome kept some hopes alive. Norman Thomas continued with the ASM annotated bibliography, which was published in due course, though the experience underlined how difficult it was for those who were not catalogers to complete even the essential fields specified.[45] John Roxborogh visited Willi Henkel in Rome, Leny Lagerwerf in Leiden, and Edith Bernard and Joseph Lévesque in Paris and sensed their frustration. They had all been deeply involved, but none had become convinced that they should give up local systems for the unrealized promise of a universal project.

ATLA's own project for referencing non-Western Christian literature also ran its course. In 1993 the International Christian Literature Documentation Project (ICLDOP) appeared in print, and then on CD as a bibliography of Third World holdings in key North American libraries.[46] It marked a move from the indexing of articles and multiauthor works to monographs and "grey literature," but the labor was considerable, and the benefits mixed. It did bring missiologically relevant literature out of the archives and into public-access catalogs, and authority files were an important component, but it became clear it was a one-off project dependent on special funding. By 1994 ATLA was moving from being primarily a publisher of printed bibliographies to a developer of online electronic databases with facilities for document delivery.[47]

---

45. Norman Thomas, ed., *International Mission Bibliography, 1960–2000* (Lanham, Md.: Scarecrow Press, 2003).

46. Douglas Geyer, ed., *International Christian Literature Documentation Project: A Subject, Author, and Corporate Name Index to Nonwestern Christian Literature* (Evanston, Ill.: ATLA, 1993).

47. "ATLA Plans for Internet Services," *ATLA Program Notes* 6, nos. 2–4 (July 1994): 1–2.

By 1995 there was online access, albeit erratic,[48] via the database for the *International Review of Mission* Cumulative Bibliography, which Christopher Smith at the Centre for the Study of Christianity in the Non-Western World at the University of Edinburgh had compiled and published in 1993 with assistance from the university computer services.[49] As with ATLA's ICLDOP, the work of establishing authority files for authors in different languages and cultures was an important outcome. It seemed that IAMS-DAB had a role in helping those involved with other providers. They could take responsibility for decisions that might be proprietary rather than global, yet still be relevant for the worldwide task. In a 1995 article Christopher Smith outlined the North American and British part of the DAB story, capturing something of its hopes, frustrations, and achievements. He noted parallel ventures by other groups and the story of GMI's work with the database after 1992.[50]

Others whose interests and commitments intersected with what the DAB project had attempted were not immune from failure.[51] As they sensed that new means of achieving the intention of the project might emerge, fears of duplication and absence of universal standardization, which were once prominent, now seemed less of an issue. It became possible to wonder, How much did it actually matter if researchers had to use more than one system, each with its own search terms and strategies?

Four years after handing the project on, DAB met again during the 1996 IAMS Buenos Aires Assembly. Stan Nussbaum reported that the GMI software was now viable, but interest in using it was fading, and it became clear that further work on it was not justified. It is hard to see whether this was lack of confidence arising from the history of the project, or whether new means of addressing the needs were proving more workable than expected.

48. Martha Smalley, e-mail to John Roxborogh, "Various," November 22, 1995.

49. Bill Watson, "Technical Note," in Smith, *International Review of Mission*, pp. ix–x.

50. A. Christopher Smith, "Mission Research and the Path to CD-ROM: Report on the Global Quest to Share Information," *International Bulletin of Missionary Research* 19, no. 4 (1995): 146–53.

51. Stephen Peterson, *Mission Studies Resources for the Future: A Report Based on the Mission Studies Resource Development Project* (Monrovia, Calif.: MARC, 1995).

At Buenos Aires DAB was aware of its need to serve the IAMS constituency in its witness to the cultural diversity and common humanity shining through the stories of a global church. Participants shared information about a Web site developed for the Overseas Ministries Study Center, a new Central Library for the Selly Oak Colleges, and the role of archives in preserving the records of First Nations in North America. A visit to the ecumenical seminary of ISEDET exposed the group to ways that the changing vocabulary of mission was being tracked through terminology used in local publications. Seeing a local documentation center newly connected to the World Wide Web in operation proved significant. The staff was passionate about the Web's importance for getting stories out, and the director of SEDOS in Rome,[52] Walter von Holzen, was thrilled to see documents appear online that he had created halfway around the world.

A survey questionnaire on documentation, archives, and bibliographic needs was distributed during the conference,[53] and responses showed that interest was well distributed globally and was shaped by location, church, and institution, as well as by the state of technology and perennial questions of resources and support. Some specialized in particular sources such as academic journals, newspapers, or faculty papers. Others focused on themes such as local theologies, women's issues, enculturation, and political missiology. Emerging questions included tracking diaspora churches, such as the Nigerian Church of the Lord, Aladura.

The Internet was being accepted as a technology that was within reach, at least of institutions. Communication was still often a matter of letters in the post, but e-mail was becoming more common. Fax was useful for many, but access to most documentation, and certainly to archives, still required a physical visit.

Less than half the respondents used a thesaurus, and only three used the Library of Congress or ATLA subject headings. Many had developed their own subject lists, and index cards were still the standard tool. Most had access to personal computers and were familiar with word processing, but less than half had modems. A

52. Service of Documentation and Study on Global Mission. See "SEDOS Rome," 2010, www.sedosmission.org/site/.

53. The survey was completed by twenty-three people (eight each from Asia/Oceania and Europe/North America, with four from Latin America and three from Africa). A copy of an analysis by Carl Dunwoody is in the IAMS-DAB archives at Yale Divinity School.

quarter had the then latest operating systems, and the same proportion had database software.

Questions raised included how to deal with oral sources, grey
literature, and stories of independent churches. The concern to
facilitate Third World access to both information about sources
and the sources themselves underlay many responses,[54] as did the
desire to take seriously the diversity of world Christianity. The
growth of postgraduate study outside Western centers created
new opportunities and demands.

## From Buenos Aires to Hammanskraal, South Africa, 2000

If the basic plea from the Buenos Aires survey was "How can we
link with other places?" then DAB needed to take seriously how
this might be facilitated. At the Executive meeting of IAMS held
in Selly Oak, Birmingham, in January 1997, it was decided that
IAMS should itself establish a presence on the World Wide Web
and, despite the "costly failure" of the DAB data-collection project,
this was entrusted to DAB.[55] As convener, John Roxborogh agreed
to be responsible, and the Web site www.iams.org.uk came into
existence, later to be replaced by the current domain, www.missi
onstudies.org (registered in 1999).

Gradually, links were discovered and noted, materials compiled, and reports added to the site. If once again a new technology proved to have a life of its own, at least this time the costs were
manageable.[56] It was not irrelevant that theological issues around
information technology were beginning to be identified, or that
access to missiological information was changing through the
mechanism of hypertext links and the power of search engines.[57]

---

54. In a plenary DAB presentation, the use of the term "Third World" was
challenged by one speaker because of its possible association with "third rate"
rather than "third force." The intention (as here) was to try to avoid defining a
large group of countries by their not being "Western."

55. "Minutes of the IAMS Executive meeting, 9–12 January 1997, at Selly
Oak Colleges, Birmingham," January 1997, p. 9, http://missionstudies.org/
archive/3exec/1997-Birmingham.pdf.

56. John Roxborogh, "The Information Superhighway as a Missiological
Tool of the Trade," *Missiology* 27, no. 1 (1999): 117–22.

57. David Lochhead, *Shifting Realities: Information Technology and the
Church* (Geneva: WCC Publications, 1997).

The next international IAMS gathering, held in January 2002 at Hammanskraal, north of Pretoria, South Africa, again found it necessary to wrestle with the role of DAB. The Web was making it feasible for small institutions to make information about their holdings, if not digitized copies of the holdings themselves, widely available. Online discussion groups were advocated by Stephen Hayes, who had been a pioneer in their development in the early days of bulletin boards and e-mail. New questions had to be faced about security and the sensitivities and ownership of material capable of misuse in the wrong hands. E-mail addresses, rare rather than unknown in Buenos Aires, were now ubiquitous, spilling over a blackboard set up to share them. Yet Africa provided evidence of the unevenness of the digital revolution, and what could later be called "broadband poverty" was becoming a new dimension of missiological concern.

If the Web meant that some of the needs that had driven the DAB database project were now being met elsewhere, the problem of resourcing for archives and documentation remained. A reminder of the social significance of this task lay in the mission of the National Archives of South Africa "to foster national identity and the protection of rights" by "acquiring and caring for records of national importance" and by promoting "efficient, accountable and transparent government."[58]

In an act of faith, it was decided to hold a further DAB conference at Rome. Outside funding would be sought. The subsequent meeting of the IAMS Executive in New York determined that the focus would be "rescuing the memory of our peoples."

## DAB Rome 2002: Rescuing the Memory of Our Peoples

The Rome 2002 consultation met from September 29 to October 6 in the International Center for Missionary Animation (CIAM) and was convened in conjunction with the International Association of Catholic Missiologists. The group was encouraged by recollections of the seminal meetings in Rome in 1980 and 1988 and the value of being exposed to the archival resources of the Roman Catholic Church and its orders. While it was not possible to repeat the

58. "About the National Archives and Records Service of South Africa," n.d., www.national.archives.gov.za/aboutnasa_content.html.

papal audience of 1980, Rome again proved to be a strategic location, and the economics manageable.

A key means to address the task of "rescuing the memory
of our peoples" centered on developing a working document
on archives management. This built on what Martha Smalley
had already done at Yale and used interaction with the more
than forty participants from twenty-five countries to develop it
as a global resource. Presentations focused on enabling participants to articulate the challenges and opportunities of their own
contexts.

Andrew F. Walls gave
the keynote address at
the DAB conference in
July 2002 in Rome.

IAMS president Paulo Suess sent a message and a flag, drawing attention to the landless workers of Brazil. Paul Jenkins enliv-
ened awareness of the hidden messages in the huge legacy of
historical photographs in mission archives. William Burrows
noted that the significance of memory for Christian mission and
archives needed to be developed alongside work on the theological dimensions of the tasks of archives, documentation, oral
history, and the rescuing of the memory of all people, particularly those at the margins. Attention was drawn to the Pontifical Commission for the Cultural Heritage of the Church and the
1997 circular letter to bishops "The Pastoral Function of Church

Archives."[59] Kwame Bediako reminded participants of the importance of archives for the recovery of Christian memory in the
post-Christian West, as well as the post-Western inculturation of
Christianity in the Majority World. Also, mission needed to take
place to and in the academy against the long amnesia in regard to
dynamic encounter with Christian faith. Archival resources were
reshaping the understanding of the New Testament in Africa, as
elsewhere, but archives were not neutral, and memories were to
be redeemed as well as rescued. Neither missionary hagiography

**Attendees at the DAB conference "Rescuing the Memory of
Our Peoples," July 2002, in Rome**

nor the demonization of mission and imperialism addressed evidence of transcendence in lives that had been lived very differ-
ently because of Christian faith.

Subsequent meetings in India, New Zealand, Madagascar,
Peru, and elsewhere took the vision of "rescuing the memory of our
peoples" into other contexts. In New Zealand it was striking that
mission executives traveled to attend a workshop because, though
they wanted to get on with the present and future challenges of
their mission, they were also faced with inquiries about their past
that they found difficult to handle. Beyond our dreams, *Rescuing the
Memory of Our Peoples: Archives Manual*, edited by Martha Smalley
and Rosemary Seton, was soon being used as a training resource. It

59. Robin Gard, "The Pastoral Function of Church Archives," *Journal of
the Society of Archivists* 19, no. 1 (1998): 53–62.

was translated first of all into French, and then into other languages and made available through the Yale Divinity School and the Overseas Ministries Study Center and their Web sites.[60]

## IAMS Port Dickson, Malaysia, 2004

The 2003 IAMS Executive meeting revisited the name of the group, settling on DABOH to maintain continuity with the group's past while giving recognition to oral history as a key dimension of its mission. Arranging for further translation and distribution of *Rescuing the Memory of Our Peoples: Archives Manual* into other languages, including Chinese and Spanish, was a major concern. In 2005 John Roxborogh relinquished his role, and the chair passed to Michael Poon, director of the Centre for the Study of Christianity in Asia at Trinity Theological College, Singapore.

Previously, oral history had frequently been spoken about but had been a gap in the actual programs of the group. Jean-Paul Wiest, who had spoken at Rome in 1988, developed this field as a special interest flowing from his work on Maryknoll in China. The contagious vision flowing from his workshops in Asia is continuing to bear fruit.

## IAMS Lake Balaton, Hungary, 2008

Many of the presentations at the IAMS assembly in Balatonfüred, located on the shore of Lake Balaton in Hungary, involved the survey of documentation. Again it was noted that, without documentation, there are no texts to archive or study. The shift from paper to e-mail had facilitated the location and sharing of documents relevant to mission, but it also had vastly changed methods of research. The implications for archives and documentation of successive generations of electronic communications are still being determined. As always, what may not appear to have missiological interest is not necessarily without missiological relevance. The records management not just of mission agencies but of all those who are in any way concerned for the mission of the church is relevant to creating archives and

60. www.library.yale.edu/div/RTMmanuallinks.html and www.omsc .org/archivesmanual.shtml.

documentation, which will be the essential primary sources for the future.

DABOH looked to commissioning best-practice manuals on grey literature and on digitalization, as well as the need to pay attention to the theology of documentation of societies in transition.

## Toward Toronto 2012

In May 2010 a planning meeting was held in Rome, hosted again by the Missionary Oblates of Mary Immaculate and the Pontifical Urbaniana University Library. It was decided to pursue a project on the theological locus of archives and the role of documentation in ministry and priestly formation. Later the IAMS Executive accepted the recommendation that Marek Rostkowski, O.M.I., be appointed co-chair, renewing and strengthening DABOH's ties with Catholic missiology, documentation, and archives.

## Conclusion

Mission studies remains concerned with the empirical life of the church worldwide, not only its theological self-understanding. The issues raised by the nature of IAMS as an association for the scholarly study of mission at the beginning of its history are still with us. If mission is to be studied scientifically, then documented sources are essential. It is still necessary to face the challenge of knowing how to identify, locate, and access written, oral, and visual evidence of Christian mission in places below the radar of conventional documentation. Technologies change and present both opportunity and temptation. If some of the DAB experience provided hard won lessons, it has also been a stimulus and an inspiration.

A broad vision of the *missio Dei* and of the interests of mission studies means that boundaries will always be widely drawn. Theologies of memory and of mission support new questions in different contexts. The technologies of the day will continue to facilitate these tasks in different ways and make their own demands. The DABOH network continues to encourage and support the practitioners and theoreticians of mission in their need to preserve and access empirical evidence of Christian mission.

Concern for memory and its record is a matter of commitment to the future as well as the past. Making it possible for new generations with new questions to find their way to primary sources of mission globally lies at the core of DABOH's identity and offers renewal. It also subverts the possibility that defining knowledge is primarily about power and dominance. Perhaps the DAB project of the 1980s needed to fail, not only to remind missiologists that some parts of God's mission are best left to others, but also to make clear that the very terms in which that mission is understood should never be captive to any one culture and its conceptual architecture.

Archives and documentation are not infallible or ever complete, but they are authentic. DABOH shares in the privilege of helping to ensure that they exist, and that they continue to speak in their own terms and in ways that address concerns of universal relevance.

# "Biblical Studies and Mission" Study Group: The First Thirty-Five Years

## John Mansford Prior

This essay looks at the birth of the BISAM study group of IAMS in the mid-1970s, the key issues that arose during its first dozen years under its pioneering coordinator, Marc Spindler, and the gradual but painful shift from classical European biblical and missiological scholarship to more contextual and intercultural readings of the Bible largely emanating from the Southern Hemisphere toward the end of the 1980s with John Pobee and, from the mid-1990s onward, with Teresa Okure and latterly John Prior. The essay concludes with crucial questions on the role of BISAM in IAMS over the coming years.[1]

## Marc R. Spindler—Pioneer and First Coordinator, 1976–88

The birth of the Biblical Studies in Mission (BISAM) Study Group of IAMS can be traced to a proposal advanced by Marc R. Spindler[2] on prospective "study projects" that might be undertaken

1. John Roxborogh graciously allowed me to make liberal use of his "History and Scope of BISAM Within IAMS: 1972–1992," in *To Cast Fire upon the Earth: Bible and Mission Collaborating in Today's Multi-Cultural Global Context*, ed. Teresa Okure (Pietermaritzburg: Cluster Publications, 2000), pp. 215–27, which has been extremely helpful; I am most grateful. The previous coordinators—Marc Spindler, John Pobee, and Teresa Okure—each responded generously to e-mail requests. Obviously opinions expressed in this present essay are my responsibility alone.

2. Marc R. Spindler (b. 1930) gained a doctorate in Protestant theology at the University of Strasbourg in 1967. He was a missionary in Madagascar (1960–74), teaching at the United Theological College, Ivato (1967–73). While director of missiology at IIMO (1974–95), Spindler was also professor of missiology and ecumenics at the State University of Leiden and State University of Utrecht. He received an outstanding Festschrift on his retirement (*Changing Partnership of Missionary and Ecumenical Movements. Essays in Honour of Marc*

by Association members.[3] This proposal was accepted in 1976 by the IAMS Executive during the Third Assembly, at San José, Costa Rica, and Spindler was tasked to commence the project. He foresaw making a new assessment of the progress of biblical scholarship in relation to mission today.

As director of the Department of Mission at the Interuniversity Institute of Missiological and Ecumenical Research (IIMO) in Leiden,[4] Spindler's original dream was to have BISAM accepted as a study project of IIMO, or at least a substantial part of an IIMO project. However, an apparently abstract study on "biblical research" was not a priority for the IIMO board. Nonetheless, IIMO approved Spindler's coordinating role for BISAM, thus allowing him use of the institute's facilities for BISAM activities, including publication of ongoing BISAM research. IIMO also approved the appointment of Frans J. Verstraelen, then Marc Spindler's deputy at IIMO, as general secretary of IAMS. For the following ten years, IIMO hosted the IAMS secretariat and the BISAM coordinator.

*Institutional support.* Spindler found he had research space under the umbrella of the Theological Faculty of Leiden University in his capacity as tutor of postgraduate students preparing for their masters. In this way he succeeded in recruiting students to research for BISAM. Peter Middelkoop compiled the bibliography *Bible and Mission*, covering the years 1960–80, and, after sixteen months as student research assistant, continued work in this field at IIMO.[5]

---

*Spindler*, ed. Leny Lagerwerf, Karel Steenbrink, and Frans Verstraelen [Leiden-Utrecht: IIMO, 1995]).

3. While the acronym BISAM has remained constant, it has variously stood for Biblical Studies and Missiology (IAMS assemblies in 1978, 1986, 2004), Biblical Studies and Mission (1982, 1992), and Bible Studies and Mission (2000). It was formerly known as a "study project" (1978) or a "working party" (1986). In 2000 the IAMS Executive clarified that groups such as BISAM are "Interest Groups" when networking between conferences, "study groups" when in session during conferences, while "projects" were limited to specific programs approved and partly financed by the Executive itself.

4. Created in 1969, the IIMO department for missiology was located in Utrecht; that for ecumenics, in Leiden.

5. Marc R. Spindler and Peter R. Middelkoop, *Bible and Mission: A Partially Annotated Bibliography, 1960–1980* (Leiden-Utrecht: IIMO, 1981). This bibliography has over one thousand entries. The IAMS Executive (London 1981) hoped this general bibliography would "stimulate the various [continenta] task-forces to compose a detailed regional bibliography on 'Bible and Mission' from within different contexts." This proposal was never realized. Further

Martin Walton was another student at the university faculty recruited for BISAM. Walton's topic was published as *Witness in Biblical Scholarship: A Survey of Recent Studies, 1956–1980*.[6] Arie L. Molendijk, yet another research assistant under the umbrella of the university, wrote a number of studies.[7] New Testament scholar Johannes Nissen, from Aarhus, Denmark, was invited by the university on a three-month scholarship (March–June 1981); he wrote a study published as *Poverty and Mission: New Testament Perspectives on a Contemporary Theme*.[8] In these ways, institutional support from both IIMO and the State University of Leiden assured the viability of BISAM throughout its first ten years.

*Initial focus.* Studies undertaken under Marc Spindler's direction indicate his interest in biblical foundations for mission and the key biblical concept of witness.[9] These concerns grew out of his earlier involvement in a consultation (Geneva 1960) organized by

---

research included studies such as that on the reception of Johannes Blauw's volume *The Missionary Nature of the Church: A Survey of the Biblical Theology of Mission* (London: Lutterworth Press, 1962) and on the use and misuse of the Bible in the Dutch branch of a nondenominational evangelistic agency; the latter study brought out the dichotomy between "scholarly uncommitted" and "missionary evangelistic" readings of the Bible (see Peter Middelkoop, *Het bijbelgebruik van het Instituut voor Evangelisatie te Doorn* [The use and misuse of the Bible in the Dutch branch of Campus Crusade for Christ International] [Leiden-Utrecht: IIMO, 1983]).

6. Martin Walton, *Witness in Biblical Scholarship: A Survey of Recent Studies, 1956–1980* (Leiden-Utrecht: IIMO, 1986).

7. Arie L. Molendijk, *Getuigen in missionair en oecumenisch verband. Een studie over het begrip "getuigen" in documenten van de Wereldraad van Kerken, de Rooms-katholieke Kerk en de Evangelicalen, in de periode 1948–1985* (Leiden-Utrecht: IIMO, 1986); "Carte Blanche voor 'Getuigen.' Ontwikkelingen in de getuigenisterminologie en theologie binnen de Wereldraad en het Vaticaan," *Nederlands Theologisch Tijdschrift* 40 (1986): 290–304; and "Carte Blanche for 'Witness': Developments in the Terminology and Theology Within the World Council of Churches and the Roman Catholic Church," *MS* 4, no. 2 (1987): 52–64.

8. Johannes Nissen, *Poverty and Mission: New Testament Perspectives on a Contemporary Theme* (Leiden-Utrecht, IIMO, 1984). Nissen recalls the 1981 Executive Committee of IAMS in London, where Walter Hollenweger (Birmingham University) gave a paper on "narrative exegesis," which triggered a lively discussion that later fed into the Bangalore Conference the following year. Thirty years later Nissen remains an active member of BISAM.

9. Later redefined as "creedal witness," that is, the expression of the Christian credo in emerging churches worldwide. The IIMO board accepted this project in 1981 and, as already noted, published several volumes.

the International Missionary Council (IMC) as it embarked on the process of integration into the World Council of Churches (WCC). Theological underpinning for this merger was spelled out in a survey of the progress of biblical studies over the previous thirty years (1930–60) undertaken by Johannes Blauw, part of a five-year IMC study project.[10] With the BISAM project, Spindler wished to go "beyond Blauw," that is, initially to undertake a follow-up survey pertaining to the period after 1960.[11] This research highlighted a key issue. As Spindler wrote a decade later, he was concerned that "a strong current in scholarship . . . insisted upon a completely disinterested, uncommitted research" among biblical scholars, resulting in "an increasing estrangement of biblical scholarship from mission studies."[12] He also observed how specialization in missiology tended in the direction of cultural anthropology and the social sciences. These concerns led to intense discussions during the first ever BISAM workshop during the next IAMS conference.

*Maryknoll workshop 1978: Biblical Foundations for Mission.* The BISAM workshop during the 1978 IAMS Maryknoll Assembly was convened by Marc R. Spindler and John S. Pobee under the theme "Hermeneutics of Mission." The workshop report opens with the following statement:

> The present trend in missiology is to . . . interpret mission via the human sciences rather than via the biblical data. . . . Conservative evangelicals . . . rightfully argue that this "collecting" task must be carried out within an agreed frame of reference—an horizon of meaning or pre-understanding, and this inescapably involves the "hermeneutical circle." All accepted that there are many different horizons of meaning: the political, sociological, economic, humanitarian, ecclesiological, eschatological, mystical and theological, and that each of these horizons has its own methodology by which to conduct the evaluative process.

The report continues: "The seemingly simple question, 'What is mission?' involves two prior questions: 'What should mission be?'

---

10. Blauw, *Missionary Nature of the Church.* The English title of the published version of Blauw's survey is too broad; his draft is more narrowly, and accurately, titled, "Mainlines of a Biblical Theology of Mission."

11. Spindler and Middelkoop, *Bible and Mission.*

12. Marc R. Spindler, "Visa for Witness: A New Focus on the Theology of Mission and Ecumenism," *MS* 3, no. 1 (1986): 51.

and 'What is mission in actual fact?'" The report concludes: "Missiology should always have a theological basis. It should also be a bridge between past ways of doing things and all future disciplines of theology and provide them with relevant data essential to realizing the fullest meaning in the life of the church."[13]

As Donald Senior noted later, interpretation of the Bible for mission depends upon our understanding of the Bible, the understanding of mission we bring to the Bible, and the recognition of the contexts in which interpretation takes place.[14] These issues gave rise to spirited debate over the years.

During the Maryknoll Assembly, proposals were made to implement the desire to go "beyond Blauw," that is, to uncover the importance for missiology of recent exegetical research. Because of an increasing awareness of the variety of intercultural readings and socioeconomic contexts, it was proposed that a task force be formed on each continent to survey what was being done and to undertake new research; only at a later stage would the findings be exchanged. Spindler nurtured a task force in Europe, but no such networks saw the light of day on other continents.[15]

*Bangalore workshop 1982: Common Witness.* At the 1982 Bangalore IAMS Assembly, the first held outside the West, BISAM attracted so much interest that the workshop had to meet in two groups. The workshop report noted that "there is a pluriform approach to the biblical theology of mission, for there is a plurality of theologies of mission within the Bible . . . a unified concept of mis-

13. Marc R. Spindler and John S. Pobee, "Hermeneutics of Mission," *Missiology* 7, no. 1 (1979): 81–85.

14. Donald Senior, C.P., "Bible," in *Dictionary of Mission: Theology, History, Perspectives,* ed. Karl Müller, Theo Sundermeier, Stephen B. Bevans, and Richard H. Bliese (Maryknoll, N.Y.: Orbis Books, 1997), pp. 44–47.

15. Marc R. Spindler and John S. Pobee, "Continental Workgroup on Exegesis and Missiology," *IAMS NL,* no. 13 (1978): 30–31; Spindler, "Biblical Studies and Missiology (BISAM). Progress Report of the European Task Force," *IAMS Newsletter* nos. 16–17 (1980): 12–13; and Spindler, "Biblical Studies and Mission," in *Study Papers for the Vth IAMS Conference, Bangalore 1982* (Leiden: IAMS, 1981), pp. 1–7. Mutual encouragement between BISAM and European biblical scholars was most evident in Germany, for instance in the work of Norbert Brox (*Mission im Neuen Testament* [Freiburg: Herder, 1982]), Miguel Rodríguez Ruiz (*Der Missionsgedanke des Johannesevangeliums. Ein Beitrag zur johanneischen Soteriologie und Ekklesiologie* [Würzburg: Echter-Verlag, 1987]), and Ferdinand Hahn (*Mission in neutestamentlicher Sicht* [Erlangen: Erlanger Verlag für Mission und Ökumene, 1999]).

sion based on the Bible is generally considered as a 'harmonizing device' and even a betrayal of the biblical data." BISAM saw its task as being "to search out those traditions and dynamics that shaped Israel's consciousness of its destiny in relation to gentiles that ultimately led Christians to proclaim the gospel to gentiles." There was a need to study how this universal mission "should be undertaken within different contexts" around the globe. At the end of the workshop, participants agreed to continue reflection via a new and restricted focus by reacting, each from his or her standpoint, to a paper, "Common Witness." This paper was circulated some four years later.[16]

*Harare workshop 1985: Context and Transformation.* The next IAMS conference was at Harare in 1985. The BISAM workshop, moderated by two African scholars, John S. Pobee and David J. Bosch, took up the theme "The Bible and Human Transformation."[17] The twenty participants hailed from eight countries: three African, three European, one Oceanian, and one North American. Six denominations were present: Anglican, Catholic, Lutheran, Presbyterian, Reformed, and Seventh-day Adventist.

On the conference theme, the workshop noted various biblical images used to describe human transformation, such as transfiguration (Rom. 12:2; 2 Cor. 3:18), new creation (2 Cor. 5:17), and regeneration (Titus 3:5; John 3:3–5; 1 Peter 1:3, 23). The report ends by asking, What characteristics and elements of human transformation can be gleaned from this mosaic of images?

Participants accepted that the Bible is always received as an interpreted text that can be understood through a dynamic and creative tension and interaction between the Bible and our various situations, which tension transcends itself to reach toward a clearer vision of God. To guard against a lopsided theology that is in captivity to a particular context, they saw the importance of reading the Bible in the context of the wider church and of being open to insights from other contexts. Every contextual reading and interpretation of the Bible needs to engage, and be engaged by, other contextual interpretations for mutual self-criticism and

16. Workshop Reports, "Workshop I: Bible and Mission," *Missiology* 10, no. 3 (1982): 348; Spindler, "Visa for Witness," pp. 51–60.

17. John S. Pobee and David Bosch, "Workshop: Bible and Human Transformation," *MS* 2, no. 1 (1985): 67–70.

mutual enrichment—that is, we need an intercultural reading of the Bible. Four major elements of the contexts in which the Bible is read and interpreted are (1) a particular people's roots, (2) post-Enlightenment culture marked by the scientific method, (3) materialism and the ethic of success, and (4) violence in situations of deprivation and degradation, anxiety, and fear.

The issue of "ordinary readings" and "scholarly readings" was raised. If there is a dynamic relation between context and text, then we also need to be mindful of how people use the Bible and what they do with the Bible. Ordinary readers need to be included in the process of interpretation.[18] A case study from South Africa that enriched this discussion was published in the same issue of *Mission Studies*.[19]

Some years later these insights, with the suggested intercultural approach, shaped BISAM sessions and projects.

*Mission as witness.* Meanwhile, discussion in *Mission Studies* returned to the theme of witness (which appeared dormant at Harare) when Spindler's paper "Visa for Witness" was published in 1986. This brought a spirited response. In arguing for the focus on witness, Spindler noted that it was a concept "which has gained increased importance in the missionary and ecumenical movement."[20]

The first response came from David Bosch, who felt Blauw had been "completely overtaken by biblical research" and that the question was caught between perceptions of the diversity of the biblical message and the failure to connect the text with mission today.[21] Biblical scholars appeared not to be interested in mission,

18. John S. Pobee, "Human Transformation—a Biblical View," *MS* 2, no. 1 (1985): 5–9.

19. J. N. J. Kritzinger, "The Bible and Human Transformation: A Case Study from South Africa," *MS* 2, no. 2 (1985): 3–7.

20. Spindler, "Visa for Witness," p. 53. A joint Roman Catholic and WCC working group had produced reports on "Common Witness" in 1970 and 1981. See Francis M. DuBose, *God Who Sends: A Fresh Quest for Biblical Misson* (Nashville, Tenn.: Broadman, 1983), and Frans J. Verstraelen, "Quest for Mission in Biblical Perspectives (BISAM PROJECT)," *IAMS Newsletter* nos. 22–23 (1983): 52–54.

21. David J. Bosch, "Towards a Hermeneutic for 'Biblical Studies and Mission,'" *MS* 3, no. 2 (1986): 65–79. Bosch's hermeneutics is discussed by J. G. du Plessis (1990), who engages with Bosch's attempt to work with both Enlightenment and postmodern models of scholarship and hermeneutics (du Plessis,

while missiologists did not understand biblical criticism. These concerns would help drive Bosch to produce *Transforming Mission*, with its explorations of paradigm shifts, which he had already begun to articulate.[22]

Bosch considered the Bangalore decision a mistake. In his view, no one biblical concept was adequate for the task, whether "witness" or "sending." He critiqued methods of interpretation that expected the exegete to bring nothing to the text for fear of misinterpreting it. A hermeneutic that does justice to the history of interpretation meant that exegetes, theologians, and missiologists could again find common ground: "It is as important to establish what a text means as it is to find out what it meant. . . . Biblical scholars help us to make sure that the meaning we attribute to a text is consonant with its original intention; for our part, we [missiologists] may be in a position to save them from turning theology into religious archeology."[23]

Understanding the Bible is a creative process generating different valid interpretations in different readers that, nevertheless, should all be consonant with the intention of the text. The only way of ensuring this valid consistency "is the ecumenical, intercultural fellowship of brothers and sisters in the faith."[24] While the practicalities of what Bosch had in mind were not explicit, clearly he wanted to return BISAM to a study of the biblical foundations of mission, albeit one in which the contextual relativities of one exegete would be compensated by the insights of others.

Lesslie Newbigin also contributed. Some themes of his *The Other Side of 1984* (1983) and *Foolishness to the Greeks* (1986) can be detected in his response. Newbigin was general secretary of the IMC when Blauw had been commissioned to undertake his survey, while "still living in the age of the so-called 'Biblical

"For reasons of the Heart: A Critical Appraisal of David J. Bosch's Use of Scripture in the Foundation of Christian Mission," in *Mission in Creative Tension: A Dialogue with David Bosch*, ed. J. N. J. Kritzinger and W. A. Saayman [Pretoria: SAMS, 1990], pp. 75–85).

22. David J. Bosch, *Transforming Mission: Paradigm Shifts in Theology of Mission* (Maryknoll, N.Y.: Orbis Books, 1991); idem, "Mission in Biblical Perspective," *IRM* 74 (1985): 531–38.

23. Bosch, "Towards a Hermeneutic for 'Biblical Studies and Mission,'" p. 75.

24. Ibid., pp. 77–78.

Theology.'"[25] Since then, the consensus of what constituted biblical theology had been lost.

In the same issue George M. Soares-Prabhu, S.J., noted that witness appeared in ecumenical discussions for sociological reasons and because of the association of mission with colonialism. Like Bosch, he called for a more sophisticated understanding of hermeneutics. Drawing on the experience of the Ecumenical Association of Third World Theologians (EATWOT), he proposed that "a more appropriate method for the study of Bible and mission might be one which would promote local discussion in well-defined cultural contexts (each with its own proper understanding of mission and its own specific way of interpreting the Bible); and only then at a second stage . . . attempt to collate their results."[26]

Spindler's paper helped expose methodological issues that BISAM had to address. The tension was palpable between a classic European approach and the more open, intercultural, and less controlled model advocated by Bosch, and more clearly by Soares-Prabhu.[27] It would take another decade for these proposals to take root.[28]

Spindler, in response, believed the study of witness was still feasible, and that the larger task visualized by Bosch was out of reach. He regarded the challenges to his vision as "formidable. However," he added, "I dare to doubt that they destroy my very small and specific enterprise." He felt that the responses had overlooked initial work by himself and IAMS on hermeneutics.[29]

Spindler believed that what was at issue was critical distance and the scholarly approach. He was concerned about "the suggestion that IAMS should endorse a new paradigm shift and help bury the Enlightenment." He felt that Newbigin's criticism of the

25. Lesslie Newbigin, "Witness in a Biblical Perspective," *MS* 3, no. 2 (1986): 80–84.

26. George M. Soares-Prabhu, S.J., "Missiology or Missiologies?" *MS* 3, no. 2 (1986): 85–87.

27. George M. Soares-Prabhu (b. 1929) died in a road accident as he was cycling to celebrate the Eucharist (July 1995). With the death of David Bosch three years earlier, BISAM lost two exceptional thinkers from Africa and Asia.

28. In the following issue of *Mission Studies* there were also contributions by Dan Beeby ("Comments on Marc Spindler's 'Visa for Witness,'" *MS* 4, no. 1 [1987]: 65–68) and John Parratt (Response to Professor Marc Spindler," *MS* 4, no. 1 [1987]: 68–69).

29. Marc R. Spindler, "Witness Under Cross-examination," *MS* 4, no. 2 (1987): 67–68.

Enlightenment was less than justified, and he saw some of this as keeping company with "blind faith-commitments like those recommended by Iranian ayatollahs or American electronic preachers. . . . I do not say that my correspondents are proposing a way of this kind. My point is only a major reservation with regard to the possibility and suitability of saying farewell to the Enlightenment in the present Western context."[30]

Spindler wrote with feeling, and his sense of what the dangers were was not entirely misplaced. At issue was how an international and interconfessional, and necessarily multicultural, body such as IAMS should study mission and the Bible. The weight of accepted cultural diversity, and the association of the Enlightenment with colonialism and cultural and theological imperialism, meant that the future for IAMS, at least, would not remain with Spindler's vision, however valuable it might prove as a contribution toward understanding a valid dimension of the Bible and mission as formulated within one particular cultural milieu.

## John S. Pobee—a Time of Transition, 1988–92

John S. Pobee had been active during the first BISAM workshop at the Maryknoll Assembly in 1978 and in all subsequent study groups (1982, 1985, 1988).[31] At the 1985 Harare Assembly he reviewed the work of BISAM and reflected on programs that might be undertaken in the future.[32] Meanwhile he also wrote articles for *Mission Studies* on the theme of Bible and mission.[33] At Harare the Executive decided to appoint one of their number as contact person for each study group to help coordinate

30. Ibid., p. 69. See also the study by BISAM member J. Andrew Kirk, *Contemporary Issues in Mission* (Birmingham, U.K.: Selly Oak Colleges, Department of Mission, 1994).

31. John Samuel Pobee attended the University of the Gold Coast (1957–61) and then Cambridge (1961–66). He was professor of New Testament studies at the University of Ghana and a director of the Program on Theological Education at the WCC.

32. John S. Pobee, "Biblical Studies and Mission (BISAM)," *MS* 2, no. 1 (1985): 121–23.

33. John S. Pobee, "Transformation: A Biblical View," *MS* 2, no. 1 (1985): 5–9; "*Skēnōsis*—the Tabernacling of the Word," *MS* 3, no. 2 (1986): 4–13; "Christian Mission Towards the Third Millennium: The Gospel of Hope," *MS* 5, no. 1 (1988): 6–14; and "Biblical Studies and Missiology (BISAM)," *MS* 5, no. 2 (1988): 132–33.

the various networks that engaged IAMS members between the every-four-years international conferences. As a New Testament scholar active in BISAM from the beginning, John Pobee was the obvious choice to represent BISAM. At the time he was IAMS vice president (1985–88).[34]

Both then and later, when he became BISAM coordinator (1988),[35] Pobee was aware of the changing demography of world Christianity that had occurred throughout the previous century. The heartlands of Christianity had shifted from the North and West to the South and East, from Europe and North America to Latin America, Africa, Asia, and the Pacific. Convinced that Christianity matters where it is alive and expanding, Pobee felt that BISAM's membership needed to represent better these vital centers of Christian faith.[36] As director of the Program on Theological Education at the WCC, Pobee was in contact with Third World scholars—in particular, biblical theologians. In his WCC work, Pobee had played a part in birthing the Circle of African Women in Theology and the Ecumenical Association of African Theologians. And thus he was able to recruit African biblical scholars of international repute such as Teresa Okure and Justin Ukpong from Nigeria. These strong, articulate voices were to lead BISAM after Pobee finished his tenure as IAMS president (1988–92).

*Rome 1988: Redefining the Scope of the BISAM Project.* In his report as BISAM coordinator at the Rome conference, Pobee paid tribute to the achievements of Spindler and the team in Leiden but called for recognition of the vision that Southern and feminist contexts could bring to biblical perspectives on mission. By the time of his report to the Executive the following year, there was further recognition that context was a key factor in the hermeneutical equation, not just Bible and mission. "In the past, biblical readings have been

34. Later John S. Pobee was elected the first IAMS president from the Southern Hemisphere. See his presidential lecture, "Mission from Below," *MS* 10, nos. 1–2 (1993): 148–70.

35. By the time of the 1988 IAMS Rome Conference, the secretariat had moved from IIMO in Leiden, where Marc Spindler was based, to Evangelisches Missionswerk in Hamburg. Joachim Wietzke replaced Frans J. Verstraelen as IAMS secretary, and John Pobee replaced Marc Spindler as BISAM coordinator.

36. Marc R. Spindler and John S. Pobee, "Biblical Studies and Missiology (BISAM) (Progress Report)," *MS* 6, no.1 (1989): 57–60.

very much northern and Latin. Now, we are aware of new read-ings and convinced that each person reads scripture through par-ticular spectacles of context and culture."[37] He highlighted the use of the Bible around the world, Southern and feminist perspectives, interfaith dialogue, and the scriptures of other religions.

During the 1988 Rome conference David Bosch contributed a paper, "The Scope of the 'BISAM' Project."[38] He noted the com-mon ground he shared with Spindler and appreciated that they were able to discuss their differences. Bosch was gracious, but challenging. To make the project manageable, he suggested focus-ing on just one New Testament author, "preferably one of the four evangelists or Paul, and reflect on what this author and the com-munity for which he wrote might have to teach us about our mis-sion today." As a first stage Bosch suggested that BISAM seek the cooperation of a number of New Testament scholars and aim at organizing teams in various parts of the world where reflection could be undertaken *in loco*. The second stage would be to set time aside during a future IAMS meeting when reflections from differ-ent regions of the globe could be presented and collated with a view to preparing a symposium volume.[39]

*Hawaii workshop 1992: The End of the Beginning.* In April 1992 Bosch died in a car accident.[40] His sudden death shocked the missiological community. Four months later the Eighth IAMS Assembly convened in Hawaii. It had been intended that David Bosch and Donald Senior would take responsibility for a BISAM workshop, with a focus on the Gospel of Mark.[41] In the event, it was left to Senior to convene the workshop. African scholars were again at the forefront.[42] However, papers were not limited

37. John S. Pobee, "Biblical Studies and Missiology (BISAM)," *MS* 6, no. 1 (1989): 57–60. On the role of Study Groups, see Joachim Wietzke, "Report of the General Secretary," *MS* 10 (1988): 125–29.

38. Two years previously Bosch had written "Towards a Hermeneutic for 'Biblical Studies and Mission.'"

39. David J. Bosch, "The Scope of the 'BISAM' Project," *MS* 6, no. 1 (1989): 61.

40. See John S. Pobee, "In Memoriam: David J. Bosch," *MS* 9, no. 2 (1992): 252–54.

41. Donald Senior, C.P., and David J. Bosch, "IAMS Project 'Biblical Stud-ies and Mission,'" *MS* 9, no. 1 (1992): 115–17.

42. Willem Saayman, Workshop Paper: "Biblical Insights on New Cre-ation and Mission in Power and Faith," *MS* 10, nos. 1–2 (1993): 83–90; and

to the Gospel of Mark but ranged over the entire Bible, from Genesis to Revelation.[43]

Nothing was heard of BISAM over the next four years. Only in 1996 was BISAM revived as a collaborative project.

*Buenos Aires workshop 1996: Economies in Conflict.* Andrew Kirk convened a biblical workshop during the Ninth IAMS Assembly, in Buenos Aires in 1996, which took up the conference theme "Economies in Conflict."[44] There were fourteen participants. They noted that the Bible speaks of money in different ways. While the worth of work is affirmed and both productivity and wealth are gifts of God, the Jerusalem temple became a locus for the corrupt use of economic power. The Scriptures give us models that inspire alternative practices. The workshop suggested areas for further research such as a study of the biblical basis for micro-economic projects, an investigation of alternative banking systems (particularly those of Islamic banks), monastic community as a model for reshaping communities, and alternatives to global capitalism arising from different faith traditions. None of these suggestions was subsequently taken up. It was also pointed out that Base Christian Communities, both Catholic and Pentecostal, are alternative ways of organizing church life, giving us new ways of reading the Bible.

*Scope and role of interest groups and study groups.* After the Buenos Aires conference, the Executive Committee clarified the purpose and position of "project work" such as that of BISAM.[45] A "study group" convenes during a conference, while an "interest group" facilitates the networking of scholars of similar study or research interest between conferences. Interest groups have a convener appointed by the Executive Committee and report to the Executive and the conference. "IAMS projects" seek to achieve in a particular time span a specific objective, be it to break new ground in a cer-

---

Teresa Okure, "Conversion, Commitment: An African Perspective," *MS* 10, nos. 1–2 (1993): 109–33.

43. Willem Saayman, "Workshop 1: Biblical Insights on New Creation and Mission in Power and Faith," *MS* 10, nos. 1–2 (1993): 171–74.

44. J. Andrew Kirk, "Workshop 1: God or Mammon: Biblical Perspectives on Economies in Conflict," *MS* 13, nos. 1–2 (1996): 80–82.

45. Klaus Schäfer, "Communications from the General Secretary," *MS* 14, nos. 1–2 (1997): 15–20.

tain area of research, have a consultation, or publish a book. IAMS budgeted both for interconference networking and for occasional consultations. Consultations would be expected to produce two to three papers for publication in *Mission Studies*.

### Teresa Okure—Revival and Redefinition, 1996–2004

At the Buenos Aires Assembly the IAMS Executive appointed Teresa Okure, the second African and first woman, as BISAM coordinator.[46] With John Pobee's oversight from the Executive Committee (1988–92) and now Okure's appointment, voices from the South that had frequently surfaced over the years came into their own. The baton was being passed to the thinking and practice of vibrant academic theologians who had long been engaged in doing theology from liberationist perspectives in collaboration with ordinary believers—in particular, with the poor.

Teresa Okure led a post–Buenos Aires conference meeting of people interested in reviving BISAM. It was proposed that each member articulate, each from his or her own context, how to understand "mission" in the Bible. This proposal led to the Durban consultation two years later.

*Durban Consultation 1998: Now, then, and where we wish to go.* After Buenos Aires, Okure began to place BISAM on a solid footing through a five-day consultation held in Durban, South Africa.[47] Concomitant with this consultation, Okure published in *Mission Studies* a proposal for the BISAM project that she drafted after the

46. Teresa Okure, S.H.C.J., of Anua, Uyo, Akwa Ibom State, Nigeria, is a member of the Society of the Holy Child Jesus (SHCJ). She studied at the University of Ibadan (1972–73), Fordham University, N.Y. (1977–81, 1983–85), where she gained a Ph.D. in scripture, and the École Biblique et Archéologique Française, Jerusalem (1981–83). Okure is professor of New Testament and gender hermeneutics at the Catholic Institute of West Africa, Port Harcourt, Nigeria. She was coordinator of EATWOT Anglophone Women's Commission (1985–97) and executive secretary of EATWOT (1986–92). She was vice president of the International Association of Catholic Missiologists (2000–2004) and on the executive committee of the Studiorum Novi Testamenti Societas (2003–5). Teresa Okure has written, edited, or co-edited nine books, thirty-nine book chapters, and twenty-six articles.

47. The consultation was financed by IAMS, the publication by Evangelische Missionswerk (EMW) and her own religious sisterhood, SHCJ (Teresa Okure, "Report on BISAM Activities: January 1999 to January 2000," *MS* 17, nos. 1–2 [2000]: 157–59).

post–Buenos Aires meeting. We are challenged: "How does one relate the Bible as enduring divine word to the Bible as limited, culturally bound human word in our contemporary multicultural communities?"[48] But it was the consultation itself, and the subsequent publication, that set in motion a long-term research project for the relaunched study group. This volume, *To Cast Fire upon the Earth* (2000), contains ten articles (pp. 33–214), a history of BISAM by John Roxborogh (pp. 215–27), and the revamped scope of BISAM, all of which is nothing less than a comprehensive research plan for the coming years, with an encyclopedic listing of issues of concern (by Okure, pp. 235–48).[49] In her introduction Okure asks,

> Can Bible studies and mission revive the spirit of an Elijah, an Amos among its members, to address issues today (dreams for a better social order)? Can it kindle fire so that it burns and destroys the divisive labels we place on those who differ from us in any way? Can the fire in the mission burn away and reduce to ashes our divisions in church, state, the new world order and transform us into Spirit filled people, filled with God's love? . . . How can Bible studies and mission help establish true communion among Christians? Would openness to the different methods used in reading the Bible and the concerns brought to it from different disciplines and social locations assist this process? (Pp. 10–11)

The dimensions of the BISAM project were to include the *contemporary situation* ("collection, documentation, analysis and interpretation of data . . . explore and interpret the different ways in which the Bible is being used as a resource in mission in their own social locations and churches"), the *historical situation* ("research the use of the Bible and the hermeneutics which governed it during the great missionary eras"), and the *biblical situation* ("explore and discover the missionary hermeneutics inherent in the Bible itself"). The fruit of the Durban Consultation, *To Cast Fire upon the Earth*, was launched during the Hammanskraal Assembly of 2000.

48. Terese Okure, "A Proposal for a BISAM Project," *MS* 15, no. 2 (1998): 167.
49. Terese Okure, ed., *To Cast Fire upon the Earth: Bible and Mission Collaborating in Today's Multi-Cultural Global Context* (Pietermaritzburg: Cluster Publications, 2000).

*Hammanskraal workshop 2000: Reader Response or Missiological Out-look?* Eighteen people participated in the BISAM study group during the Hammanskraal Assembly. They looked at how they read the Bible from the perspective of mission within their diverse multicultural global contexts. The preconference proposal—that participants read selected texts within the context of the biblical authors, the reader's own social location, and the global village—had not been acted on.[50] In fact, there was little consensus in the group. Some sought to do Bible study from within different life contexts, cognizant of ways a biblical text converses with the readers' experiences in his or her social location ("reader-response"), while others were more concerned with how the Bible functions in mission studies ("missiological outlook"). Small-group readings of Matthew 13:1–23 (the parable of the sower) brought out the ambivalence of biblical texts, issues of accountability, valid and invalid readings, the balance between community readings and individual readings, academic readings, and readings with and by a congregation.[51]

*Geneva Consultation 2002: Missiological Readings.* Two years after Hammanskraal, eleven BISAM members who had written up missiological readings of the Bible held a consultation in Geneva, run jointly by the BISAM coordinator and Jacques Matthey, secretary of the Commission on World Mission and Evangelism (CWME) of the WCC. The papers were published before the consultation.[52] The eleven missiological readings (four on Wisdom literature, two on Colossians, five on Matthew) were written by BISAM members based in Britain, Denmark, Ecuador, Indonesia, Netherlands, Nigeria, Philippines, South Africa, and Switzerland. These activists formed a BISAM "core group" throughout Teresa Okure's tenure.

Daniel Patte, present at Geneva, together with Teresa Okure

50. Teresa Okure, "IAMS Conference 2000: Study Group 'The Bible in Mission,'" *MS* 15, no. 2 (1998): 161–63.

51. Teresa Okure, "Report on Group 7: The Bible and Mission Studies," *MS* 17, no. 1 (2000): 128–33.

52. Jacques Matthey, ed., "Bible Studies and Mission," *IRM* 91, no. 360 (2002). CWME not only published the papers in *IRM* but also sponsored the Geneva consultation.

and three other co-editors, conceived the idea of compiling the *Global Bible Commentary*. Although it was not a BISAM project per se, nevertheless eight of the seventy-one contributors were active in BISAM, including the general editor himself. This is but one example of how the BISAM network feeds into other academic networks to which members belong.[53]

At the Geneva consultation another project was decided on: the composition of a methodological handbook for a culturally conscious reading of the Bible, with an emphasis on mission. The study was conceived as a collection of short texts with questions for readers revolving around the general themes of "power" and "the other." Within a couple of months proposals by each of sixteen prospective authors were e-mailed to the others for comments and suggestions. Owing to the wide divergence of methods used by the authors, the project was held in abeyance until the next IAMS conference.

*Port Dickson workshop 2004: Integrity of Mission.* At the Port Dickson BISAM workshop a dozen papers from all six continents honed in on the conference theme of the integrity of mission, underlining issues of credibility, accountability, and contextual challenges.[54] The twenty participants worked in smaller groups. Teresa Okure, the BISAM coordinator, endeavored to focus conversations on the light of the Gospel—the life and work of Jesus Christ. Tension between a broad dialogical understanding of mission and an understanding commencing with, and centered upon, the person of Jesus Christ has been present in BISAM almost from the

---

53. Daniel J. Patte, Severino Croatto, Nicole Wilkinson Duran, Teresa Okure, and Archie Chi Chung Lee, eds., *Global Bible Commentary* (Nashville: Abingdon Press, 2004). This work in turn gave birth to the series of commentaries "Texts & Contexts," published by Fortress Press. Other examples of "spin-offs" would be BISAM contributions to the *Lexikon missionstheologischer Grundbegriffe*, ed. Karl Müller and Theo Sundermeier (Berlin: Reimer Verlag, 1987), including that of Marc Spindler, "Bibel," pp. 50–53, and the ongoing study on contextual Bible interpretation by the Society of New Testament Studies (SNTS) with BISAM members such as Daniel Patte, Teresa Okure, Hans Kvalbein, and Johannes Nissen.

54. Since Brill began publishing *Mission Studies*, the reports and plans of study groups are no longer available in the IAMS journal. The rest of this essay is culled from reports, documents, and e-mails in possession of the author.

beginning. In such creative encounters the study group displays its value and importance.

## John Mansford Prior—Continuity in the Cyber Age, 2004–12

*Post–Port Dickson core group meeting 2004.* At the commencement of the core group meeting held immediately after the Port Dickson Assembly, the IAMS general secretary, Birger Nygaard, asked the group to choose a new BISAM coordinator. The choice fell not on an internationally regarded Bible scholar, as were the three previous coordinators, but on an intercultural theologian living on a small island in eastern Indonesia. The energy of a dynamic convener was to be followed by a quieter, lower-profile presence.

During this two-day meeting, now chaired by John Prior, the 2002 Geneva project "Exercises in Missiological Readings of the Bible" was revised. The idea of a handbook with questions for readers and instructions for study was abandoned. Essays were now to be culturally conscious readings of both the biblical context and the author's context, with an emphasis on mission. The audience was to be the readership of *Mission Studies*. The aim was for a "representative" selection of biblical books read in the context of "power" and "the other." A diversity of approaches, whether textual or intertextual, would be respected. Under the new guidelines eleven essays were submitted. It was an unenviable task to select six of them for publication.[55] There were three essays on the Old Testament (Genesis, Joshua, Jonah), and three on the New Testament (Acts, Romans, Corinthians). The authors, three women and three men, hailed from Argentina, India, Indonesia, Nigeria, the United Kingdom, and the United States.

Three other projects were drawn up. Eight participants were eager to write up and publish reflections generated during the Port Dickson BISAM workshop on the theme of the integrity of mission. Prospective readership would be animators and cross-cultural missioners, thus helping bridge the gap between mission academics and practitioners. It was also proposed that research be done into how the Bible has been used in ecumenical texts since Edinburgh 1910. Yet another project approved was to compile a

---

55. Lalsangkima Pachuau, ed., *"Power" and "The Other": Missiological Readings of the Bible* (= *MS* 23, no. 1 [2006]).

preliminary bibliography on the use of the Bible in grassroots communities. Three members volunteered to coordinate these projects. However, despite the energy palpable during the meeting, each of the volunteer coordinators eventually withdrew because of pressing commitments, and none of these projects saw the light of day. The BISAM coordinator learned that a single project between conferences coordinated by himself was the most that could be realistically expected from the busy, though spirited, membership.

There was one interesting spin-off from one of the abandoned projects, that of the use of the Bible in grassroots communities. Veteran BISAM member Johannes Nissen informed BISAM coordinator John Prior about Hans de Wit's intercultural reading of the Bible project from Vrije Universiteit, Amsterdam.[56] Since then, Prior has been actively involved in the Vrije Universiteit project, becoming a member of the Advisory Board of the Intercultural Bible Collective when the second phase was launched in 2010. Once again, link-ups between networks and projects of members beyond BISAM are proving to be mutually enriching.

*Balaton workshop 2008: Human Identity and the Gospel of Reconciliation.* No fewer than thirty members attended the BISAM workshop at Balaton, Hungary. A majority of papers, however, were not biblical in nature, although all were on the conference theme. The problem was that, unusually, the IAMS secretariat simply apportioned conference participants, more or less equitably, to each workshop. Of the biblical papers, three were recommended for publication in *Mission Studies*, two of which saw the light of day.[57]

*Bible, Nation, Empire: 2009–11.* The final session of the Balaton workshop consisted of a BISAM business meeting. A single postconference project was proposed on the theme "Bible, Nation, Empire: The Use of the Bible by Scholars and by Local Congregations." The rationale explained that "today at local, regional and global levels we are working to rediscover and re-create community as

56. Hans de Wit, Louis Jonker, Marleen Kool, and Daniel Schipani, eds., *Through the Eyes of Another: Intercultural Reading of the Bible* (Amsterdam: Vrije Universiteit, 2004).

57. Elizabeth Glanville, "Missiological Reflections on Difference: Foundations in the Gospel of Luke," *MS* 26, no. 1 (2009): 64–79; and John Mansford Prior, "Integration, Isolation, or Deviation: Reading Galatians 3:27–28 in Indonesia Today," *MS* 27, no. 1 (2010): 71–90.

some nations are merging into larger blocs and others seem to be systematically failing, all this happening within the tentacles of a global economic and political 'empire.'" The question is, "How do we understand specific biblical texts within their own nation/empire contexts in the light of our own nation/empire contexts?" By 2010 three papers on the theme had been submitted from Argentina, Denmark, and Ghana, while a further four papers on other biblical themes were sent in from Australia, Guatemala, and Kenya. Papers were circulated among the other authors for comment. After reediting, authors returned their papers to the BISAM coordinator, who submitted them to *Mission Studies* for consideration; meanwhile, they have been posted on the BISAM page on the IAMS Web site.

*Executive and Web page.* In January 2009 the IAMS secretary e-mailed questions from the Executive Committee to each of the study group coordinators asking whether they were willing to continue as coordinators, requesting information on forthcoming plans, giving news of the new IAMS Web site then in preparation, with separate pages for each study group, reminding coordinators that an annual budget can be claimed if needed, and conveying the willingness of the Executive to help coordinators in any way possible. Apart from not needing an annual budget, the BISAM coordinator responded positively to all points.

Since 2004, communication among members had been carried out through e-mail.[58] In 2005 BISAM opened its own blog, giving information on current research projects. The blog linked to the BISAM page on the IAMS Web site, but it was abandoned when IAMS upgraded its Web site in mid-2009, allowing the coordinator access to edit and upload material on the page himself.[59]

## BISAM 1976–2011: A Fragile Flower

BISAM, like other study networks involving international cooperation, has been subject to many vicissitudes. Not all that has been attempted has been completed. And yet for all its fragility in prac-

58. The annual subvention budgeted by the IAMS treasurer for BISAM activities has not been requested since 2004.

59. See http://missionstudies.org/index.php/study-groups/bisam/bible-nation-empire/.

tice, the flowering of a vision of what can and needs to be learned about biblical studies in mission through a sharing of insights and experiences among a network of committed members of academia and people from the grassroots, from different cultures and social and gender contexts, and from a whole range of ecclesial confessions, still captures the imagination. A few students and colleagues of Marc Spindler from the late 1970s are still part of the network, while younger scholars from Latin America, Africa, Asia, and Oceania now openly converse with more seasoned academics both within and between cultural domains. Ecumenical Protestants, evangelicals, and Catholics now exchange insights with Pentecostals and Independents. Study sessions during the quadrennial assemblies are necessarily spirited, while, understandably, collaborative projects between conferences tax the energy and perseverance of the coordinator.

Looking back, the drawn-out crisis as BISAM shifted from the classical heartlands of biblical scholarship and mission thinking in the outward-looking churches of Europe and North America toward a whole range of daring, liberative, intercultural readings in the South simply mirrored the changing membership of IAMS—and of Christianity—as a whole.

One term not referred to in BISAM documentation is "postcolonial," and yet key characteristics of postcolonial readings of the Bible seem to pinpoint what engages BISAM, namely, multicultural readings by academics and congregations that emerge from both local and global contexts, readings that bring out inconvenient truths that recognize the complex nature of studying the Bible in mission. As BISAM enters its thirty-sixth year, so it is quietly playing its part in "de-centering universal and trans-historical values of Western categories of knowledge," while articulating readings from the margins, together with those of the mainstream.[60] To quote John Roxborogh: "What we all demonstrate is that no matter how committed [we may be] to a view of theology that does not privilege western conceptual frameworks, we cannot actually get rid of it. . . . BISAM is central to working through what it means to be local and universal and to face the challenges of competing hegemonies of method and conclusion. Perhaps it does not hurt

60. R. S. Sugirtharajah, *Exploring Postcolonial Biblical Criticism: History, Method, Practice* (Oxford: Wiley-Blackwell, 2012).

for those of us doing our best to do and reflect on mission, to know we are not only among the doctors, we are also patients with the diseases of our cultural particularities."[61]

On the BISAM Web page, we read that the study group

> seeks to investigate collaboratively, in the true spirit of mission, various ways in which the Bible is used today in mission, and the multifaceted questions which it raises among peoples of different race, gender, class, culture, creed, faith and social location; as such BISAM operates on an inter-disciplinary basis.
>
> The BISAM network is conscious of the need for deepening awareness of the interpretive methods we use; of the need for ongoing studies of how the Bible is actually used in specific contexts by faith communities; and of the need for the development of creative imagination in "weaving together" the story of Jesus with stories of people in a particular context.

In June 2011 there were 60 contacts on the BISAM e-mail list, divided among Europe (18), Africa (15), Asia (9), Latin America (9), North America (6), and Oceania (3). There are 13 women and 47 men.

Collaborating as an international, multicultural team from within the whole spectrum of Christian denominations, while operating on an interdisciplinary basis, BISAM has learned that the overriding need is to listen deeply from the cave of the heart, to be open to the Spirit in others who start from a quite different position. The enduring dynamic between mission and the Bible in changing contexts points to the value of the study group, but it also raises crucial questions: What projects bring that into view? How can the insights of the BISAM story be communicated to younger generations? How can people be prepared for new contexts, questions, and refined methodologies—or even quantum changes?

*For all that has been, thanks. For all that will be, yes.*
—Dag Hammarskjold

---

61. Roxborogh, e-mail message to author, April 5, 2011.

# "Healing/Pneumatology" Study Group

## Christoffer H. Grundmann

Ever since 1986, the International Association for Mission Studies has included a study group on the subject of healing. The following essay tells about the origin and evolution of this group during the past quarter century.

## Beginnings: The Church as a Healing Community

The beginnings of the IAMS study group "Healing/Pneumatology" lie in Africa, at the Sixth IAMS Assembly, held January 8–14, 1985, in Harare, Zimbabwe. During this conference Hans-Jürgen Becken, who had researched the healing activities of African Independent/Indigenous Churches (AIC), offered a workshop "The Church as a Healing Community."[1] The topic reflected the importance of healing in the African religious context, to which years before Bengt Sundkler had drawn attention.[2] The theme of the workshop also aligned well with concerns of the Christian Medical Commission (CMC, formed in 1968) of the World Council of Churches (WCC). Becken was a member of the CMC advisory study group,[3] to which he made explicit reference in his work-

1. Besides his other published material, see Hans-Jürgen Becken's doctoral dissertation on the theology of healing in the African Independent Churches in South Africa, published as *Theologie der Heilung. Das Heilen in den Afrikanischen Unabhängigen Kirchen in Südafrika* (Hermannsburg: Verlag der Hermannsburger Mission, 1972), and his articles "African Independent Churches as Healing Communities," in *Afro-Christian Religions and Healing*, ed. G. C. Oosthizen (Leiden: Brill, 1979), pp. 227–39, and "Ekuphakameni Revisited: Recent Developments Within the Nazaretha Church in South Africa," *Journal of Religion in Africa* 9, no. 2 (1978): 161–72.

2. Bengt Sundkler, *Bantu Prophets in South Africa* (London: Lutterworth Press, 1948; 2nd ed., 1961), and its sequel *Zulu Zion and Some Swazi Zionists* (London: Oxford Univ. Press, 1976).

3. See J. McGilvray, *The Quest for Health and Wholeness* (Tübingen: German Institute for Medical Missions, 1981), p.116. McGilvray, who was the first

shop description, which appeared in *Mission Studies* before the conference.[4] Thus the workshop combined local distinctiveness and overarching global perspectives in its theme, as well as in its moderator. Realizing the importance and vastness of the subject and its missiological challenges, the participants felt the need for a more intensive study of the issues raised.[5] Sensing that the IAMS constituency, which is not defined by church affiliation, offered an ideal body with potential for in-depth study of the phenomenon in a truly global community and for going beyond the merely anecdotal, those present suggested continuation of the workshop. Three people—E. Rizzo de Oliveira (Brazil), Becken, and Christoffer Grundmann (both from Germany)—were asked to draw up a plan of action to be presented to the Executive Committee for consideration. This was done immediately so that a decision could be taken by the Executive in its next meeting, scheduled for June 13–16, 1985, at Ventnor, New Jersey, where the proposal became an agenda item.

The minutes of this meeting read:

> Proposal for a continuation of Harare workshop on *The church as a healing community*. The IAMS exec[utive] c[ommit]tee looked into the general proposal and referred it back to the initiators . . . with the request:
>
> • to define what kind of research they envisaged IAMS to do that is not yet done by other groups;
> • to present a more detailed plan of action (content, participants, structure, activities, financial implications [etc.])
> • to present an outline for such a working party to the next IAMS ex. ctee.[6]

---

director of the CMC, tells the well-documented history of the origin of the CMC, its focus of work, and its theological concerns. The principal document for the topic "The Church as a Healing Community" is *The Healing Church* (Geneva: WCC Publications, 1965), the report of a consultation held in 1964 at the German Institute for Medical Missions, Tübingen, sponsored jointly by the WCC and the Lutheran World Federation.

4. "The Church as a Healing Community," *MS* 1, no. 2 (1984): 35–43.

5. For a report on the workshop, see "The Church as a Healing Community," *MS* 2, no. 1 (1985): 82–84 (identical with *Christian Mission and Human Transformation: Report of the Sixth IAMS Conference, Harare, 8–14 January 1985*, ed. F. J. Verstraelen [Gweru, Zimbabwe: Mambo Press, 1985], pp. 82–84).

6. IAMS Executive Committee meeting, Ventnor, N.J., United States, June 13–16, 1985, p. 6, http://missionstudies.org/archive/3exec/1985-Ventnor.pdf.

The small group submitted a revised proposal in January 1986.[7] In its meeting in Rome that year (April 20–24), the Executive Committee, while acknowledging that "The Church as a Healing Community" is "a relevant subject to deal with," was still reluctant to take on the project. The minutes of that meeting record that questions were raised, such as, Is this really a missiological project breaking new ground? Do we need to start on a new structure? Does this project concentrate on the South or the North?

Thanks to the advocacy for the matter by committee member Frans J. Verstraelen, who had met with representatives of the group a month earlier at 's-Hertogenbosch, Netherlands, on the occasion of a seminar with the charismatic African healer Emmanuel Milingo, former Roman Catholic archbishop of Zambia,[8] it was resolved "to start this new project on the following conditions: 1 – The study group is requested to work out more specifically the objectives and means of implementation of the project. 2 – There should be a close cooperation with regional and ecumenical groups . . . ," especially the CMC, and, "3 – The task force should be made more representative," mainly by including members from Africa.[9] In the Association's journal the "formal approbation" of this study group was greeted as a "sign of healthy vitality of our Association."[10]

## Development: Beyond the Ecclesiological Focus

Once officially adopted as a study project, healing became a familiar theme within IAMS, figuring regularly in its journal, *Mission Studies*, appearing consistently on the agenda of its Executive Committee meetings, and being a topic of workshops during General Assemblies. However, the present familiarity of the topic

7. Some details of the refined proposal can be gleaned from the report "The Church as a Healing Community (HEALING)," in *MS* 5, no. 2 (1988): 146–47.

8. On this meeting, see H.-J. Becken and Christoffer Grundmann, "Cultural Emancipation and Healing in the Third World," *MS* 3, no. 1 (1986): 61–62.

9. Minutes of IAMS Executive Committee, meeting in Rome, April 20–24, 1986, p. 4, item 1.5, http://missionstudies.org/archive/3exec/1986-Rome.pdf. The persons suggested were Bishop Peter Sarpong and Kofi Appiah-Kubi, both from Ghana, and Obed Kealotswe from Botswana. Kofi Appiah-Kubi became a member of the group in 1987 (see *MS* 5, no. 2 [1988]: 148).

10. *MS* 3, no. 1 (1986): 77.

within IAMS did not happen overnight. Rather, it has come from the unrelenting efforts of group members to keep missiology alert to the need for serious reflection and research of the phenomenon of healing, and more recently also on the discernment of spirits, or pneumatology.

When H.-J. Becken resigned as convener of the study group because of his retirement in 1987, the Executive Committee unanimously elected Christoffer Grundmann to be the new convener.[11] While Becken took responsibility for running another workshop, entitled "The Church as a Healing Community,"[12] at the Seventh IAMS Assembly, held in the Augustinianum in Rome, June 29–July 5, 1988, Grundmann became responsible for designing and preparing the study group's exposure program, featuring encounters with people and institutions engaged in the healing ministry, as well as visits to historic places of healing in the Eternal City.[13] He also was entrusted with organizing and moderating the postconference meeting of the group. During the discussions in the postconference meeting, it became clear that, if the project was going to stay relevant, the research focus had to be broadened beyond its ecclesiological confines to embrace the phenomenon of healing in its entirety.[14] Such widening of the scope was felt necessary in order to accommodate the wide-ranging variety of healing phenomena observed within and outside the church. This renaming would also enable rigorous scholarly inquiry not restrained by dogmatic reservations, and it would make genuine interdisciplinary discourse with medicine, ethnomedicine in particular, psychology, and anthropology easier.[15] Henceforth the study group

11. Minutes of IAMS Executive Committee, meeting in Rome, November 26–29, 1987, p. 9, item 7, http://missionstudies.org/archive/3exec/1987-Rome.pdf.

12. For a report on this workshop, see M. Mary Moore, "Workshop 2: 'The Church as a Healing Community,'" *MS* 5, no. 2 (1988): 99–101.

13. People visited and talked with were Msgr. E. Milingo and Msgr. F. Angelini, the Pro President of the Pontifical Council for Pastoral Assistance to Health Care Workers (*Dolentium Hominum*); places visited were Tiber Island, where the Greek Asclepius cult was once officially introduced to Rome, today the site of the hospital of the Do Good Brothers, and the Clinica Gemelli. See F. A. Sand, "Exposure Programme 'Healing,'" *MS* 6, no. 1 (1989): 52–55; see also her paper "Healing as Kerygma," *MS* 7, no. 1 (1990): 97–100.

14. The key article "Healing as a Missiological Challenge," by Christoffer Grundmann, appeared some time earlier in *MS* 3, no. 2 (1986): 57–62.

15. See H.-J. Becken, in *MS* 10, pp. 146–49.

was called simply Healing, and its members set out to pursue ambitious research goals.

The first goal was that of finding "the adequate rendering of 'healing' into French, Italian, and other languages," as well as terms for witch doctor, fetishist, magic, and so forth—that is, for the technical terms in the various cultures. These issues were to receive top research priority because to come to some consensus here was felt to be "a vital issue and a prerequisite for the communication among the members."[16] Also, every member of the group, as opportunity allowed, was encouraged to become engaged in or continue field studies and to systematically collect bibliographic data and documentation. The group also recognized the need for developing an appropriate format for making comparisons.[17] Finally, the IAMS members present at the post-conference meeting expressed their conviction that "the entire efforts and thrust [of the group] should go towards the development of a 'theology of healing' (or: 'theologies of healing')," which—as they realized—would require considering issues of "lifestyle and authority, the discipline of prayer, charism(a) and institution, . . . medicine and drugs as participation in creation, [and] recreation[, as well as] healing, redemption, and reconciliation; evil[,] disease[, and] illness; [and] discernment of spirits." In short, it was soon realized that studying healing entails addressing also a host of related issues.

As could be expected, implementation of these goals happened only in part and never to the extent anticipated or wished for. Nevertheless, something did come about, not just in the way of individual studies done by members (too many to be listed here), but—as will be shown later—in the sense of a genuine learning experience for the group overall. When the IAMS Executive Committee in its meeting at Bossey, Switzerland, January 12–16, 1989, reviewed the Rome Assembly report of the study group, it expressed the conviction that "the Healing project has developed into a genuine IAMS project with a global perspective and a wide local participation," meeting "the lack of theological reflection to be observed" elsewhere. The Executive Committee also urged estab-

---

16. Christoffer Grundmann, "Aspects of Further Research Within the Study Project 'Healing,'" *MS* 6, no. 1 (1989): 72.
17. Ibid.

lishing "contacts with CMC . . . in order to avoid duplication."[18] Heeding this counsel, the convener instituted contact with officers of CMC and added their names to the project mailing list, a practice observed ever since.

The next significant changes happened during the Ninth Assembly, at Buenos Aires, April 10–19, 1996. These changes affected the leadership of the group, the structure of its working, and the content of its particular research focus. At the Buenos Aires conference Godelieve Prové, M.D., S.C.M.M. (Netherlands), assisted by Robert Schreiter, C.PP.S. (U.S.A.), took over responsibility for group facilitation. It was also agreed that the group should be known as an interest group.

The most remarkable change at that time, however, had to do with the research focus, since by then it had become clear to those seriously pursuing the study of healing missiologically that "it is not possible to work on a 'theology of healing' in the strict sense," simply because "healing and salvation are not identical and are not to be confused. . . . Healing and salvation do overlap . . . but they differ significantly, too." Consequently, the task to which this particular group is dedicated is "to identify the overlapping as well as the diverging fields." It was also regretfully noticed that "one of the still unfulfilled tasks of the project group [is] to develop a common format" for reporting about healing experiences, about healing procedures, and about actual practical healers that would be reliable enough to allow drawing meaningful "conclusions on the basis of qualified material." Furthermore, the study group members had come to understand that "any missiological/theological reflection on healing has to tackle the question of the body," that is, "the lived body, especially the . . . wounded" body, which would also require addressing "the underlying anthropological model" operative in any therapeutical context. Since this aspect touches upon "the prevalent neglect of the body in the history and practice of missions," group members began to realize the far-ranging consequences of any follow-up along this line of inquiry—namely, that such a quest would sooner or later pose "a qualified challenge to long-established patterns of missiology." The group was beginning to realize that the very under-

18. Executive Committee, meeting January 12–16, Bossey, p. 4, http://missionstudies.org/archive/3exec/ 1989-Bossey.pdf.

standing of the Gospel itself is at stake, the Gospel that "bears witness to God incarnate and bodily resurrection," over against a practice of mission that all too often focuses on the salvation of the "eternal soul" at the expense of the "merely temporal body," thereby contradicting the Good News of God incarnate in Jesus Christ.[19]

The comprehensive project report for the period stated that, on the whole, "the understanding of the phenomenon of healing got deepened and can now be addressed more adequately than before," including the communal and socioeconomic aspects. It is now clear that healing movements all around the world must be interpreted "more in light of traditional cultures coping with the clashes and changes caused by transition into modernity and cultural pluralism than in light of an 'age of the spirit,'" as has been claimed for long by many working in foreign missions. The report noted further that "other theological and missiological topics which demand substantial discussion and qualified research like questions of christological, pneumatological, and anthropological character" were raised as well.[20] This breadth of discussion made group members aware that, when studying healing in the perspective of mission, a host of related issues surface that also deserve proper missiological attention.

## Continuation: From Buenos Aires (1996) to Port Dickson (2004)

To properly understand the development of the IAMS group dedicated to the missiological study of healing, we must note a major change made by the Association. After the assembly at Kaneohe, Hawaii, August 4–11, 1992,[21] IAMS decided to open membership to nonacademicians, reflecting "a strong feeling that missiology cannot be purely an academic exercise but has to be done from a position of actual involvement in missions. This suggests rethinking our membership criteria and [being] more open to groups actively involved in frontier missionary work. Neither the missiologist nor the missionary activist

19. "Project Report Healing," *MS* 13, no. 1 (1996): 335–37.

20. Ibid., p. 337.

21. For the workshop offered at that conference, Healing as a Sign of New Creation, led jointly by José Miguel de Angulo, Godelieve Prové, Eric de Rosny, S.J., and Christoffer Grundmann, see the brief report by M. Mary Moore and Ed Schroeder in *MS* 10, nos. 1–2 (1993): 206–7.

should reflect and operate in isolation. Both are in need of creative exchange of theological convictions and missionary experiences."[22]

Experiencing the influx of nonacademic missionary membership and working with a less rigorous scholarly agenda, the "interest group Healing" found that its main activity consisted of keeping some momentum going by staying in contact with one another in between the quadrennial conferences and in preparing a workshop for the general gathering of the IAMS constituency. The workshop offered at the conference at Hammanskraal, South Africa, January 21–28, 2000, adapted the conference theme "Reflecting Jesus Christ: Crucified and Living in a Broken World" in the phrasing "Reflecting Christ: Crucified and Living Healer." Its twenty-one participants wrestled with theological and practical issues, some of which were acute in the local setting, like the questions of an appropriate Christian response to the HIV/AIDS crisis and the churches' ministry of reconciliation in post-Apartheid South Africa. The explicitly theological themes discussed included the relationship between healing and salvation. Where do they intersect? What is their difference? The group's report on this point noted that the "relationship between healing and salvation needs further research and dialogue." Participants also expressed interest in the theme "Theology of Healing for the New Millennium." The group reported, "Having entered deeply into the reality of disease, illness, evil, healing and reconciliation, having experienced both the powerlessness of humankind and at the same time the strength of human beings in peace in spite of AIDS, the power of painful and at times flawed reconciliation rituals, the beauty of the seemingly impossible—perpetrators and victims shaking hands—we explored the elements for a new theology of healing." But in the final paragraph Dagmar Plum, S.C.M.M., and Godelieve Prové, the group's facilitators, who also served as workshop reporters, wondered "whether we really need a theology of healing for the new millennium or rather a theology in which healing takes a central place. Should healing be a theme for one of IAMS future conferences?"[23] So far this has not happened. It is noteworthy, however, that the motto of the Tenth Assembly of

22. See Joachim Wietzke, "Brief Historical Sketch of IAMS," p. 2, http://missionstudies.org/archive/0manual/3%20history.htm.

23. See the group report "Reflecting Christ: Crucified and Living Healer," *MS* 17, no. 1 (2000): 120–24.

the Lutheran World Federation, held in Winnipeg, Canada, in July 2003, was "For the Healing of the World."[24] Also, the Thirteenth World Mission Conference of the Commission on World Mission and Evangelism (CWME) of the WCC, held in Athens, Greece, in May 2005, convened under the theme "Come Holy Spirit: Heal and Reconcile!"[25] Both conferences received a lot of input from IAMS members engaged in the study of healing.[26]

The Hammanskraal workshop report closed with a note on the group's prospects for continuation, for the conveners felt a certain lack of active participation by members who had indicated interest but did not contribute in one way or another.[27] However, when asked about the future of the Healing group, "participants expressed a strong consensus for the group's continuation in order to collaborate in research, to share ideas and experiences, to prepare for the next IAMS conference, to exchange relevant healing rituals and liturgies, etc."[28] The final sentence reports that four persons were interested in steering the interest group: Stuart C. Bates (South Africa), Bernhard Ugeux (France),[29] Dagmar Plum (Germany), and Godelieve Prové.[30]

## Taking On an Additional Topic: Pneumatology

As was the case with previous assemblies, the group studying healing again prepared a workshop for the assembly held July 31–

24. *For the Healing of the World: Study Book, LWF Tenth Assembly, Winnipeg, Canada, 21–31 July 2003* (Geneva: LWF, 2002).

25. See *Come, Holy Spirit—Heal and Reconcile*, thematic issue of *IRM* 92, no. 372 (Jan. 2005); Michael Kinnamon, "Report on the World Mission Conference, Athens 2005," *IRM* 94, no. 374 (July 2005): 387–93; Jacques Matthey, ed., *"Come Holy Spirit, Heal and Reconcile!" Report of the WCC Conference on World Mission and Evangelism, Athens, Greece, May 2005* (Geneva: WCC Publications, 2008).

26. See the letter by Godelieve Prové, dated May 3, 2002, Amsterdam, in *MS* 19, no. 2 (2002): 199–200, and the reports mentioned in n. 25.

27. Besides G. Prové's letter mentioned in n. 26, see also the minutes of the IAMS Executive, January 29–February 4, 2002, Prague, p. 5, item 4.2.3, http://missionstudies.org/archive/3exec/2002-Prague.doc; and minutes of the IAMS Executive meeting in Paris, January 28–February 2, 2003, p. 7, item 4.2.3; http://missionstudies.org/archive/3exec/0_archive.htm, scroll down to 2003, click January 28–February 2, 2003, Paris, France.

28. *MS* 17, no. 1 (2000): 124.

29. See his article "The New Quest for Healing: When Therapy and Spirituality Intermingle," *IRM* 96, nos. 380–81 (Jan.–Apr. 2007): 22–40.

30. *MS* 17, no. 1 (2000): 124.

August 7, 2004, at Port Dickson, Malaysia, under the title "Reconciliation and Healing," with G. Prové serving as its facilitator.[31] In a letter dated June 16, 2004, addressed to the enrolled participants and mailed before the assembly, Prové spelled out the task of the workshop: "Confronted with the human yearning for health, healing and wholeness as a universal phenomenon encountered in every culture, the mission study group wants to see more clearly what the Christian mission of healing and reconciliation has to offer: What belongs essentially to a mission of healing and reconciliation in the light of the Gospel? This seemingly simple question needs careful discernment and the courage not to shy away from the difficulties we will encounter."[32] The workshop enjoyed input from Jacques Matthey, director of CWME, who shared a "Statement on Mission as Reconciliation," a preparatory paper for the World Mission conference at Athens the following year. Birgit Weiler, S.C.M.M., shared a narrative of her experiences with the Truth Commission in Peru, while Paul J. Bhakiaraj from India presented a paper "Reconciliation and the Integrity of Mission," and Christoffer Grundmann reflected upon the topic "Inviting the Spirit to Fight the Spirits? Pneumatological Challenges for Missions in Healing and Exorcism."[33] Although much of the material was made available for study electronically before the conference, several workshop participants reported that they struggled with "too much content within the time available." Some also felt that "healing had been somewhat marginalised at the cost of reconciliation, justice or pneumatology." At the same time, they also expressed a desire that "the IAMS Interest group Healing would continue to exist in between conferences."[34]

31. Also in this year G. Prové published her important study on the history of the Medical Mission Sisters (SCMM), *Becoming Human: A Story of Transformation Through Conflict and Healing* (Delft: Eburon, 2004).

32. The letter is available online at www.missionstudies.org/archive/conference/4miss.study.groups/study_group02_healing_introduction.htm.

33. In *IRM* 94, no. 372 (Jan. 2005): 51–73.

34. The quoted words are from the unpublished report "Healing and Reconciliation," by Dagmar Plum, Godelieve Prové, and Birgit Weiler, Mission Study Group IAMS Conference 2004, p. 4. According to the "Editorial Note" in *MS* 21, no. 2 (2004), the Executive Committee planned the edition of "a special volume of proceedings [of the Eleventh IAMS Assembly] that will be published within the next year" by its then president. This, however, did not happen. Three years later only the plenary addresses of the Port Dickson conference were published in *MS* 24, no. 2 (2007). The study group report, however, is available from the author of this chapter.

The Port Dickson Assembly yielded one rather surprising result affecting the future work of the interest group, namely, the taking on of an additional missiological research topic: pneumatology. The reason for doing so was more pragmatic than academic, even though healing is very often interpreted as being the outcome of physical workings of the (Holy) Spirit, especially in Pentecostal and Charismatic traditions. The general theme of the assembly was "The Integrity of Mission in Light of the Gospel: Bearing the Witness of the Spirit." In conversations and discussions triggered by the plenary presentations, pneumatology came to the attention of many as an issue of missiological neglect. This led to a spontaneous roundtable brainstorming session involving not less than thirty-one participants, facilitated by Christoffer Grundmann in the afternoon of August 5. The ninety-minute session yielded as a practical result the recommendation "to initiate a respective IAMS study group to be called: Mission, Pneumatology, and the Spirit Worlds." This move "was felt necessary in order to visually put a topic on the agenda of international mission studies . . . which otherwise is feared to get lost sight of completely, as happened in the past." Four people would monitor the group's activities—Christopher Oshun (Nigeria), Wai Man Yuen (Hong Kong, China), Victoria Paegler (U.S.A.), and Christoffer Grundmann— with Grundmann "asked to set [the project] afloat."[35]

The thirty-one participants (from eighteen different countries) in that memorable meeting identified several research topics, including the following:

- analysis of the reasons for the pneumatological deficit in mission studies past and present;
- "Spirit"-talk and "Spirit"-signs in missions, esp. with reference to Pentecostal and charismatic mission work;
- the Holy Spirit and the readings of the "signs of the times";
- comparison of biblical and nonbiblical spirit-worlds;
- spirit-worlds and the overall worldview they entail (including valuation of the respective morals, the assessment of evil, fate, and diseases);
- discernment of spirits;
- spirit, mind, and Holy Ghost.

35. Letter containing the group-session report by the facilitator to the participants of the roundtable talk, dated October 25, 2004, Valparaiso, p. 1, a copy of which was sent to the IAMS Executive Committee and the then IAMS president Darrell Whiteman.

As with the Healing project, so here it was felt necessary to compile a somewhat comprehensive bibliography. Kirsteen Kim (Birmingham, U.K.) offered to begin such a resource.[36]

This proposal was sent to the IAMS Executive by the liaison person who on April 7, 2005, received the following e-mail reply from Frans Dokman, then secretary of the Association: "Your plan to initiate an IAMS study group 'Missiology & Pneumatology' has been approved by the IAMS Executive Committee. On behalf of the Ex.Com., I'd like to express the great appreciation for your initiative. . . . A large number of the IAMS members have great interest in this topic. Inside/outside IAMS 'missiology and pneumatology' offers a field for dialogue between North and South, and so it contributes to the aims and mission of IAMS: thank you!!"[37] This encouragement indicated a promising future, for the secretary also mentioned that the Executive Committee had made available a small budget for project expenses, to be administered by the group's convener.[38]

Changes in the IAMS secretariat, however, as well as diversion of interests of group members, many of whom were already heavily engaged in preparation for the Edinburgh 2010 centenary celebrations, led to a very slow progress of the work, if any at all. Kim, as promised, sent her bibliography on Spirit/spirits,[39] which was then augmented by materials collected by the facilitator before he mailed a draft compilation to the members of the group. The accompanying letter of February 8, 2007, clearly acknowledged the shortcomings, of which the compiler was fully aware. He pointed to the fact that the draft was hardly comprehensive—"it lacks important elements like multilingual indexing, issue related organization, and a unified system of cataloguing." He asked for input, pleading that all would "work here together

36. Ibid., p. 2.

37. A hard copy of this e-mail is with the author of this article.

38. "The Ex.Com. doesn't like to give you only moral support. For your information, there is a budget available of $500 for every Study Group. You can contact me or our Treasurer . . . on this" (ibid., third paragraph).

39. Based mainly on the materials used for her dissertation, published as *Mission in the Spirit: The Holy Spirit in Indian Christian Theologies* (Delhi: ISPCK, 2003). See also K. Kim, *The Holy Spirit in the World: A Global Conversation* (Maryknoll, N.Y.: Orbis Books; London: SPCK, 2007), and *Joining In with the Spirit: Connecting World Church and Local Mission* (Peterborough: Epworth Publishing, 2010).

as the community of scholars to which we all belong and are part of in one way or the other." He mentioned the need for "an adequate . . . terminology, which will help us as a meaningful tool in communicating about the issues at hand without having to avail of . . . derogatory language and concepts," as well as the value of examining "the makeup of different rationalities."[40] While this great missiological challenge was consciously recognized, active participation did not live up to expectations, causing the liaison person to remark, "In closing, I would like to express my hope that there will be some more feedback than before so that we can generate a genuine momentum for the Budapest conference," which, as it come about, was actually held in Balatonfüred, Hungary, August 16–23, 2008.

In the meantime, the convener of the Healing interest group, G. Prové, resigned, leaving the appointment of a successor to the Executive, which asked its treasurer, Allan Anderson, to take care of the matter. Anderson turned to Christoffer Grundmann for help, asking him whether he would be willing to serve as a workshop (now called "parallel group session")[41] facilitator for "Pneumatology and Healing" during the upcoming conference. The task this time was not to pursue a particular quest but to accommodate as well as possible topics offered by colleagues in the field of their studies that were somehow related to healing and pneumatology and to provide a forum for sharing. This led to a most diverse set of contributions and did not allow for an overarching ongoing discourse because of the constant shifting of audience. In the postconference meeting of the interest group, however, those attending expressed—again—a strong interest in seeing the study/interest group on healing and pneumatology continue, believing it could serve as a forum for exchange and reflection within IAMS. Also, the group asked that a workshop or parallel group session definitely be provided during the next conference. This expectation

40. IAMS study group "Missiology and Pneumatology," 2nd link letter, February 8, 2007, in the file of the group facilitator.

41. In an e-mail communication of October 30, 2007, to the group facilitator, then Executive Committee member Allan Anderson explained that the "only difference is terminology—our case, one of only two or three actively working study [!] groups in IAMS will be called a 'parallel session' in next year's conference and will be more structured and academically rigorous than the workgroup format of previous years." (Hard copy of this communication is with the author of this article.)

was publicly shared in the final plenary at Balatonfüred and communicated to the Executive Committee.

This is as far as the history of the Healing/Pneumatology IAMS group can be told and documented at the time of this writing, other than to note that preparations are under way for a workshop during the next conference, scheduled for August 15-20, 2012, in Toronto, Canada.

## Assessment

After having surveyed the nonlinear, contingent history of the IAMS Healing project, an assessment is in order here. The development of the study group Healing/Pneumatology doubtless reflects as much the charismas and active input of those engaged in it as it does the overall changes within IAMS as these took shape over the years, including its policy decisions and the modifications of the Association's journal. During the first years of its publication *Mission Studies* served mainly the purpose of communication for the IAMS constituency, but it does so no longer. This is certainly a side effect of the steady increase in electronic networking, which tends to replace the conventional ways of sharing information but, not discounting its conveniences, results in a growing fragmentation of continuity, not to speak of the lack of qualified documentation, making it extremely difficult to keep proper track of relevant developments.[42]

Furthermore, the reality that IAMS is an international association with a rotating Executive and has suffered from frequent changes of its secretariat has also left a mark, as is noticeable in the inconsistency of terminology—study group, interest group, project—and the shift of focus from issue orientation in conference workshops to providing opportunities for individual research presentations in parallel groups. These circumstances did not allow for systematic growth or a coherent process; the only continuity seems to have been the permanence of change in objectives, policies, and, of course, people. Despite these challenges, IAMS identified with this project throughout the years, providing protection and moral support.[43] This endorsement is far less trivial than it first

---

42. The time from which this change is noticeable for IAMS is the Eleventh Assembly, at Port Dickson, Malaysia, 2004. See n. 34.

43. To my knowledge, the IAMS Executive never spent monies on the

appears, because it is in the fields of healing and of spirits that people of the East and the West, the North and the South realize severe conflicts in meaningful communication, conflicts mainly provoked by a practice and theology of mission steeped in Enlightenment rationalism or in reactionist opposition to it—each claiming to be biblical. But healings and spirits cannot be contained, nor can they be properly understood by the established way of doing theology and missiology. It is here that the special contribution of this study group comes into its own.

Writing about Pastor Johann Christoph Blumhardt (1805–80), renowned for his healing ministry,[44] Karl Barth (1886–1968) once remarked that Blumhardt "was not to be studied but . . . to be experienced." Barth acknowledged that Blumhardt's theology might seem primitive in form, but it is "at any rate also knowledge, and in substance [it] is original and important. . . . Academic theology has its limitations with regard to history and substance where it has to be unacademic if it is not to become immaterial. . . . Theology is concerned with a subject about which theories can be made only on the basis of its revelation of itself [i.e., God in Jesus Christ], but not otherwise. This limitation to the possibility of theorizing must become visible in theology itself by theology not taking up too rigid an academic position. . . . All too often decisive things have been recognized and stated precisely at these boundaries of theology as a discipline."[45] This remark made in 1947 did not find a hearing in its time.[46] Instead, the way of doing theology that became dominant in the Western world turned into strict academic scholarship that severed the ties with life and faith as actually lived and experienced. It lost sight of the existential importance of healing and of discerning the spirits. This, finally, had the effect of treating healing and discernment of spirits—against the unambiguous witness of Scripture—as theologically irrelevant.

Things changed somewhat in the latter half of the twentieth century as familiarity grew with healing activities in indigenous

---

project group, despite its commitment (see n. 38), most probably because it was never asked to do so.

44. See Dieter Ising, *Johann Christoph Blumhardt, Life and Work: A New Biography*, trans. M. Ledford (Eugene, Ore: Wipf & Stock, Cascade Books, 2009).

45. Karl Barth, *Protestant Theology in the Nineteenth Century: Its Background and History* (Valley Forge, Pa.: Judson Press, 1976), pp. 643–44.

46. The first edition appeared in 1947 (Zollikon: Evangelischer Verlag); a revised second edition was published in 1952.

Christian churches around the world, notably in Africa, Latin America, and Asia. The clash between the rational, nominalist way of doing theology in the West and the embodied, experience-based way of doing theology by people from the so-called Third World became manifest in the formation of the Ecumenical Association of Third World Theologians (EATWOT) in 1976 at Dar es Salaam, Tanzania. The signatories of EATWOT's founding document programmatically declared, "We reject as irrelevant an academic type of theology that is divorced from action. We are prepared for a radical break in epistemology which makes commitment the first act of theology and engages in critical reflection on the praxis of the reality of the Third World."[47]

Responding to this challenge, academic theology admitted that today the once so-called "nontheological factors" represent the most exciting fields for theological inquiry.[48] It has made "liberation theology" or other indigenous theologies the preferred, almost exclusive, subject of study,[49] while IAMS dared to focus on other hot topics, namely healing and pneumatology. In this way IAMS contributed and, slowly but steadily, continues to contribute to forging a new way of doing nonpartisan missiology beyond any particular academic, theological, or cultural preference. Unlike other missiological issues, the nonacademic character of healing and of the discernment of spirits poses exceptional scholarly challenges. The Healing and Pneumatology group, while not claiming to have mastered these challenges, sees that it has identified and addressed important issues, helping to make them more accessible to others for further investigation.

---

47. *The Emergent Gospel: Theology from the Underside of History; Papers from the Ecumenical Dialogue of Third World Theologians, Dar es Salaam, August 5–12, 1976*, ed. Sergio Torres and Virginia Fabella (Maryknoll, N.Y.: Orbis Books, 1978), p. 269.

48. See Trutz Rendtorff, "Universalität oder Kontextualität der Theologie. Eine 'europäische' Stellungnahme [Universality or contextuality of theology: A "European" statement], in *Zeitschrift für Theologie und Kirche* 74 (1977): 241.

49. For the terminology, see Gustavo Gutiérrez, *A Theology of Liberation* (Maryknoll, N.Y.: Orbis Books, 1973); Joseph Cardinal Ratzinger, "Liberation Theology: Preliminary Notes," in *The Ratzinger Report* (San Francisco: Ignatius Press, 1985); and Jürgen Moltmann, *The Gospel of Liberation* (Waco, Tex.: Word Books, 1973).

# Appendixes

# Appendix 1
# General Meetings: Themes, Locations, and Presidents

| Year | Theme | Place | Presiding Officer/ President |
|------|-------|-------|------------------------------|
| 1955 | Preliminary meeting | Hamburg, West Germany | W. Freytag (chair) |
| 1966 | Preliminary meeting | Hamburg | H.-W. Gensichen (chair) |
| 1968 | European consultation | Selly Oak, U.K. | H.-W. Gensichen (chair) |
| 1970 | European conference | Oslo, Norway | H.-W. Gensichen (chair) |
| 1972 | I. Mission in the Context of Religions and Secularization | Driebergen, Netherlands | H.-W. Gensichen |
| 1974 | II. Mission and Movements of Innovation in Religion | Frankfurt, West Germany | H.-W. Gensichen |
| 1976 | III. Tradition and Reconstruction in Mission: Where Are We in Mission Today? | San José, Costa Rica | Arnulf Camps, O.F.M. |
| 1978 | IV. Credibility and Spirituality in Mission | Maryknoll, N.Y., U.S.A. | Arnulf Camps, O.F.M. |
| 1982 | V. Christ's Mission with [or to] the Multitude: Salvation, Suffering, and Struggle | Bangalore, India | Johannes Aagaard |

| 1985 | VI. | Christian Mission and Human Transformation | Harare, Zimbabwe | Gerald H. Anderson |
|---|---|---|---|---|
| 1988 | VII. | Christian Mission Towards the Third Millennium: A Gospel of Hope | Rome, Italy | Joan Chatfield, M.M. |
| 1992 | VIII. | New World—New Creation: Mission in Power and Faith | Kaneohe, Hawaii, U.S.A. | John Pobee |
| 1996 | IX. | God or Mammon: Economies in Conflict | Buenos Aires, Argentina | Michael Amaladoss, S.J. |
| 2000 | X. | Reflecting Jesus Christ: Crucified and Living in a Broken World | Hammanskraal, South Africa | Chun Chae Ok |
| 2004 | XI. | The Integrity of Mission in the Light of the Gospel: Bearing the Witness of the Spirit | Port Dickson, Malaysia | Paulo Suess |
| 2008 | XII. | Human Identity and the Gospel of Reconciliation: An Agenda for Mission Studies and Praxis in the 21st Century | Balatonfüred, Hungary | Philomena Njeri Mwaura |
| 2012 | XIII. | Migration, Human Dislocation, and the Good News: Margins as the Center in Christian Mission | Toronto, Canada | Jonathan J. Bonk |

# Appendix 2
# Officers and Editors

## Presidents

| | |
|---|---|
| 1972–74 | H.-W. Gensichen |
| 1974–76 | Arnulf Camps, O.F.M. |
| 1976–78 | Arnulf Camps, O.F.M. |
| 1978–82 | Johannes Aagaard |
| 1982–85 | Gerald H. Anderson |
| 1985–88 | Joan Chatfield, M.M. |
| 1988–92 | John S. Pobee |
| 1992–96 | Michael Amaladoss, S.J. |
| 1996–2000 | Chun Chae Ok |
| 2000–2004 | Paulo Suess |
| 2004–6 | Darrell L. Whiteman |
| 2006–8 | Philomena Njeri Mwaura |
| 2008–12 | Jonathan J. Bonk |

## Vice Presidents

Arnulf Camps, O.F.M.
Stanley J. Samartha
Johannes Aagaard
Gerald H. Anderson
Joan Chatfield, M.M.
John S. Pobee
Michael Amaladoss, S.J.
Ana Langerak
Paulo Suess
Darrell L. Whiteman
Philomena Njeri Mwaura
Jonathan J. Bonk
Mika Vähäkangas

## General Secretaries

| | |
|---|---|
| 1972–74 | Olav G. Myklebust (Oslo) |
| 1974–76 | Andrew F. Walls (Aberdeen) |
| 1976–86 | Frans J. Verstraelen (Leiden) |
| 1986–95 | Joachim Wietzke (Hamburg) |
| 1995–2000 | Klaus Schäfer (Hamburg) |
| 2000–2004 | Birger Nygaard (Copenhagen) |
| 2004–6 | Frans Dokman (Nijmegen) |
| 2006–8 | Jan van Butselaar (Nijmegen) |
| 2008– | Cathy Ross (Oxford) |

## Treasurers

| | |
|---|---|
| 1972–74 | Olav G. Myklebust (Oslo) |
| 1974–88 | Paul R. Clifford (Selly Oak, U.K.) |
| 1988–97 | Martin Conway (Selly Oak, U.K.), with Marcella Hoesl, M.M. (1989–90), and J. Andrew Kirk (1991-97) |
| 1997–2004 | J. Andrew Kirk (Selly Oak, U.K.) |
| 2004–8 | Allan Anderson (Selly Oak, U.K.) |
| 2008– | David Emmanuel Singh (Oxford) |

## Editors of *IAMS News Letter*
| | |
|---|---|
| 1973–74 | Olav G. Myklebust (Oslo) |
| 1975–76 | Andrew F. Walls (Aberdeen) |
| 1976–83 | Frans J. Verstraelen (Leiden) |

## Editors of *Mission Studies*
| | |
|---|---|
| 1983–86 | Frans J. Verstraelen |
| 1986–89 | Thomas Kramm |
| 1990–96 | Horst Rzepkowski, S.V.D. |
| 1997–2004 | Stephen B. Bevans, S.V.D. |
| 2005–12 | Lalsangkima Pachuau |

## Associate Editors of *Mission Studies*
| | |
|---|---|
| 1986–89 | Joachim Wietzke |
| 1990–96 | Joachim Wietzke, Klaus Schäfer |
| 1997–2004 | Robert J. Schreiter, C.PP.S., Klaus Schäfer, Birger Nygaard |
| 2005–12 | Catherine Rae Ross, J. Jayakiran Sebastian, Paulo Suess, Susan Smith, J. Kwabena Asamoah-Gyadu, Mika Vähäkangas, Mariel Deluca Voth, Michael Poon |

## Book Review Editor of *Mission Studies*
| | |
|---|---|
| 2001– | Paul V. Kollman, C.S.C. |

# Appendix 3
## Conference Participants and Membership

| Conference | Registered Participants | Total Members (Individual/Corporate) |
| --- | --- | --- |
| I. Driebergen (1972) | 123 | 244 (205/39) |
| II. Frankfurt (1974) | 141 | 323 (273/50) |
| III. San José (1976) | 100+ | 383 (329/54) |
| IV. Maryknoll (1978) | 160 | 544 (488/56) |
| V. Bangalore (1982) | 120 | 576 (518/58) |
| VI. Harare (1985) | 187 | 622 (564/58) |
| VII. Rome (1988) | 206 | 565 (488/77) |
| VIII. Kaneohe, Hawaii (1992) | 179 | 570 (497/73) |
| IX. Buenos Aires (1996) | 129 | 533 (459/74) |
| X. Hammanskraal (2000) | 222 | 608 (523/77, 8 associate) |
| XI. Port Dickson (2004) | 200+ | 424 (361/46, 12 associate, 5 honorary) |
| XII. Balatonfüred (2008) | 234 | 400 + |

# Appendix 4
# Guidelines for Appointment of
# Honorary Life Members

The Executive can appoint IAMS Honorary Life Members as a tribute to outstanding accomplishments in missiology and dedicated services to IAMS.

## 1. Criteria
Honorary Life Members are appointed on the basis of the following criteria:
1. Exceptional services to missiology
2. Exceptional services to IAMS
3. Candidates should be retired from official posts
4. Candidates are to be appointed by a unanimous decision of the Executive.

## 2. Entitlements
Honorary Life Members are entitled to free membership in IAMS and free subscription to *Mission Studies.*

## 3. Nomination
Any two members of IAMS can nominate a person for Honorary Life Membership. A nomination shall be submitted in writing to the Executive with a motivation for the nomination.

## 4. General guidelines
1. Appointment of Honorary Life Members will take place according to a restrictive policy in order to limit the number of such members.
2. The Executive shall seek to provide a proper continental balance in its appointments. Pursuit of such balance is, however secondary to the stated criteria (see 1. above).

3. Newly appointed Honorary Life Members will be presented in *Mission Studies*.
4. On the IAMS Website each Honorary Life Member will be portrayed.

These guidelines shall be made known to IAMS members via the IAMS Web site.

# Appendix 5
# Honorary Life Members

Gerald H. Anderson, U.S.A.
Joan Chatfield, M.M., U.S.A.
Jan A. B. Jongeneel, Netherlands
C. René Padilla, Argentina
John S. Pobee, Ghana
Willem Saayman, South Africa
Frans J. Verstraelen, Netherlands/Zimbabwe
Andrew F. Walls, Scotland[1]

**Deceased Honorary Life Members**
Stanley J. Samartha, India (deceased July 22, 2001)
Olav Guttorm Myklebust, Norway (deceased November 29, 2001)
Paul Rowntree Clifford, England (deceased January 19, 2003)
Arnulf Camps, O.F.M., Netherlands (deceased March 5, 2006)

1. This list of honorary life members is complete as of the conclusion of IAMS's Twelfth General Assembly, Balatonfüred, Hungary, August 2008.

# Appendix 6
# Constitution and Byelaws

## Constitution of the International Association for Mission Studies (IAMS)

### 1. Name
The name of the Association shall be "The International Association for Mission Studies" (hereafter referred to as the Association).

### 2. Objectives
The Association is an international, interdenominational and intercultural body committed to the scholarly study of issues related to Christian mission.

The main objectives of the Association shall be:
- (a) to promote the scholarly study of theological, historical and practical questions relating to the mission of the Church;
- (b) to disseminate information concerning mission among all those engaged in such studies and among the general public;
- (c) to relate studies in mission to studies in theological and other disciplines, through the encouragement of interdisciplinary research programmes and other appropriate means;
- (d) to promote fellowship, cooperation and mutual assistance in mission studies, especially among national, regional and denominational mission study associations and equivalents;
- (e) to organize international conferences of missiologists;
- (f) to encourage the creation of centres of research;
- (g) to stimulate publications in the area of the Association's interest, including an international journal and bibliography.

### 3. Membership
Individuals, institutions and likeminded associations and networks wishing to further the aims of the Association may be admitted to the Association by vote of the Executive Committee.

### 4. Finance
The resources of the Association consist of:
  (a)  Subscriptions from members,
  (b)  Subsidies and donations.
Every member shall pay an annual subscription determined from time to time by a General Meeting of the Association.

### 5. Officers and Executive Committee
The officers of the Association shall be a President, a Vice President, a General Secretary, a Treasurer, and the Editor of the journal of the Association. The President and Vice President shall be elected, and the General Secretary, Treasurer and Editor shall be approved by a General Meeting of the Association for a period of four years or until the General Meeting next after the expiry of that period.

The Executive Committee manages the affairs of the Association between general meetings of the Association. The Executive Committee shall consist of the officers with five other members elected by a General Meeting of the Association to represent continental regions for a period of four years or until the General Meeting next after the expiry of that period.

The Executive shall normally meet once a year. Officers and members of the Executive Committee shall be eligible for re-election. The elections shall be governed by byelaws.

### 6. General Meeting
The Executive Committee shall convene a General Meeting of the Association about every four years.

All individual members, and one representative of each corporate member, shall have the right to attend and vote at General Meetings of the Association.

At each ordinary General Meeting the Executive Committee shall submit for the approval of the Meeting a report of its activities since the last ordinary General Meeting and its proposals for advancing the objects of the Association.

## 7. Headquarters
The Executive Committee shall have the power to determine the location of the Headquarters of the Association. Usually, the location of the General Secretariat is regarded as the Headquarters of the Association.

## 8. Funds
The funds of the Association shall be held in the United Kingdom but if at any time the members resolve at a General Meeting that the funds should not be so held the Executive Committee shall inform the Charity Commissioners of the terms of the resolution.

## 9. Byelaws
Byelaws may be approved by a majority of members present and voting at any duly constituted General Meeting of the Association.

## 10. Alterations to the Constitution
Additions and alterations to the Constitution shall be made only by resolution of the General Meeting, carried by a majority of not less than two thirds of those voting. No amendment may be made which shall cause the Association to cease to be a charity in law.

Adopted 29 August 1972
Amended 31 July 1974
Amended 24 August 1978
Amended 28 January 2000

*Amended by the XIth Quadrennial General Assembly, 3 August 2004*
*Amended by the XIIth Quadrennial General Assembly, 20 August 2008,*
*Balatonfüred, Hungary*

# Byelaws: The Executive Committee

### §1
"The Executive Committee (of the International Association for Mission Studies) shall consist of the officers with five other members elected by a General Meeting of the Association for a period of four years or until the General Meeting next after the expiry of that period" (Const. §5).

### §2
The duties of the Executive Committee are:
- (a) To approve the membership applications of individuals and institutions to IAMS (§3).
- (b) To determine the date and convene a General Meeting of the Association about every four years (§6).
- (c) To determine the location of the Headquarters of the Association (§7).
- (d) Between General Meetings to be responsible for furthering the objects of the Association as listed in §2 of the Constitution of the Association.
- (e) To obtain financing through subsidies and donations and to set up a permanent system of financing the work of the Association.
- (f) Between General Meetings to be the Executive group which has the power to determine all things except those expressly reserved to the General Meeting.

### §3
The presence of at least four members of the Executive Committee is necessary for a legal meeting. The President or Vice President must always be among the four.

### §4
A simple majority vote of those present and voting will be required for the passage of any act of the Executive Committee while in session.

### §5
These byelaws may be amended by the ordinary voting procedures explained in §4 above. Changes take effect immediately. They must be presented to the General Meeting of the Association

at its next gathering for subsequent approval according to §9 in the
constitution.

*Approved at the IAMS General Meeting 24 August 1978.*
Amended by the Executive Committee 28 January 2001 according
to the Hammanskraal constitutional changes.

# Byelaws: General Meeting of the Association

Procedure for the election of President, Vice President, and other
members of the Executive Committee

### 1. Setting up of a Nomination Committee
The election process will be guided by a Nomination Committee
comprising the following persons: the outgoing President of IAMS
together with one representative from each of the regions of Africa, Asia, Europe, Latin America/Caribbean, North America and
Oceania, nominated by Regional Meetings in their first session.

The Nomination Committee will constitute itself after the first
regional meeting. It will elect its own chair. It may, if deemed necessary, seek the advice of the previous Executive Committee.

### 2. Preparation of Slate for the Election of President, Vice
President and Executive Committee
The Nomination Committee will from names proposed by the
Regional Meetings plus the current Vice President prepare one
slate of candidates for consideration by the General Meeting for
the positions of President, Vice President, and five Executive Committee members.

The current Vice President will normally be nominated for President. However the General Meeting may request the Nomination
Committee to propose an alternative.

The six regional areas are represented by the Vice President and
five Executive Committee members.

## 2.1. Proposals from Regional Meetings
Regional Meetings are required to nominate three persons to be considered for election to the Executive Committee. These are to be listed and take into account the criteria listed in 2.2.

Regional Meetings must obtain the consent of persons they propose for election.

The Nomination Committee has the right to return to all the Regional Meetings to request an additional person be proposed by each region.

## 2.2. Criteria
Regional Meetings and the Nominating Committee are required to ensure that those proposed for election and included in the final slate of candidates represent a good mix and balance of persons, taking into account considerations relating to continuity, geographical and denominational representation, gender, skills, regional leadership and availability to participate in the work of IAMS.

## 3. Voting process
The Nomination Committee will present its nominated slate at a General Meeting of IAMS.

## 3.1. Right to vote
Only full IAMS members present at the conference are eligible to vote and to stand as candidates for election.

Corporate members of IAMS, represented in the Conference, have one vote.

Each individual person has only one vote, either as individual member of IAMS or as representative of a corporate member.

## 3.2. Secret ballot
The voting will be conducted by means of a secret ballot.

### 3.3. Majority
The IAMS General Meeting is entitled, by simple majority vote of members present at the meeting, to accept or reject the slate proposed by the Nomination Committee. The meeting may also make suggestions and require the Nomination Committee to present an amended slate.

*Adopted by the XI Quadrennial Assembly, Malaysia, 3 August 2004*

# References and Resources

Aagaard, Johannes. Obituary. *MS* 24, no. 1 (2007): 7–8; *IBMR* 31, no. 3 (2007): 141.

Amaladoss, Michael. "My Pilgrimage in Mission." *IBMR* 31, no. 1 (2007): 21–24.

Anderson, Gerald H. "Introducing a New Journal." *MS* 1, no. 1 (1984): 2–3.

———. "My Pilgrimage in Mission." *IBMR* 29, no. 3 (2005): 139–43.

Anderson, Gerald H., and Arnulf Camps. "Open Letter of Special Greetings and Congratulations." *MS* 12, no. 1 (1995): 3–4. On the occasion of Myklebust's ninetieth birthday and Gensichen's eightieth birthday, recalling their formative role and contribution in the establishment of the IAMS.

Beaver, R. Pierce. "The Meaning and Place of Missiology Today in the American Scene." Paper delivered at the consultation at Selly Oak, Birmingham, April 1968, mimeographed; copy in the Billy Graham Center Archives, Wheaton, Illinois.

Bosch, David J. Obituary. *IBMR* 16, no. 3 (1992): 108; see also John S. Pobee, "In Memoriam: David J. Bosch," *MS* 9, no. 2 (1992): 252–54.

Burrows, William R., Mark R. Gornik, and Janice A. McLean, eds. *Understanding World Christianity: The Vision and Work of Andrew F. Walls.* Maryknoll, N.Y.: Orbis Books, 2011. See especially chap. 6, by Jonathan J. Bonk, "Changing the Course of Mission and World Christian Studies," pp. 61–77.

Camps, Arnulf. "Ökumenische Initiativen auf internationaler Ebene (IAMS, EATWOT, WCRP)." *Zeitschrift für Missionswissenschaft und Religionswissenschaft* 70 (1986): 248–60.

———. "My Pilgrimage in Mission." *IBMR* 20, no. 1 (1996): 33–36.

———. *Arnulf Camps: Pelgrim en Missioloog. Levensweg van een Nijmeegse hoogleaar* (Arnulf Camps: Pilgrim and Missiologist. Life of a Nijmegen Professor). Edited by Vefie Poels. Nijmegen: Valkhof Press, 2006. See pp. 236–41.

———. Obituary. *MS* 23, no. 1 (2006): 5–7; *IBMR* 30, no. 3 (2006): 151.

Clifford, Paul Rowntree. *An Ecumenical Pilgrimage*. London: West Ham Central Mission, 1994. See pp. 135–36.

———. Obituary. *MS* 20, no. 2 (2003): 6–7; *IBMR* 27, no. 2 (2003): 75.

"De eerste europese consultatie van missiologen in Selly Oak, April 16–19, 1968." *De Heerbaan* 21, no. 4 (1968): 205–32. Articles by J. Verkuyl, J. M. van der Linde, and A. Camps, reporting on the European Consultation on Mission Studies, held at Selly Oak, Birmingham, in April 1968.

Gensichen, Hans-Werner. "My Pilgrimage in Mission." *IBMR* 13, no. 4 (1989): 167–69.

———. *Invitatio ad Franternitatem: 75 Jahre Deutsche Gesellschaft für Missionswissenschaft (1918–1993)*. Münster: Lit Verlag, 1993.

———. Obituary. *IBMR* 23, no. 3 (1999): 119. There was a brief editorial notice of his death in *MS* 17, no. 2 (1999): 1, which said that the next issue of the journal "will carry a longer tribute to the memory of this great missiologist and scholar," but due to an editorial oversight, it never appeared.

Glazik, Josef. "The Meaning and the Place of Missiology Today." *IRM* 57 (1968): 459–67. Paper given at the European Consultation on Mission Studies held at Selly Oak, Birmingham, April 1968.

Henkel, Willi. "My Pilgrimage in Mission." *IBMR* 31, no. 2 (2007): 84–86.

Horner, Norman A. "The Association of Professors of Mission: The First Thirty-Five Years, 1952–1987." *IBMR* 11, no. 3 (1987): 120–24.

*IAMS Governance Manual*. On the IAMS Web site, www.missionstudies.org.

*IAMS Matters*. Official [electronic] newsletter of IAMS. No. 1 (September–October 2011); bimonthly.

*IAMS News Letter*. Occasional, then semiannual, 1973–83 (nos. 1–23).

Kirk, J. Andrew. "My Pilgrimage in Mission." *IBMR* 28, no. 2 (2004): 70–74.

Lande, Aasulv. "The Legacy of Olav Guttorm Myklebust." *IBMR* 31, no. 3 (2007): 142–46.

McGavran, Donald A., ed. *The Conciliar-Evangelical Debate: The Crucial Documents, 1964–1976.* South Pasadena, Calif.: William Carey Library, 1977. This is an expanded edition of *Eye of the Storm: The Great Debate in Mission* (Waco, Tex.: Word Books, 1972). Contains three papers on the theme "Presence and Proclamation as Forms of Mission," by Max Warren, Donald McGavran, and Hans J. Margull, given at the European Consultation on Mission Studies held at Selly Oak, Birmingham, in April 1968. The paper at the consultation by R. Pierce Beaver, "The Meaning and Place of Missiology in the American Scene," was not published.

*Missiology* 7, no. 1 (1979). Special issue with papers, workshop reports, and main addresses from the IAMS assembly at Maryknoll, New York, August 21–26, 1978.

*Missiology* 10, no. 3 (1982). Special issue devoted to papers and reports, including the presidential address by J. Aagaard, from the IAMS assembly at Bangalore (Whitefield), India, January 4–9, 1982.

*Mission Studies: Journal of the International Association for Mission Studies* (successor to the *IAMS News Letter*). Semiannual, 1984–.

Myklebust, Olav Guttorm. *An International Institute of Scientific Missionary Research.* Oslo: Egede Instituttet, 1951.

———. *The Study of Missions in Theological Education.* 2 vols. Oslo: Egede Instituttet, 1955–57.

———. "On the Origin of IAMS." *MS* 3, no. 1 (1986): 4–11.

———. "My Pilgrimage in Mission." *IBMR* 11, no. 1 (1987): 22–23.

———. "Message to IAMS members." *MS* 5, no. 2 (1988): 4.

———. Obituary. *MS* 19, no. 2 (2002): 12–13; *IBMR* 26, no. 2 (2002): 75.

Okure, Teresa, ed. *To Cast Fire upon the Earth: Bible and Mission Collaborating in Today's Multicultural Global Context.* Pietermaritzburg: Cluster Publications, 2000. Includes a chapter by John Roxborogh on the history of BIAMS.

Samartha, Stanley J. "Mission and Movements of Innovation." *Missiology* 3, no. 2 (1975): 143–53. Keynote address at IAMS Frankfurt Assembly, July 30, 1974.

Shenk, Wilbert, and George R. Hunsberger. *The American Society of Missiology: The First Quarter Century*. Decatur, Ga.: ASM, 1998.

Smith, A. Christopher. "Mission Research and the Path to CD-ROM: Report on the Global Quest to Share Information," *IBMR* 19, no. 4 (1995): 146–52.

Sundkler, B. G. M. "The Meaning, Place, and Task of Missiology Today." Paper delivered at the consultation at Selly Oak, Birmingham, April 1968, mimeographed; copy in the Billy Graham Center Archives, Wheaton, Illinois.

Verstraelen, Frans J. "Het eerste intercontinentale missiologencongres. Driebergen, 19–23 augustus 1972." *Wereld en Zending* 1, no. 5 (1972): 371–74.

———. Interview with Gerald Anderson, March 30, 2005.

Walls, Andrew. Interviews with Gerald Anderson, November 10, 2004, August 18, 2008, and November 2, 2011.

Whiteman, Darrell. "Message from . . . President." *IAMS Electronic News Letter*, March 2005.

Wietzke, Joachim. "Brief Historical Sketch of IAMS." Mimeographed, January, 1993; included in the *IAMS Governance Manual* at www.missionstudies.org.

See inside cover of *MS* 1, no. 1 (1984), also inside cover of *MS* 2, no. 2 (1985), for list of IAMS publications. See also the list of IAMS "Interest Groups" in *MS* 14, nos. 1–2 (1997): 18ff.: BISAM, DAB, Healing, Patristics and Mission, Women in Mission.

# Contributors

**Gerald H. Anderson**, Director Emeritus of the Overseas Ministries Study Center, New Haven, Connecticut, was a Methodist missionary on the faculty of Union Theological Seminary in the Philippines (1961–70). A former president of the American Society of Missiology (1973–75), he was president of IAMS (1982–85).

**John Roxborogh** practiced as an electrical engineer before training for the Presbyterian ministry. After doctoral studies in Aberdeen he served in parish ministry and theological education in Malaysia and New Zealand. He was convener of the Documentation, Archives, and Bibliography (DAB) Study Group from 1992 to 2005, and a member of the IAMS Executive Committee from 1992 to 1996. Currently retired in Dunedin, New Zealand, he maintains his interests in technology, archives, and mission and is involved in various writing projects relating to Christianity in Southeast Asia.

**John Mansford Prior**, born in the United Kingdom, is a member of the Society of the Divine Word (SVD) and has been living in Indonesia since 1973. After fourteen years in pastoral work, he has been lecturing at St. Paul's Institute of Philosophy, Ledalero. He is active in evangelization and in the interreligious and social communications offices of the Federation of Asian Bishops' Conferences.

Since 2004 he has been coordinator of the Biblical Studies in Mission (BISAM) Study Group of IAMS and, since 2009, a member of the Advisory Board of the Intercultural Bible Collective, Amsterdam.

**Christoffer H. Grundmann** is the John R. Eckrich University Professor in Religion and the Healing Arts at Valparaiso University, Valparaiso, Indiana. Born in Germany, he studied theology and received Lutheran ordination. He has worked in Caracas, Venezuela, and from 1978 to 1983 taught at the Tamilnadu Theological Seminary in Madurai, India. Returning to Germany, he served as theological consultant, hospital chaplain, and study secretary of the German Institute for Medical Missions in Tübingen.

# Index

217

MacInnis, Donald E., 115
Mackie, Steven G., 5
Malloy, Robert, 27n1
Maluleke, Tinikyo Sam, 81
Mammon, 66–67, 71–72
Mananzan, Mary John, O.S.B., 53
Mandela, Nelson, 79
MARC. *See* Mission Advanced Research and Communication Center; Machine Readable Cataloguing
Marchisano, Francesco, 89
Margull, Hans-Jochen, 4, 6
Martin, Marie-Louise, 60
Masson, Joseph, 4
Matthey, Jacques, 172, 187n25, 188
Mbwana, Martin, 60
McGavran, Donald, 4, 12n1
McGilvray, J., 179n3
Melanchthon, Philipp, 111
Metzler, Josef, O.M.I., 6
Middelkoop, Peter R., 25, 158, 159n5, 160n11
Míguez, Néstor, 67
Míguez Bonino, José, 74
Milingo, Emmanuel, 181, 182n13
Missio Aachen, 141
*missio Dei*, 13, 100, 155
*Missiology* (ASM), 9, 25
Missio Munich, 141
mission, from below, 61–62, 167n34
Mission Advanced Research and Communication Center, 136
*Missionalia* (SAMS), 9, 140–41
Missionary Research Library (New York), 137
*Mission Studies: Journal of the IAMS*, 35, 37–38, 55, 65, 75, 85, 90, 122, 124, 126; and desire for a journal, 1, 8, 14, 18
Miyamoto, Ken Christoph, 116
Mokofeng, Takatso, 42
Molendijk, Arie L., 159
Moltmann, Jürgen, 194n49
Monti, Emilio M., 84
Moore, M. Mary, 182n12, 185n21
Morgan, Robin, 76
Moritzen, Niels-Peter, 6
Mosothoane, E. K., 18
Mugabe, Robert, 36n2
Müller, Karl, S.V.D., 97
Muller, Robert, 23
Munthe, Ludwig, 97
Murray, Jocelyn M., 64–66, 97
Mushete, A. Ngindu, 32, 141–42
Mveng, Engelbert, S.J., 38
Mwaura, Philomena Njeri, 81–82, 94, 98, 104, 106, 109, 114–15, 117
Myklebust, Olav Guttorm, 1–6, 8, 14, 38, 54–55, 62–63, 83, 97, 127–28, 140

Nagasaki, attack on, 61n4
National Archives of Zimbabwe, 43
National Council of Churches (South Korea), 113

Prior, John Mansford, S.V.D., 124; history of BISAM, 157–78
Program on Dialogue with People of Living Faiths and Ideologies (WCC), 12, 30
Project for New Religious Movements, 9
Promper, Werner, 6
Prové, Godelieve, 184–88, 191
Provisional Committee (IAMS), 6, 135–36

Ranson, Charles W., 2, 8, 54
Ratzinger, Joseph Cardinal, 194n49
Rayan, Samuel, S.J., 5
readings of the Bible, 159n5, 163, 167–68; intercultural, 157, 161, 177; missiological, 172–74; postcolonial, 177
reconciliation: church as mediator of, 94, 188; gospel of, 104, 107, 109–12, 175; of human wounds, 82, 112; in national healing, 41, 113–14, 186
Reilly, Michael Collins, 23
Rendtorff, Trutz, 194n48
*Rescuing the Memory of Our Peoples* (M. Smalley and Seton), 89, 133, 153–54
Reyburn, William D., 7
Robeck, Cecil, 108
Rosny, Eric de, S.J., 185n21
Ross, Andrew C., 115
Ross, Catherine (Cathy) Rae, 84, 90, 100, 109, 116, 118–19, 122–24
Rostkowski, Marek, O.M.I., 123, 155
Roxborogh, John, 63–64, 66, 79–80, 88–89, 117, 157, 171, 177–78; history of DAB(OH), 133–56
Ruiz, Jerjes, 72–73
Ruiz, Miguel Rodríguez, 161n15
Rzepkowski, Horst, S.V.D., 55–56, 58, 64, 66, 72, 74–75, 83

Saayman, Willem, 76–77, 87, 168n42, 169n43
Sacks, Jonathan, 112
Samartha, Stanley J., 4–5, 8, 12–14, 19, 29–31, 87, 97, 112
Samuelson, A., 58
Sand, F. A., 182n13
Sanneh, Lamin, 87
Saracco, Norberto, 110n4
Sarpong, Peter, 181n9
Scannone, Carlos, S.J., 69
Schäfer, Klaus, 67–68, 70, 72–74, 77–79, 84, 89–90, 101, 169n45
Scherer, James, 37
Schipani, Daniel, 175n56
Schoonhoven, Evert Jansen, 6, 72
Schreiter, Robert J., C.PP.S., 75, 85, 112–13, 184
Schroeder, Edward, 72, 76, 185n21
Scott, Michael, 38
Scottish Institute of Missionary Studies (Aberdeen), 14
Sebastian, J. Jayakiran, 90
Second Vatican Council. *See* Vatican II
secretariat (IAMS), at: Aberdeen, 14; Leiden (IIMO), 20, 45; Hamburg (EMW), 45, 67, 79, 84; Copenhagen (Aeropagos), 86, 89, 102; Nijmegen, 101–3, 105, 108, 121; Oxford, 119, 121
SEDOS (Rome), 149
Seminarium Indicum, 7
Senior, Donald, C.P., 61, 161, 168